Start reading at
('Prologue' best sk



DAVID WATKINS

# PALESTINE

## An Inescapable Duty

Alhani

Alhani International Books - 1992
London

First published in Great Britain in 1992
by Alhani International Books Ltd.
102, Crawford Street
London W1H 1AN



**ISBN 1-873765-06-1**



British Library Cataloguing in Publication Data

Watkins, David
***Palestine, an Inescapable Duty***
I. Title 956.9405092

Printed in Great Britain by
Biddles Ltd, Guilford, Surrey

‘ There is a clear duty upon all we
who have known for so long
so much about these problems
to continue to hold the standard high ’

**Rabbi Elmer Berger**

*Geneva, 21 August 1984.*

**ABOUT THE COVER...**

I wondered how can a lifetime struggle of a people be reduced to fit a 60"x40" canvas. My intuition urged me to start at the roots, and I began at the lower right corner. The arrow points to the year 1917 (١٩١٧), imposing a question mark about justice and truth. The uniqueness of the historical case of Palestine evokes a resounding exclamation mark.

On the lower left side, a set of roots extends deep into the soil. It grows upward to form the olive tree, symbol of long life and peace. On the right, other shoots converge from without, spreading over the body of Palestine. They form a hand that grabs the trunk of the tree, distorting its growth.

The conflict intensifies, two claims over one body. Rage spreads, while the heart, Jerusalem, calls for attention, sending its own luminous signals.

The conflict generates two forces that hover over the land. The black arrow, the negative force of hatred, mistrust and pain heads downwards. Eventually, it is bound to decline. The white positive force of truth, duty, tolerance and justice supports the land, starting as a small patch on the left. It spreads inevitably gaining more volume, more recognition. Once it reaches the right border of the painting, it escapes beyond it, collecting more energy and rejoining the canvas once more.

The white force sweeps upwards, ultimately lifting the body towards peace. The olive tree is revived: Two branches, two distinct identities still share the tree. They both extend to the top of the canvas where a healthy glowing phase begins, and unfolds beyond the painting.

This **'Conflict Over One Body'**, I dedicate to a just solution.

***Lamis, 1992***

*To the late Eddie Wigham and Betty,*

*friends through thick and thin.*

## CONTENTS

# FOREWORD

To have a book with both a prologue and a foreword may seem like carelessness, if I may adapt the words of Oscar Wilde's famous character Lady Bracknell. But every book on the contemporary Middle East is inevitably overtaken by events and the reason for this late-written foreword is to set the book in the context of rapidly changing events during the time of its gestation.

The original text was completed and delivered to be published in the autumn of 1990. It was intended as a memoir of the author's time as director of CAABU from 1983 to 1990, combined with an analysis of the Middle East in the nineteen-eighties, a decade which may come to be regarded as one of the most significant of the century. Unfortunately, unexpected delays in publication were encountered and the text was overtaken by the Gulf War of early 1991. It was revised in the summer of that year to take account of the changes, with hopes for publication in autumn 1991. However, it again became necessary to update the text to take account of the Madrid Conference. At that stage, I gave serious thought to moving Chapter 5, which deals with the subject of an international peace conference, to a later part of the book, because the Madrid Conference provided a suitable cut-off point. In the event, I decided against doing so. It will be for readers to judge whether or not that was the right decision.

Even as this foreword was being written in January 1992, events were developing rapidly with the decision of the Israeli government to deport twelve more Palestinians and to increase still further the colonizing settlements in the occupied territories. These actions were not new in themselves, for both were in continuation of a long established policy in breach of the Fourth Geneva Convention governing the conduct of occupying powers, but coming at a crucial stage in the attempted peace negotiations initiated at Madrid, they were a calculated attempt to wreck the "peace process" and a snub to the entire international community. There was shamefully little international reaction to the colonizing proposals but the deportations of the Palestinians brought strong protests from the USA, the European Community, Britain, Russia, China and other countries. However, the question remained as to what extent the high contracting parties to the Geneva Convention would be prepared to fulfil their obligation under international law to exercise power to curb this defiance of the Convention and of civilized international conduct. The extent to which member states of the United Nations will be prepared to observe their legal duty, to say nothing of their moral obligation to curb such conduct, is one of the subjects discussed in this book.

As the final revision was being completed in late December 1991, the Soviet Union was being dissolved, to be replaced by the new Commonwealth of Independent States. However, it remains referred to as the Soviet Union, because that is what it was throughout the period covered by the book. Another of the principal themes, that East-West co-operation is essential for the resolution of the Palestinian problem, is not invalidated.

I want to express my thanks to Mrs. Ayubi of Ithaca Press, who was the first to undertake to publish the book. I also want to thank Mr. Samir Shawa and his colleagues in Alhani, for their generous offer to publish the book, an offer I was delighted to accept.

I thank Mrs. Lamis Shawwa for the picture she painted specially for the cover and for her notes on the picture. Contained within her painting is all the tragedy of Palestine, all the resilience and all the aspirations of Palestine's indomitable people.

**London, January 1992** **David Watkins**

# PROLOGUE

# INTO SOMETHING VERY DIFFERENT

# 1

## TRAUMATIC DAYS

In 1983, my seventeen years in the house of Commons came to a grinding halt. It was on Thursday, 19 May that I finally knew that my parliamentary career was finished and that for the first time in my life, at the age of fifty-seven, I would be unemployed. Then, on Thursday, 16 June, one week after the general election of that year, the Executive Committee of CAABU - the Council for the Advancement of Arab-British Understanding - unanimously invited me to accept the Directorship of the Organization, which I took up in September. I had been associated with CAABU since its early days in 1967 and had served as an executive committee member, a vice-chairman and for the last four years as a joint chairman. CAABU in 1983 was not in good shape. There had been no Director for nearly two years, funds had dried up and the organization was facing demise. It had been kept ticking over mainly through the efforts of Douglas Collard, a part-time employee of CAABU and Director of the Arab-British Centre (the building in which CAABU is housed) and by Michael Adams, the authority on the Middle East who, in the early days, had been CAABU's first Director. When it first began to be known that my parliamentary career was in jeopardy, Douglas Collard had suggested that I might be appointed Director and the idea had gained strong support. When I was appointed, my brief, in the first place, was to ensure the very survival of the organization and then to restore it to its former glory and more. Before going further, it is appropriate to recount something more of the circumstances of how I came to leave Parliament.

The Consett Division of County Durham, which I had represented since 1966, was abolished in the boundary redistribution which came into effect for the 1983 election. The constituency was split in two; one part, comprised of the town of Consett and its environs, went into the new constituency of Durham North West, while the other part, comprised of the town of Stanley and environs, went into the new constituency of Durham North. Although there were major boundary revisions, Durham was to be left with the same number of county constituencies. All the old seats were Labour held and it was likely that the new ones would also be Labour. Thus the situation was that every sitting Member who wished to stand again could be accommodated, subject to selection as candidate in one of the new constituencies. The Labour Party rules were that every sitting Member who had been previously re-selected for his old constituency had an automatic right to be short listed for the candidature in every new constituency of which his old one formed a part. All over the country, amicable arrangements had been made among constituency Labour Parties and MP's to ensure that sitting MP's who wished to stand again could be accommodated. On paper, there was every reason to suppose that the sitting Members in Co. Durham could also be so accommodated. However, the Rt. Hon. Ernest Armstrong had other ideas.

Ernest Armstrong had been the Member since 1964 for the old Durham North West Division, which would form the geographical bulk of the new Durham North West although, in the new division, the heaviest concentration of electors would be in the Consett area. Armstrong had served as a junior minister in the Labour governments of the 1970's and had been a whip both in government and opposition. He had been ambitious to be made Government Chief Whip when James Callaghan succeeded Harold Wilson as Prime Minister in 1976 and he was angry when he was not given the job. In 1982, he was appointed as one of the three Deputy Speakers. By that time, I had been a Member of the Chairmen's Panel (experienced Members who Chair Standing Committees on the detailed discussion of bills) for four years and my own name was considered alongside his, the post eventually going to him because he was older - eleven years - than me.

Under the Labour Party rules applying to the redistribution of constituency boundaries, he had automatic rights to be short listed for the new Durham North West as well as for the new Durham

Division and for the new Sedgefield. Had he opted for Sedgefield, there would have been no problems in accommodating all the sitting County Members. Alternatively, as he was then already sixty-eight years of age, he could have retired with honour and would almost certainly have gone to the House of Lords, thereby fulfilling another long-term ambition. But, during office as a deputy Speaker, he had acquired an ambition to move up to become the Chairman of Ways and Means, who ranks second to the Speaker and who, given the right circumstances, has a good prospect of going on to become Speaker. The Chairmanship of Ways and Means was to become vacant after the general election and in the North East, inspired rumours began to circulate that he could become "County Durham's first Speaker." There were two additional, relevant, circumstances in the situation. Nothing of course, is ever certain in politics but the first circumstance was that it was not beyond the bounds of possibility that had I been in Parliament after the election, I might myself have become Chairman of Ways and Means. The second circumstance was that Armstrong's daughter, Hilary, had parliamentary ambitions and was expressing a strong interest in the candidature in the new Sedgefield Division. If I were to be eliminated from Parliament, Armstrong might well become Chairman of Ways and Means and have his daughter in the House. He calculated correctly that he could outvote me in Durham North West and he knew, as I and everyone else knew, that in the only alternative available to me, in Durham North, I would be heavily outvoted by Giles Radice, Member for the Chester le Street Division which, like Consett, was to be extinguished.

In the spring of 1983, these matters were heavily exercising the minds of the MP's and constituency Labour Party activists who were involved. Publicly, Armstrong equivocated about his intentions to the last possible minute and he absented himself when meetings of the Co. Durham MP's were called to try to resolve the situation. The selection conference for the Durham North West candidature was held on Saturday, 7 May at Tow Law which,at a little over a thousand feet above sea level and exposed to the elements on every side, is one of the coldest and bleakest towns in all England, made temporarily famous in earlier years for having a "giant-killing" football team. Armstrong was selected. Afterwards, one of the prominent members of the old Consett Constituency Labour Party, who had become an officer of the new CLP, who had not always seen eye to eye with me but who had supported me, remarked (not to me) that "David was the better man on the day." It did not, of course, make the slightest difference. As one of my women supporters said immediately after the meeting "Whatever you said or did made no difference, the meeting might just as well never have been held, the result was decided before it took place." That was of course exactly the situation. Armstrong, as he had calculated he could, had been able to have a majority there who would vote for him regardless.

Short of surrendering to the situation. there was no choice except to proceed to oppose Giles Radice in Durham North. The selection conference was held one week later in Pelton, in the climatically more hospitable lowlands of the county. The meeting was a much larger one than at Tow Law, packed of course with Giles's supporters. I opened by expressing my regrets that Armstrong's conduct should have made the contest necessary at all and went on to make substantially the same speech that I had made at Tow Law. If I say so myself. I made one of the best speeches of my life and handled all the questions well. "Tremendous performance!" remarked the Deputy Regional Organizer of the Labour Party to me as we mounted the platform for the announcement of the result after the ballot. Giles himself told me that his own supporters had told him that I had outclassed him. Of course, that made no difference to the outcome, but Armstrong would never have made such a gracious concession. One factor which helped to improve my "performance" was that I was relaxed in the knowledge that, whatever the quality of my speech, it would not affect the result. Seventeen years earlier, when I had appeared before the Consett selection conference as a stranger and an outsider, I had also made one of the best speeches of my life, then also relaxed through believing that I had no real chance. On that occasion, against all the odds, I had carried the day triumphantly. There is some irony in that the first and last speeches I made to active Labour Party members in the North East were, for similar reasons, among my best although with opposite results.

When the Tow Law result had been decided, moves were initiated for a fall-back position to nominate me for the Sedgefield candidature. After the meeting at Pelton, this was activated immediately and I was nominated by the appropriate District Committee of my trade union, the AEU. I arrived back in the North East on 19 May for the selection conference, to discover on arrival that I had not been short listed. Hilary Armstrong was not short listed either. The constituency party selected Tony Blair, a very able young barrister who quickly went on to make a strong impact in the House. I returned to London and within days, went to the House of Commons to clear my desk, terminate the employment of my secretary and my research assistant and remove my possessions. My feelings were to sever all association with the place as quickly as possible and never to go there again. Over the years, I had witnessed how some former MP's seemed unable to disassociate themselves from Parliament and were regularly to be seen rather pathetically hanging about the place. Whatever the future might hold - and at that time it was very uncertain - I was absolutely determined not to become like them. Subsequently, my job as Director of CAABU regularly took me there but it was a full two years before I was able to enter the building without feelings of extreme distaste, made the more difficult by the warm greetings which I always received from former colleagues - and by no means only in my own party.

Armstrong's conduct did him little good. In the 1983 election, many of the marvellous band of Labour and trade union activists who had always worked so hard for me, refused to work for him, a number went to work for other candidates in other constituencies. There was also a strong reaction among the general public. I received many expressions of support and many Labour supporters abstained from voting, although I urged them not to do so. It was of course a disastrous election for Labour anyway but even so, he only held what should have been a strong seat on a minority vote in a three-cornered contest with an embarrassingly small majority. A comment on his standing in the area which sticks in my mind was made some two years later by a retired Consett steel worker whom I knew well and with whom I kept in touch until his death in 1988. He was Matt Connor, a widely known figure in the British Legion, a down-to-earth, common-sense, unassuming man who sought no personal glory or public recognition but who quietly did an immense amount for the disabled and disadvantaged and for the community in general, and who had often sought my advice and help. "Since you left" he said, "Consett has been represented by a silent and invisible MP."

There was a furious reaction against Armstrong in the Parliamentary Labour Party, where it was made absolutely clear to the leadership that he would not be tolerated as Chairman of Ways and Means. On 24 June, *The Guardian*, in an article headed "Surprise over deputy speaker," carried a photograph captioned

"Ernest Armstrong: not popular with colleagues." The report stated that he had been understood to be "in line" for the post of Chairman of Ways and Means but that Labour Whips had told Michael Foot (then in his last weeks as Labour Party Leader) that "Mr Armstrong was not popular." The post went to Harold Walker, who was an old AEU friend. Harold had been Member for Doncaster since 1964 and we had known each other, through the union, since well before either of us were MP's. He was more or less literally dragged from his dinner one evening by Michael Cocks, the Chief Whip, and told that he had to make an immediate decision to accept nomination as Chairman of Ways and Means. Michael Cocks, Member for Bristol South 1970-87,( later Lord Cocks of Hartcliffe), was another old friend from my earlier days in Bristol and, indeed, in 1983, I was still a registered elector in Bristol and retaining my Labour Party membership in his Constituency Labour Party, which I had joined in 1950.

Ernest Armstrong was reappointed as a Deputy Speaker junior to Harold Walker. who had no previous experience of chairmanship in the House. If I had been demeaned in such a way, I would not have accepted the lesser position, but that was one of the differences in our respective approaches. He retired at the next election and was succeeded by his daughter, who was selected for the candidature by a single vote. The AEU nominated David Clelland, Leader of Gateshead Council. By so narrowly missing the candidature, he actually arrived in Parliament earlier, subsequently being selected as candidate and elected at the Tyne Bridge by-election on the death of the sitting Member, Harry Cowans, in 1985.

## 2

# A WEEK IN POLITICS

A substantial part of this book is comprised of articles, papers and speeches I produced on Middle East issues during my time as Director of CAABU, but the first article is from the earlier period when I was in Parliament and its purpose is to indicate how different a life I then led. The original was written in December 1977 and published in *Voice of the Arab World* in February 1978 as one in a series of diary features called *One Man's Week*. The original was edited and slightly shortened by *Voice*, while in this version the original is edited and slightly lengthened! It is not an absolutely literal account of the particular week it refers to but it is an accurate indication of how I was then occupied. It was before I was appointed a Member of the Commons Chairmen's Panel. The article now needs to be set against the backdrop of the situation and events at the time it was written.

There was a Labour government in office and James Callaghan was Prime Minister. Menachem Begin had not long since become Prime Minister of Israel and was visiting Britain. Anwar Sadat was President of Egypt and had just made his famous visit to Jerusalem. Jimmy Carter was President of the United States. The events leading to Camp David and the Egyptian-Israeli peace treaty were still in the future. Said Hammami was the outstanding first representative in London of the Palestine Liberation Organization. In January 1978, between the writing of my article and its publication, he was murdered in his office by the Abu Nidal group. The meeting he addressed, referred to in the article, was the last time I saw him, I recall that he gave a vivid address on the PLO's reaction to Sadat's policy.

## ONE MAN'S WEEK

*** *Monday***

Drive from my home in Richmond to the House of Commons. I would prefer to travel by the Underground but there is no alternative to driving because it is often after midnight when Parliament finishes work and there is then no public transport to get home. London in December, cloudy and cold, although not so cold as my constituency, which I have visited at the weekend and which, nearly three hundred miles (four hundred and eighty kilometres) north of London and on high ground, endures long winters with severe frosts and snowfalls. I have held my regular interview session for constituents during the weekend and today's first task is to represent to Ministers and officials the cases which have been brought to me. As usual, there is also a heavy post bag. Dictate many letters and give a great deal of work to my secretary, Fiona MacDonald. This is the time of Menachem Begin's visit to London and the post includes abusive Zionist letters because I have stated publicly that his record as a war criminal makes his visit unwelcome to many people in Britain. The post also includes letters of support, including one from a survivor of the atrocity which Begin masterminded in 1946 at the King David Hotel in Jerusalem.

In the evening, there is a meeting organized by CAABU on the theme "A Homeland for the Palestinians: Britain's Message to Begin. " Excellent speeches from Christopher Mayhew and Dr. Mohammed Mehdi, both founder members of CAABU, Sir Anthony Nutting, who resigned as Minister of State at the Foreign Office and gave up a potentially brilliant political career over Suez in 1956 and was another founder member of CAABU, and from John Reddaway the Director of CAABU. The main business in the House is an important emergency debate on alleged corruption in Crown Agents, who handle a great deal of worldwide business on behalf of the British government and, in the middle of the CAABU meeting, the Members of Parliament present have to leave to vote in a division - a common occurrence.

*** *Tuesday***

Accept telephoned invitation from BBC radio to record, on Thursday, a discussion with a Conservative and a Liberal MP for the world service, on the controversial bill currently before Parliament on direct elections to the Assembly of the European Economic Community. Tyne Tees Television, who broadcast in the Northern Region of England where my constituency is situated, telephone to invite me to take part with a Conservative MP in their weekly current affairs discussion on Friday. Regretfully have to decline because of other commitments. Tyne Tees are good on these sort of programmes and they once made a programme on the Middle East, in which I debated with three other MP's, all more or less hostile.

For this parliamentary session, I am chairman of the English Northern Regional Group of Labour Members of Parliament and our regular fortnightly meeting is this afternoon. After chairing it, I go straight on to chair the annual general meeting of the Labour Middle East Council (LMEC). A well-attended meeting reviews the past year's work, takes a ballot vote to elect a new executive committee which, in turn, will elect the officers at its first meeting, and takes an important policy decision to encourage the setting up of comparable organizations in the Socialist parties in other European countries. Membership of LMEC is open to all individual members of the Labour Party who accept the aims and objects. There is a good attendance from among the fifty MP's who are members and many of the others present are influential figures - councillors, trade union officers, church people and so on. We end with a characteristically well-informed and incisive address from Said Hammami, the London representative of the PLO.

*** Wednesday**

Wet, foggy and miserable. As I drive over Westminster Bridge, the Houses of Parliament look like one of Monet's impressionist paintings. Such a busy day that I do not get into the debating chamber until late evening, even though it is Foreign Office question time, at which I am normally a regular and active attender.

Start by visiting, with other Labour Members, the headquarters of the British Insurance Association, where we have a lively discussion which continues through a working lunch. I have been interested in the worldwide British insurance industry since I piloted my own first piece of legislation through Parliament, my Private Member's Bill which became the Employer's Liability (Compulsory

Insurance) Act 1969. Back to Parliament and straight to chairing a two hours meeting between the Northern Group of Labour MP's and the chiefs of the Northumbrian Water Authority, who are responsible for water supply and conservation in our region. From that, I go straight to an all party meeting of MP's to reconstitute the British-Libyan Parliamentary Group. Am elected chairman and, while appreciating the honour of this further expression of confidence from colleagues, begin to hope that I shall not come to resemble the character in the Gilbert and Sullivan opera who was chairman of practically everything, Next, comes a briefing from my research assistance, Christopher Inman, in readiness for the next engagement, which is a meeting of concerned persons about Liddle Towers, a man from a constituency adjoining mine, who died as a result of injuries received while he was in police custody. Go there, as chairman of the Northern Group, to support my parliamentary colleague who represents the constituency and who is pressing for a public inquiry.(1)

Throughout the eight and half hours that I have been involved in this series of engagements, urgent messages have been arriving from my constituency, from government departments and elsewhere. My secretary has been handling them as far as possible but now I have to deal with those which require immediate, personal attention. Without the marvelllous support of my secretary and my research assistant, of June Ward, the executive secretary of LMEC and of Eddie Wigham, the Labour Party agent in my constituency, I could not possibly cope with the volume of work.

**** Thursday***

The Prime Minister announces a Public Inquiry into the Crown Agents scandal which was debated on Monday. Note an article in *The Times* newspaper complaining that few MP's were in the debating chamber for yesterday's proceedings on the Scottish Devolution Bill. Wonder if the writer put in as hard a day's work as I did.(2)

Walk, as I always do if time and distance permit, to the studios to

---

(1) This was a famous civil liberties case. The constituency was Chester le Street and the MP was Giles Radice. The case has never been satisfactorily resolved.

(2) The Scottish Devolution Bill occupied a vast amount of time and was ultimately abortive.

record the BBC World Service interview about which they telephoned on Tuesday, then return for a brief visit to a pre-Christmas party organized by Members' secretaries and House of Commons staff. Members of Parliament, including Cabinet Ministers and Opposition Shadow Ministers, mix informally with secretaries and staff at this pleasant annual event. Have to leave early to attend the weekly meeting of the Parliamentary Labour Party and then go on to the first meeting of the newly formed London Committee for Democratic Government, where we discuss possible courses of action to encourage democratic government in Pakistan. Recall that, last week, a reporter telephoned me about this new committee and that I detected the usual tendency of the British media to belittle rather than to report factually.

Reflect that there are so many definitions of democracy. My own view is that no one has ever bettered Abraham Lincoln's immortal "government of the people, by the people, for the people" although, in the seemingly more complicated world of the late twentieth century, there are conflicting definitions both of "democracy" and of "people". Slip into the chamber, intermittently, to follow the debate, which is on the complex difficulties of Northern Ireland. Enjoy a late dinner in the Members' dining room with a fellow Labour Member who shares my views on the Middle East and a Cabinet Minister who does not. Leave the House at about eleven o'clock for King's Cross Station, to take the sleeping car train to Newcastle Upon Tyne.

***** *Friday***

When I leave the train at half-past seven in the morning, it is still some time before daylight but Newcastle, northernmost of the big industrial cities in England and capital of the northern region, is teeming with life, with thousands of people on their way to work or on their way home after having worked through the night. I have hardly slept at all but revive over an excellent if expensive breakfast in the British Railways hotel which is part of the station. After breakfast, meet a representative of one of the local radio stations and record an interview on current regional affairs, then walk the short distance to another leading hotel for the main business that has brought me from London. This is a meeting between the Northern Group of Labour MP's and members of the Northern Regional Council of the Confederation of British Industry. Although representatives of nationalized industries are present, most of these men are capitalists and proud of it and, with deep differences between us, there are what are usually described as "frank exchanges" but it is all courteous and good humoured and valuable to both groups.

Return to the south on one of British Rail's most famous inter-city expresses, "The Aberdonian" which, at its Newcastle stop, has already covered about a half of its long, high-speed run to London from Aberdeen, Britain's oil capital on the north east coast of Scotland. Get home at about seven in the evening and watch television, the first opportunity of the week to do so, but nature catches up on me and I fall asleep in front of the television set.

*** *Saturday***

Drive to Northampton, a nerve racking hour and a half on the crowded M1 motorway, for a meeting of the trustees, of whom I am one, of Industrial Common Ownership Finance Ltd. (ICOF). Common ownership, or as they are also known, self managed enterprises, are co-operatives which are democratically owned and controlled by the people who work in them. My second piece of Private Member's legislation was the Industrial Common Ownership Act 1976, an important measure to encourage this type of development. ICOF is recognized by the government as an agency to administer the modest loan fund provided by the Act for financing developments. There are now over fifty such enterprises in Britain and their numbers are increasing, a small but vital sector in the economy, pointing the way to replace Britain's dying capitalist system.(3) At the meeting, we have many applications for loans to consider and difficult decisions to take. We also devote much time to proposals to reconstitute ICOF itself to meet its growing responsibilities and the meeting lasts, with an hour for lunch, from ten-thirty in the morning until five-thirty in the afternoon. Common ownership and the Middle East are my two great passions in politics. I have a dream that they will come together when the new Palestine is established, in that at the centre of its system of economic organization, Palestine will have this democratic system for the ownership and control of its industries by its people.

---

(3) By the end of the 1980's, there were well over one thousand such co-operatives.

### *** Sunday**

The one day of the week free for relaxation, something absolutely essential after a week at such pressure. Get up early and go to the local baths as soon as they are open for a long swim before the pool gets too crowded, then home for breakfast and a leisurely morning reading newspapers and listening to music. I enjoy listening to music and have a collection of records ranging from the contemporary masters of jazz to the classics. If I have a favourite composer, it is Beethoven, whose enormous genius I find truly awe-inspiring, the more so in the knowledge that for much of his life he was totally deaf, which did not prevent him from composing some of the greatest music ever composed by anybody.

Later, turn on the television for the early evening news and am profoundly shocked to hear that David Holden of the *Sunday Times*, an outstanding journalist and authority on the Middle East, has been found murdered in Cairo. The last time we met was two months ago, in October, at a conference on the Middle East at Ditchley Park in Oxfordshire. Now, he is yet another victim of the Middle East and the last time I ever saw him is a poignant memory. It was on the lovely autumn afternoon when we were both leaving at the end of the conference and we exchanged friendly farewell waves across the car park. Sadly turn off the television and put the finishing touches to this article which I have been jotting down on odd scraps of paper throughout the week.

# 3

## COMMONERS AND LORDS

There are certain days when everything seems to happen at once and Thursday, 16 June 1983 was such a day. The executive committee of CAABU, of which I was then one of the two joint chairmen, were meeting at 11.00 a.m. I deliberately absented myself because they were to discuss the vacant directorship and it was as near as anything ever can be to certainty that they would invite me to accept it. Before 9.30, events seemed set to be important but predictable. By midday, I felt irresistibly reminded of the opening words of Georges Simenon's novel *The Man from London*, of which a very free translation is "At the time, these seem to be hours like any others but, afterwards, they can be seen to have been quite exceptional". To go from the excellent to the lesser, I can also perceive in retrospect an element of one of Jeffrey Archer's awful novels in which Members of Parliament spend a lot of time beside the telephone, waiting for calls to announce their appointment to the high office which is depicted as their sole motivation for entering politics.

The telephone first rang at about half-past nine. I was surprised to hear "This is General Shazly speaking from Algeria." Saad El-Shazly was the Egyptian Chief of Staff who masterminded the crossing of the Suez Canal in the 1973 war in the Middle East. The purpose of the war was a limited one, to try to force international action through the United Nations to resolve the Palestinian situation, but the brilliant initial success went to President Sadat's head and he thought that he could go on to defeat the Israeli army. There was never any prospect of that, as the General Staff strongly and repeatedly advised him. The result of his foolishness was much unnecessary loss of life and a near defeat. Relations between him and Shazly became very strained and in 1974, Shazly was appointed as Egyptian Ambassador to Britain, largely to get him out of Cairo, where he was a popular and respected figure whom Sadat saw as a threat to himself. Shazly devoted himself to his new diplomatic post with great ability, he was the first really effective Egyptian Ambassador in London. His stay though was all too short and in 1975, following a military takeover in Portugal, he was made Ambassador to that country, possibly on the basis that a general was thought to be needed to talk to colonels. In 1978, he was dismissed after publicly criticizing Sadat over his Camp David policy and he subsequently went to live in Algiers. I had not had contact with him since he left London in 1975.. He now asked me if I had read his book - *The Crossing of Suez, the October War (1973)* (Third World Centre, London, 1980). I had not and, without explaining, he indicated that "one of his men" would get a copy to me that day. Something was obviously afoot of which I ought to have known more.

Within twenty minutes, another phone call came from a Mr El-Shahat, speaking from an address in London. He was obviously "the general's man" whom the general must have telephoned immediately after speaking to me. He said that he would like to make arrangements to get the book to me that day. At 6.30 that evening, I was due to chair a meeting of CAABU members and their guests in one of the smaller rooms at Central Hall, Westminster and we agreed that Mr El-Shahat would meet me there and hand over the book. I gathered that there was a move in Egypt to bring General Shazly to trial over the contents of the book and that I could help his defence with a statement in his support. At that stage though I was still rather vague about the whole thing.

At 11.15, the telephone rang again and that call really staggered me. It was (Sir) Tom McCaffery from Michael Foot's office at the House of Commons, to say that Michael was anxious to put my name forward in the Dissolution Honours List and would I accept. This was totally unexpected but my instinctive reaction was that I would not accept. Confused, and thinking stupidly on the lines of an MBE or some other equally pointless bauble. I asked what Michael had in mind. "A life peerage" said Tom. That took away the last breath of such wind as was still left in my sails. I have always been against the House of Lords and, already, in answering two friends, Jack Taylor a business acquaintance and Jack Hill a Labour Party colleague, who had inquired as to my reactions if such an offer were to be made, I had said that an offer was extremely unlikely and that I would refuse it in any case. I stated my views about the Lords to Tom McCaffery. "It would bring you back" he replied. "I know that" I said and, the politician in me coming out, I added, more desperate to play for time than anything else, "Rather than think aloud, could I call you back either later today or tomorrow morning?" He replied that it was essential for him to know by the next day at the latest.

Very few things have thrown me so completely as that telephone call. I was too agitated to think straight, quite literally, I started pacing up and down in my flat, something I had never done before, trying to sort out a mind that had suddenly been put in turmoil. I had to talk to somebody. After about half an hour, I tried to call my former secretary, Fiona MacDonald, at the House of Commons. She was not at her desk and the recorded answering service gave me the number at which a message could be left. At that number, nobody answered. I shudder to think what people with urgent messages for MP's, Ministers and Officials of the House must think of such infuriating incompetence at such a level.

At 12.15 a.m, I was still in turmoil when the phone rang again. It was Douglas Collard at CAABU, to tell me that the executive committee, by a unanimous decision, had decided to invite me to accept the directorship. I said that I would of course accept. I told him about the call from Parliament and he promptly showered me with congratulations. I said that I wanted to talk with Anthony Nutting, then one of the two vice-chairmen of CAABU, who had been my staunchest advocates for the post. Douglas told me that Anthony would call me back from the more private telephone in his (Douglas') flat in the Arab-British Centre. The instant I put down the phone, it rang again. It was Paul Flowers, a Methodist Minister who was a longstanding member of the CAABU executive committee and also of the executive of the Labour Middle East Council (LMEC) of which I was then still chairman. Like Douglas Collard and Anthony Nutting, Paul had been working to support my appointment to the directorship. He was ringing to offer his congratulations because, he told me, the executive committee had appointed me with enthusiasm. I just had to tell him about the offer from Michael Foot. He had no doubt - I should accept. Anthony Nutting came through immediately I put the phone down. Douglas had already told him my news and he was clearly, genuinely delighted, as much about that as about my appointment to the CAABU directorship. So far as he was concerned, any idea that I might not want a peerage simply had to be dismissed. He stressed that it would not be incompatible with the directorship (a matter which had been exercising my mind considerably) and he made the point that it would give me an important platform for speeches about the Middle East.

I have always found that, in the midst of momentous events, more mundane things continue to happen with an awesome inevitability. Within minutes, Mr John Barrett, a senior executive with the Equitable Life Assurance Society, telephoned about a private pension to supplement my frozen and of course reduced through my premature departure, although index-linked, parliamentary pension. I had talked about such a pension with Fiona and she had been in touch with him, he being the representative with whom we had negotiated her own pension in conjunction with the parliamentary fees office. He had one particular and very understandable anxiety, which he sought to express as diplomatically as possible. "Will you be taking up any consultancy work?" he asked, a shade diffidently. "I can assure you" I told him "that I shall have an income from which to pay the premiums" and we arranged an appointment to discuss arrangements.

Fiona telephoned at about two o'clock to find out the news from CAABU. I told her that I was appointed and also about the call from Tom McCaffery. Knowing my views on the House of Lords, the peerage and the Establishment in general, she simply dissolved into helpless laughter. It was a great relief, I joined in. "Henceforth, my future is with the Establishment" I said. "You said that last night" she retorted. It was true, I had said it at a Wine Society Dining Club dinner where she, Paul Flowers and Chris Inman, my former research assistant, had been my guests. It had been, as always, a dinner jacket affair and we had been joking about that over aperitifs. Fiona had drawn attention to my normal reluctance to wear a dinner suit and had alleged that, now, "you couldn't keep me out of one" to which I had replied with the Establishment crack although, in honesty, it was not the first time I had used it. Fiona had no doubts, I must accept the offer of a life peerage and must call back to Tom McCaffery as soon as possible to say so.

I telephoned Tom at 2.45 and said that I would accept my name going on the list, as well as to say again how unexpected it had been and that I wanted my warmest thanks conveyed to Michael Foot for thinking of me. Of the three Labour Party leaders I served under in my seventeen years in the Commons, he was the only one who ever did. Tom then told me about and we discussed what was in the event to prove a celebrated row over the 1983 Dissolution Honours List. Labour is very much under represented in the Lords and whatever views one takes about its existence, so long as it does exist, it is necessary to have representation there. Therefore, it was proposed to submit a list of twenty five or so names but it was known that Margaret Thatcher, the Prime Minister, who ultimately controlled the situation, would be predictably against any effective Labour representation in the Lords and she would refuse to accept any except a very limited list. It was proposed to make an issue of this and it would be a number of weeks before the matter would be resolved. It was a relief, I was happy for my name to be placed well down the list, among likely refusals.

The CAABU meeting I was to chair at Central Hall, Westminster was at 6.30 p.m. I arrived about ten minutes early, to find Mr El-Shahat talking to Michael Adams. He had copies of General Shazly's book for Michael and myself and Michael had presumably been approached in the same way. It transpired that the General was being charged with revealing Egyptian military secrets in his book. It was a ludicrous allegation. It was getting on for ten years since the war, four years after the signing of the Egyptian-Israeli treaty and it was three years after the book had been published. Saad El-Shazly was seeking references from friends and had stated that, provided the trial was a properly conducted one in open court, he would return from exile to answer the charges. I promised Mr El-Shahat that I would let him have a statement by the following Monday, as he requested. I was going to Bristol the following day, Friday, to spend the weekend with my aged father and stepmother but I would be able to get the statement in the post from there by Saturday midday.

Before the CAABU meeting started I had a brief talk with Cyril Townsend MP, my joint chairman. He had chaired the executive committee and had tried to telephone me but with my phone so constantly engaged, he had been unable to make contact. He kindly invited me to lunch at his flat, the following Tuesday, to talk about the directorship and about appointing a successor to me as joint chairman. I had not intended to say anything to him about the offer of a life peerage but suddenly found myself blurting it out. He was clearly surprised and somewhat at a loss to comment. I knew though that I could rely absolutely on his discretion. For all our basic political differences, I held - and hold - Cyril in high regard. Subsequently, he remained senior joint chairman throughout my seven years as director and ours was at all times a warm and fruitful relationship.

The meeting went well. The speaker was Peter Mansfield, the internationally renowned writer and authority on the Arab World and a vice chairman of CAABU. In 1956, like Anthony Nutting, he had resigned over Suez, in his case from the Foreign Service, giving up a potentially brilliant diplomatic career on an issue of principle. As expected, he gave the meeting a superbly factual and well delivered address on the current Middle East situation, under the title "Syria - the Scapegoat?" There was a good audience of about ninety people and a very good discussion. Michael Adams took me by surprise with a warm tribute to my former service in Parliament, which evoked loud and prolonged applause (which was not my reason for thinking well of the discussion). There was a lump in my throat but I think I managed to disguise it in responding.

From the meeting, I went to the Lansdowne Club to have dinner with Jack and Freda Taylor. Jack Taylor was a businessman from Darlington, whom I had first met in the late nineteen sixties, during my early years in Parliament, when he was manager of a then major engineering plant. At that time, I was actively involved with industrial health and safety, he was a leading figure in the subject in the North East and had asked me, a couple of times, to address meetings. Subsequently, he left engineering and founded his own company in the business of labour recruitment and executive search. In 1981, he reconstituted the company and invited me to join the board, of which I remained a member until 1987. When I had gone to the North East to discover that I was not short listed for the Sedgefield candidature, I had stayed with Jack and Freda, their hospitality and kindness during traumatic and bitter days is something I shall always remember. Our dinner at the Lansdowne Club was to discuss company business. I told them of the confirmation of my appointment as Director of CAABU and hinted at a possible life peerage, something which we had previously talked about in an abstract and light hearted way. They reacted strongly in favour, Jack remarked that it was "good to see me smiling again." I was aware of experiencing a reaction I had known before - a sudden feeling of exhilaration after a period of great tension and anxiety. I got home at about 11.30 and went to bed at once, taking General Shazly's book with me. After about thirty or forty minutes, I was too tired to go on reading but had scanned sufficient to have in mind an outline of a statement in his support. It seemed an appropriate way to end as eventful a day as any I have known.

The treatment of General Saad El-Shazly remains a sordid episode in modern Egyptian history. Two years before this particular development, he and eighteen others had been "tried" in their absence by a secret court which deprived them of their civil rights and confiscated all their possessions in Egypt. Their offence was that they had organized the Egyptian National Front to oppose President Sadat because of his treaty with Israel. In the new trial, he, who had fought for Egypt with great distinction in five wars, was accused of treason in that he had revealed Egyptian military secrets in his book. The Egyptian government did not inform him that he was to be tried or what the charges were against him. No lawyer of his choice was allowed to represent him, see any evidence or even attend the trial. The court appointed its own lawyer to represent him but he was someone who had never met Shazly and whose knowledge of the case was restricted to reading the papers prepared by the prosecution. When Shazly, who had been deprived of his citizenship, applied to go to Cairo to face the charges in person, he was not allowed to enter the country ,[(4)] hence his request to myself, among others, for statements in his support. I have never bothered to check up on the outcome of this travesty but it was an honour to respond to the request from such a distinguished friend who could have become a distinguished President of Egypt - which was, of course, why he was treated as he was by lesser but more powerful figures.

The statement obviously had to be as diplomatic as possible and, in opening, I made the point that I had no desire to intervene in internal controversy in a friendly country but felt that I must express a personal testimony in support of the General. He had come to London in 1974, when I first met him, with the justified reputation of one of the greatest soldiers in the Arab World. He had quickly proved also to be an outstanding diplomat who had brought to the

---

(4) Reports, Kuwait News Agency (KUNA), July 1983.

Egyptian representation in London a forcefulness and standing which it had not known previously and he had laid the firm foundation upon which no less able successors had been able to build.[5] With reference to the alleged betrayal of military secrets. I drew attention to the lapse of time between the war and the publication of the book, which had in any case come out after the signing of a peace treaty with the enemy country, while much of what the book described had appeared in the world press, where the war had been the subject of detailed examination years before the book was written.

I pointed out that in military history, the book was a work of importance and also in its discussion of relationships between soldiers and politicians. These were almost always difficult, in all countries, in war and in peace and any book which discussed them , as this one did, was to be welcomed as an important contribution to the art of government. (This was a delicate point but since it was the heart of the matter, it could scarcely be avoided). Finally, I made the point that to make any sort of scapegoat of one of Egypt's greatest soldiers, who also became one of its most effective diplomats, would reflect discredit on Egypt whereas, if he could be welcomed back, that would reflect great credit on the country, on its government, institutions and people. I signed the statement as "Member of Parliament 1966-83; Chairman, the Labour Middle East Council; Director-Designate, CAABU." It was perhaps only a gesture but it was a gesture that had to be made.

Meanwhile, the matter of the life peerage trundled along its pre-ordained course and, in idle moments, I even toyed with possible titles. My former parliamentary colleague, Tudor Watkins, was already there and called "Lord Watkins" so I would have to look for an alternative. I looked through the cast of Gilbert and Sullivan's *Iolanthe* to see if it contained anything I could use but had to conclude that it would probably be preferable not to be "Lord Tolloller" or "Lord Mountararat." I was initially disinclined to take any title associated with Consett or district because it would almost certainly result in letters from people there putting their complaints as if I were still their MP. I did think about "Lord Bedminster," partly because it sounds slightly silly to people who do not know Bristol, but more so because Bedminster is the

---

(5) This was not mere diplomatic talk. Shazly was followed by a succession of able and effective Ambassadors

working class district where I was born. The populous, nineteenth century Bedminster was built around long since closed coal mines, in one of which my father worked for a time after the first world war. It was my vividly recalled, boyhood recollections of seeing disabled ex-servicemen of the first world war begging in the streets of Bedminster in the 1930's that first made me a Socialist.

During a weekend in Bristol, I looked up Bill and Eileen Copestake, who are literally my very oldest Labour Party friends. In 1950, they were near neighbours when I was not long back from national service in the RAF and still living with my parents, and Bill and Eileen were active and locally well known in the Labour Party. It was on their door that I went and knocked to apply to join the party and Bill was later my election agent when I was a candidate for the City Council. Bill's real name is Herbert Stanley and he an example among others I have come across of persons who, for reasons which I have never been able to fathom, are known by first names other than their real ones. Another case in point was my regular pair when I was in Parliament, Jerry Wiggin, the Member for Weston Super Mare, whose real first names are Alfred William. When I mentioned the possibility of a life peerage to Bill and Eileen, they, as I hoped they would, dissolved into laughter, Bill suggested as a title "Lord Watkins of the Malago" and it held some attractions. The Malago is a small stream which flows through Bedminster, where it use regularly to cause flooding before the construction of the storm water system which was one of the major projects undertaken by the City Council in the 1950's, at the time when I was a member of the council. Cotswold Road, where I was born, overlooks the Malago just before it disappears into culverts and the stream also flows close to the former Beasley French engineering factory where I was working until I entered Parliament. The little river seemed to have quite a lot going for it for possible ennoblement..

A couple of weeks later, however, I began to revise ideas about a possible title, at the suggestion of two other very dear friends, Eddie and Betty Wigham. Eddie was the secretary of the Consett Constituency Labour Party throughout the period when I was the MP and he was my election agent in all the five elections I contested there. During July 1983, Eddie and Betty came to stay overnight with me in the course of visiting their son Peter, an officer in the Metropolitan Police Force and his wife Sandra, whose son had just been born, Eddie and Betty's first grandchild. It was the first time I had seen Eddie and Betty since the days preceding the election and I told them for the first time about the proposal to include me in the Dissolution Honours List. Like so many whose opinions I valued, they were amused, although not so hilariously as Fiona MacDonald or Bill and Eileen Copestake. We discussed possible titles and they were firmly of the opinion that I ought to take something connected with the North East and, notwithstanding my earlier reservations about that, I could see the sense, especially since, as Eddie pointed out, many staunch Labour friends in the north would be disappointed if I did otherwise.

Eddie died of cancer in October 1989. He was a sportsman who was both physically and mentally active all his life and he neither smoked nor drank. His sadly premature death confirms my personal conviction that there is no such thing as 'natural justice' in the course of nature. There is even less so in the course of human affairs, where all justice and all injustice is created by human beings. When I first met Eddie, he was a fitter in the colliery at Craghead, Co. Durham. With the closure of, eventually, all the local pits, he went into engineering in other fields and finally into social service in which. at the time of his death. he was deputy warden of an old people's home. He was a deeply caring person who was widely and rightly respected. At his funeral service, the Methodist Church in Lanchester, Co. Durham, including the vestry, was packed to capacity and a large congregation who could not be accommodated stood in tribute outside. One of the most moving tributes of all was that by a large contingent from the old people's home where he worked, who insisted on being present and many of whom were so frail and infirm that they had to be assisted into the church.

By the time of Eddie and Betty's visit to me in July 1983, the whole question of the life peerage was becoming increasingly academic. For several weeks there had been, exactly as Tom McCaffery had anticipated in that first telephone call, a major public row over Michael Foot's list, which contained twenty-seven names. Margaret Thatcher had refused absolutely to accept more that a handful. The saga finally ended on Wednesday, 20 July, when I received a letter from Michael indicating that my name could not go forward because of Thatcher's restrictions. It was not unexpected and my feelings were more of relief than anything else. Had I been on the final list, I was committed to accept and it was a relief not to be included because I had begun to feel increasingly that I had accepted against my better judgement. The list was finally made public on 22 July and I gained some amusement from the snide comments in *The Times* and *The Guardian*. The latter stated that Michael had "demonstrated political compassion ... those chosen are clearly men whose careers would have been greatly at risk outside Parliament." I had a pretty shrewd idea which ones were meant. Hardly Harold Wilson, who had retired from the Commons and who headed the list, but "no names, no pack drill".

## 4

# DISASTER IN LEBANON

Events in the Middle East in mid 1983 were in a state of escalating tension. The Israelis, with American backing, were in occupation of a large part of Lebanon, following their invasion of 1982. The then American President had put forward the "Reagan Plan" in September 1982, which had included an adumbrated form of Palestinian self-government - the most fundamental issue of the whole Arab-Israeli conflict - in association with Jordan. The then Israeli Prime Minister, Menachem Begin, the former and unrepentant Irgun Zvai Leumi terrorist with a record as a war criminal in Palestine in the 1940's as well as in Lebanon in the 1980's, had instantly rejected the Reagan Plan. Then had come the massacre of hundreds of Palestinian men, women and children in the refugee camps at Sabra and Shatilla, by the pro-Israeli Lebanese Phalange, with the open connivance of the Israeli army.

Those events of 1982 had injured Israeli-American relations but the Israelis, with their powerful lobby in the USA working flat out in their support, were already moving effectively to retrieve the situation. One consequence of their moves was that on 17 May 1983, the USA had manoeuvred Amin Gemayel, the President of Lebanon, into a preposterous and unworkable agreement with Israel for the withdrawal of foreign forces from his country. The Israelis, having signed, then refused to withdraw, even conditionally, unless Syria also withdrew unconditionally. The Israeli view of the agreement was that it was a follow up of the earlier ceasefire, of which their interpretation was that the other side should stop fighting while they continued their advance into more and more territory. Not surprisingly, the Syrians refused to withdraw from Lebanon on such grotesque terms. They had already been deceived over the original ceasefire and they had not been a party to the 17 May "agreement." They had not been consulted, they had originally been invited into Lebanon by an earlier Lebanese government and they could see signs of an impending Israeli attack against their own territory.

There was a collective sense of Arab shame because they had proved so incapable of doing anything in the face of the Israeli invasion of Lebanon. Syria, the only country which had resisted the Israelis, was, together with Libya, actively fomenting opposition to Yasser Arafat and the PLO. The PLO had been tricked by the Americans into evacuating Beirut and allowing themselves to be dispersed around the Arab World, and Syrian contempt for the PLO leadership over that gave birth to the mid-1980's Syrian attempt to create a Syrian controlled alternative to the PLO. The Reagan administration in the USA regarded the Middle East as a major sector in the front line of its strategy of global confrontation with the USSR and, in pursuance of its strategy, was trying to pressure the Arabs in general and the Syrians in particular to give the Israelis the free hand they wanted to control the whole region, control which was thought to be in America's interest. Because Syria was not amenable to pressure and was supported by the Soviet Union, there was a major propaganda offensive to try to put the blame for all the turmoil in the Middle East on the Syrians (hence the title "Syria - The Scapegoat?" of Peter Mansfield's address to the CAABU meeting in London on 16 June - see pages 27-28. The Syrians, in turn, were not exactly helping their own case.

All through 1983, that dangerous situation of the midsummer continued to deteriorate. On Sunday, 23 October, one hundred and ninety one United States marines, part of a four power multinational force stationed in Lebanon, were killed in a suicide bomb attack on their headquarters and twenty-three French soldiers were killed in a similar attack on the same day. Those events were exploited with great success by the Israelis in reconsolidating their alliance with the USA. On 29 November, Yitshak Shamir, who had replaced Begin as Prime Minister, making a special visit to Washington, made an agreement with the United States President which lifted American Support for Israel to a level unprecedented in the entire, long standing and close association between the two countries.

Under the terms of that agreement, there was to be joint military planning, joint naval manoeuvres in the Mediterranean, intelligence sharing and the stockpiling of American military supplies in Israel. In July 1982, the American administration had banned the shipment of cluster bombs to Israel because of the extensive Israeli use of them against civilians in Lebanon but, under the November agreement, shipments were to be resumed immediately. It was in this agreement also that the arrangement was entered into whereby, from October 1984, the military aid supplied to Israel by the USA would cease to be on loan and would be in the form of outright grants. Israel was then in the preliminary stages of building its new Lavi fighter bomber aircraft and production was to be heavily subsidized by the US, one result of which was that the plane would be in strong and American subsidized competition in world markets with the products of America's own aircraft industry. The final feature of the agreement was that there would be a free trade agreement which would exempt Israeli exports to the USA from all tariffs, an unprecedented arrangement which the USA did not have with any other country. The total cost to the USA amounted to $2.61 billion (which was subsequently increased so that it reached an annual rate of around $3.5 billion).

In return, Israel made absolutely no concessions. Shamir made it clear that his government was totally against any freezing, leave alone dismantling, of the illegal Israeli settlements in the occupied West Bank, which President Reagan, taking a phrase from the European Community's Venice Declaration of 1980, had described as "an obstacle to peace." Neither did the Israelis make the slightest withdrawal of their opposition to any deals in weapons between the United States and any Arab countries, notwithstanding that American policy was stated to be to develop military ties and consultations with all friendly states in the region - including of course Egypt, which had a peace treaty with Israel.

The one-sided and dangerous nature of American policy was graphically demonstrated within days. Only a few days after the agreement between Reagan and Shamir, President Gemayel of Lebanon visited Washington, to receive very different treatment. If there was ever to be peace and if the faction-torn Lebanon was ever again to become a governable country, a revision of the 17 May "agreement" was essential. It was to seek such a revision, which only the United States could bring about, that Gemayel had gone to Washington. The American administration refused point blank to help. Then, the American component of the multinational force stationed in Lebanon, supposedly to keep the peace, attacked Syrian forces, without any consultation with Britain, France and Italy, America's partners in the multinational force; an attack which came near to creating direct confrontation with Syria's ally, the Soviet Union. It proved to be the beginning of the end of that disastrous phase in American policy, involving the withdrawal of the French, Italian and British contingents of the multinational force and finally, in early 1984, a humiliating American withdrawal.

A number of events flowed from the American policy of that period and especially from the Israeli-American treaty of 29 November 1983. The Israeli Lavi aircraft was eventually abandoned after furious lobbying in Washington by the American aircraft industry, whose own interests were so seriously affected, which caused Israel to turn to its other close ally, apartheid South Africa, to seek the production of the aircraft in that country. Otherwise, the flow of American support to Israel increased steadily. American intelligence and help with aircraft refuelling was a vital factor in the Israeli attack on Tunis on 1 October 1985, while Israeli intelligence backing was a key factor in the American attack on Tripoli and Benghazi in April 1986. The results of the Middle East policy of Ronald Reagan, the trigger happy, Hollywood cowboy President in the nineteen eighties, long continued to impede progress to peace and justice.

## 5

# FRUSTRATION IN TUNIS

Although my appointment as Director of CAABU was in June 1983, by mutual agreement, I did not take up the post until September. It was, however, necessary to give urgent attention to the parlous financial situation because bankruptcy and closure were staring CAABU in the face. My appointment was widely welcomed and the then Director of the Arab League in London, Khalil Al Azhari, arranged for me to visit Tunis, to meet the Secretary-General, to discuss the Middle East situation and also CAABU's role and its finances.

Khalil Al Azhari had been posted to London in February 1982. One of the nicest men I have met, he was a Palestinian who had previously been Arab League Director in Tokyo for a number of years. He had been looking forward to a final posting at headquarters in Tunis or in another Arab country for a few years before retiring but, instead, found himself in London on a "temporary" basis, that is to say that he was only appointed for one month at a time, a situation which lasted altogether for thirty-two months until he finally left London for Tunis in September 1984. That put him in an impossible situation, both in his home and family life and in his post, where he had no power to take any decision of any importance and that in one of the most important of all the Arab League's outposts. After he had been in London for some time and with no signs of any change in the terms of his appointment, he did suggest to headquarters that, as he had then familiarized himself with the requirements of the London posting, he would be prepared to forego his cherished ambition to finish his career at headquarters or in another Arab country and stay in Britain until he reached retirement, but he received no positive response. It was one example of what is known to everyone familiar with the Arab World, that - to say the very least - efficient administration is not an Arab strong point! - something which was to be brought home to me even more strongly than before during the visit to Tunisia.

I arrived in Tunis on the evening of Monday, 4 July. due to return home the following Friday. As promised, I was met at the airport and conducted to the Hilton Hotel. On arrival at the hotel, it was clear that no reservation had been made but there was, fortunately, no problem in getting a room. Having got me registered, my escort, a young Palestinian, left me to my own devices and with the understanding that I would be contacted from the League Headquarters the following morning. I never saw him again. By the middle of the following morning, nothing whatever had happened. I telephoned the Arab League and after being passed through four different people, finally found myself talking with an English speaking lady in Adnan Omran's office, who quickly comprehended the situation and told me that Adnan would telephone me, himself. Adnan Omran was a senior official, a deputy secretary-general and head of the political department. A Syrian, he had previously been an effective Syrian Ambassador in London, which was when I had first got to know him.

By half past three in the afternoon, nothing had come from the League so, leaving a message in the manner prescribed by the hotel as to my whereabouts, I went to spend a pleasant couple of hours at the hotel swimming pool. At about seven in the evening, with still no message from the Arab League, I went down to dinner and in the hotel lobby, by a welcome stroke of luck, came across Adnan Omran, who was there on other business. He greeted me enthusiastically and told me that he had telephoned the hotel but had been told that I was not answering the phone in my room, that they could not locate me and that they assumed that I must be out! Adnan was upset at the failure of communication and at my wasted day. He asked if I would mind waiting by the telephone in my room the following morning, when he would personally make arrangements for me to be telephoned, collected and closeted with the Secretary-General.

The following morning, I breakfasted early and was back in my room by half past eight. The telephone rang at 10.20. It was Adnan, who said that an appointment had been arranged for me to see the Secretary-General at ten o'clock, that a car had called for me and that the driver had been told that I was not answering the telephone in my room and they did not know where I was. By that time, my patience was wearing thin and Adnan was pretty angry too. New arrangements were made then and there and within half an hour an Arab League car called to pick me up. I made sure that I was at the hotel entrance to meet it and to try to avoid any more farce. At headquarters, I was ushered into the Secretary-General's office by embarrassed and apologetic officials. I had already met Chedli Klibi briefly, during one of his visits to London. Now. we talked for almost two hours, through an interpreter.

He reflected the profound gloom felt by the Arabs and which I shared. He wanted a "European initiative" and also, interestingly, greater support among the Western European Socialist Parties, through the Socialist International. I entirely agreed as to the desirability of both but I had to tell him of the grave difficulties of accomplishing either in the climate of the times. Following her 1983 election victory, Margaret Thatcher was trying to extend her policy of the satellitisation of Britain in orbit around the United States by working with Helmut Kohl, the then relatively inexperienced, right wing Chancellor of West Germany who had been elected to power the previous year, to try to line up the whole European Community in subservience to the requirements of American policy. As for the European Socialist Parties, while it was true that the deep seated Zionist influence they had experienced for decades was declining, more so in some countries, Britain for example, than in others, there was still, at that time, no prospect of any concerted action on their part.

Following my long discussion with the Secretary-General and spread over the remaining two days of my visit, I had several meetings with Adnan Omran and with other senior League officials. It emerged, among other things, that the Secretary-General had been angry over the incompetence and discourtesy of the arrangements for my visit. However, his displeasure made not the slightest difference to the arrangements themselves. When my visit ended, a middle ranking League official was supposed to come to the hotel to escort me to the airport. By midday, when it was necessary to leave, neither he nor anyone else had arrived, although the car which had been placed at my disposal, with a very competent and helpful driver, had arrived two hours earlier. There was no choice except to go to the airport. I then discovered on checking out, that the Arab League had made absolutely no arrangements. The hotel receptionist telephoned the League (he said) who (he said) denied any knowledge of any Mr Watkins staying on their account. There was no choice except to settle my own bill. I told the unfortunate hotel staff exactly what I thought about the administration of both the hotel and the Arab League.

The driver was as annoyed as I was. He took me to the airport and promised to go straight to the League to report what had happened. It so happened that a fellow passenger on the plant was Clovis Maksoud, the Arab League's Permanent Observer at the United Nations in New York, whom I had known since earlier days in London. The driver had been as good as his word in reporting to the League and Clovis, who had gone to the airport via the League offices, was also very angry. "One of our greatest friends, and this is how we treat him" he said. He told me that the London office had been telexed to make arrangements to reimburse me at once. Within half an hour of arriving home, Khalil Al Azhari telephoned from the London office. He was terribly embarrassed. In Arab culture, it is one of the ultimate sins to insult an honoured guest and Khalil was very conscious of the enormity of what had happened. There was a final touch of farce. He had gone to the airport to meet me, after receiving the telex from Tunis, but the plane had been twenty minutes early, he had been delayed in the Friday afternoon traffic jams and he had missed me.

In addition to discussing the Middle East situation, the object of my meeting with the Secretary-General had been to discuss CAABU's role and its finances. I had told him that I wanted to make CAABU the most effective "pro-Arab" organization in the western world and that to do so would require financial support. We would need a budget of £250,000 for 1984 (which was pretty modest) with a rolling programme of financial backing keeping two to three years ahead, so that we could function properly and plan ahead without having to dissipate so much of our time and effort on raising money. He listened attentively, made notes and said it would be considered. It was considered and some help did materialize but it dried up within a year, although it has to be said in fairness that the Arab League was experiencing its own severe financial problems.

We also looked elsewhere for support. British companies doing business with the Arab World showed no willingness whatever to help, a position which should perhaps be set in the context of the Euro-Arab Dialogue, which had been instituted earlier between the Arab League countries and those of the European Community and which had broken down because the European side was concerned only with furthering its commercial interests. Anthony Nutting became Treasurer of CAABU and he wrote a frankly worded letter which we hand delivered to all the Arab Ambassadors in London and, after discussions with the Ambassadors, a committee was set up in February 1984 to consider CAABU's position. The committee consisted of the two Joint Chairmen of CAABU (Cyril Townsend MP and John Cartwright MP), together with myself and with the Kuwaiti Ambassador and the Arab League Director. The committee was due to meet on 12 March but was postponed by the Arab side. The meeting was rearranged for 8 May, when the same thing happened. The committee eventually met on 8 June and produced no result.

Eventually, we were helped over our immediate difficulties through the good offices of a group of Arab businessmen in London and, finally, CAABU finances were put on a firm basis through the good offices of, among others, Sheikh Nasser Almanquour, the very able Saudi Arabian Ambassador and Dean of the Arab Diplomatic Corps in London. He arranged for a visit to CAABU by one of his country's most dynamic ministers, Dr Abdul-Rahman A. Al-Zamil, the Deputy Minister of Commerce and that was when things finally started moving to some effect. Sheikh Nasser also arranged for a visit by the officers of CAABU to Saudi Arabia, where we met, among others, leading members of the Council of Saudi Arabian Chambers of Commerce and Industry. CAABU's finances were finally put on a sound basis through their good offices and especially through those of their Secretary-General, Abdullah Dabbagh and their Chairman, Suleiman Al Olayan, a remarkable man who started life as a truck driver with ARAMCO (Arab-American Oil Company) and who became one of his country's most successful businessmen, with extensive interests in London and New York, as well as in Riyadh.

My first six months as Director of CAABU were spent in ensuring the very survival of the organization, the next twelve months in putting things on a sound basis and in doing everything possible to ensure that the organization would never again face extinction through lack of funding. The unhelpful attitude of British institutions meant that we had to look largely to the Arab World and it was in a time when they were becoming much more circumspect in financial matters than in the "oil boom" years of the nineteen-seventies. One thing we always did, as CAABU always has done, was to emphasize our independence. CAABU has never, ever taken money from any quarter with conditions attached to it. Its donors have always respected that and have helped because they supported the work and felt trust and confidence in the way the work was carried out. In measuring the effectiveness achieved, where better to turn than to the forces of Zionism? The Israeli Defence Forces Journal, in its issue of Spring 1988, described CAABU as "one of the most active and important non-Arab pro-Palestinian organizations."

# 1

# THE CAABU YEARS: RECURRING ISSUES

By its constitution, CAABU is required to hold an annual general meeting of members every November. The Director's report is a major item on the agenda and, in presenting it, my regular practice was to survey the situation in the Middle East as well as to report on activities. The following essays are closely based in the reports presented on the dates indicated. In retrospect, it emerges strikingly how certain basic issues recur year after year, notably the need for a stronger British policy, a stronger European policy and for an international peace conference. That so little progress was made with these issues for so long provides an appropriate commentary on the nineteen-eighties. The protracted delay in gaining official acceptance for a peace conference, in particular, shows how entrenched minority power can so successfully delay progress which is necessary for the common good. At the time of the final report on 29 November 1990, a month before my retirement as Director, everything was dominated by the crisis created by the Iraqi invasion of Kuwait on 2 August and by the American led build up for the attack on Iraq in January and February 1991, to which I shall return in the final section of this book.

*24 November 1983*

This year has been the most difficult in the history of CAABU. We have experienced shrinking financial resources whilst faced with horrendously difficult developments in the Middle East. The title CAABU means Council for the Advancement of Arab-British Understanding and although the Middle East has naturally been in the forefront of our minds and work during the year, we have also been concerned, as we must be, with all Arab countries. It has always been, and it remains, CAABU policy not to interfere in internal developments in Arab countries and not to take a stand for or against any particular Arab country in its relations with others of the Arab World or elsewhere[(1)]. What is paramount is that we do have a deep sense of involvement and concern for every Arab man, woman and child. We have an interest in the hopes and aspirations of the entire Arab nation and we are turning increasingly to the human rights question and to how CAABU can play an even larger role in this field.

As regards the Middle East and the fate of the Palestinians, the picture could hardly be more depressing. The question "what can be done about it?" is often posed with an air of hopelessness, with an assumption that little or nothing can be done, but it is that very sense of hopelessness which we must resist and which we must encourage our friends to resist. It is true that in Tripoli, in Lebanon, there are over thirty thousand UNRWA refugees and that all UNRWA operations there stopped on 3 November. It is true that what Zionist propaganda and the Israel invasion of Lebanon failed to do, namely to destroy the Palestine Liberation Organization, some Arab forces now seem determined to achieve. The internecine struggle which continues can only give comfort to the enemies of peace and justice. In this confused and tragic situation, CAABU has tried to maintain and to provide a balanced view, keeping in mind always that Israel invaded Lebanon which Syria did not do. Yet Israel expects to withdraw with gains from aggression at the expense of an Arab country which was not an agressor.

It has always been argued in CAABU that a much stronger British policy is required, that it must be a main purpose of British policy to influence European countries towards a more concerted effort for a Middle East settlement, and that there must be a

(1) A policy which frequently put us in the position of walking on a tightrope suspended over a minefield!

European policy more independent of the United States and more frank in exerting pressure on the United States to change its policy of total support for Israel at the expense of the rest of the countries of the Middle East. Furthermore, CAABU has always insisted that the Soviet Union must be involved in any peace settlement if such is to be effective and lasting. In furtherance of those policies, CAABU officers have called on Ministers of the Crown three times during the year. There were two calls on Mr Francis Pym when he was Foreign Secretary and these were followed by a visit to Mr Richard Luce, Minister of State responsible for Middle East matters. On each of these occasions, it was emphasized that the situation was becoming ever more threatening and that the only solution was along the lines just indicated. We have continued our work in providing Members of Parliament and others - of all parties, regularly and frequently - with information to enable them to be well armed for any public discussion. In this, we have worked in close association with the Labour, Conservative and Liberal Middle East Councils and with the British section of the Parliamentary Association for Euro-Arab Co-operation.

Among the tragic results of the Israeli invasion of Lebanon was the subsequent detention of thousands of prisoners in the El Ansar prison camp and elsewhere. The Israelis refused to treat them as prisoners of war or to provide them with the minimal protection which that status would afford them under the Geneva Conventions. It is perhaps the cruellest irony of all that Israelis will not treat them as prisoners of war because they regard them as "stateless terrorists" when Israel itself is responsible for their having no country and no democratic rights. We are waging a specific campaign on this issue. This very morning has come the dramatic news of the release of some six thousand prisoners. We can legitimately claim the release as evidence of the success of the campaign for the prisoners' rights in which CAABU has played such an important part. We shall continue to campaign for the restoration of the human rights of the released prisoners, some of whom, it must be noted, are being deported overseas and not returned to their homes and families. We shall also continue to campaign for the restoration of the rights of the sorely oppressed Palestinians in Israel and in the occupied territories.

During the year, we have constantly kept under review the treatment given by Israel to the teachers and students of Bir Zeit University. There was a new and cruel twist to Israeli persecution of Bir Zeit in the middle of November when twenty expatriate teachers, including two British, were actually accused of forging work permits and the Principal of the University was accused of "conspiracy." When this occurred, we set aside our other work and concentrated immediately on protesting and drawing the attention of our own government to what had happened and calling for action.

***6 December 1984***

Nineteen eighty-four opened with the Middle East in renewed turmoil as a direct result of USA policy in the region. On 29 November 1983, an agreement had been made between President Reagan and Prime Minister Shamir for far greater support for Israel even than previously. Not much more than hours later, an appeal for help in Lebanon by President Gemayel was curtly dismissed by President Reagan. Within days came the commencement of open hostilities against Syrian forces in Lebanon by the United States. Those events set in motion the withdrawal of the multinational force stationed in Lebanon, supposedly to keep the peace, including the withdrawal of the small but effective British contingent, which had performed impeccably well in extremely difficult circumstances. In total, those events led to the collapse of American policy in the region.

Early in the New Year, our own Foreign Secretary, Sir Geoffrey Howe, made a strong statement in Saudi Arabia, reasserting that the European Community's Venice Declaration of 1980 remained the basis of British policy. He added that Palestinian rights remained at the core of the Arab-Israeli conflict and that the PLO should be associated with peace negotiations subject to its recognizing Israel, and that the Israelis should cease their colonizing operations on the West Bank. It requires to be said, here, that the Venice Declaration is much more than a pious declaration of principles, for, in an often overlooked section, it announced the intention of the EC countries to make contact with all parties to the conflict, with a view to determing the form for an EC peace initiative. The sad fact is that, neither in Britain nor elsewhere in the EC, has there been any effective follow up to that declaration. Neither has there been any other major statement or any public initiative.

With the collapse of American policy in the early months of the year, events in the Middle East seem to have been viewed in official circles in Britain and in the West generally, as being frozen while the world waited for, first, the outcome of the Israeli and then the American elections. In reality, of course, events in the Middle East have been far from frozen. The Israeli settlements policy and de facto annexation of the West Bank and the Gaza Strip has continued apace, as has the subjugation and persecution of the people of occupied southern Lebanon. These developments appear to be backed by the United States, whose Middle East policy now seems to be controlled by Israel. The elections in both countries have come and gone and have made no basic difference. Once again, as in the past, they have been excuses for western inertia while the Israeli policy of hegemony in the region has been consolidated and strengthened.

For most of 1984, the PLO has been engaged in unsuccessful efforts to regroup and to regain power to influence events. Eventually, the Palestine National Council was able to meet in Amman in November, although it is too early to assess the likely outcome of the important decisions taken at that meeting, especially as they have to be interlocked with a number of other factors, including pan-Arab, European and American reactions. Meanwhile, in the Gulf, the war between Iraq and Iran has entered its fifth year and shows no sign of ending. So 1984 draws to a close in a setting of western inaction in the face of a Middle East situation which remains as horrendous and as dangerous as ever.

At the 1983 conference in Geneva of governments and non-governmental organizations (of which CAABU was one), the call was made for an international peace conference under United Nations auspices and the proposal was subsequently endorsed by the General Assembly in Resolution 38/58C. The roots of that proposal go right back to Security Council Resolution 338 of 1973, which set up the Geneva Conference under joint USA-USSR chairmanship, to bring together all parties to the dispute. Sadly, Geneva broke down through Israeli wrecking tactics and the joint superpower approach was subsequently breached by the unilateral Camp David so-called 'peace process' which proved to be no peace process. The plain fact is that there has been more war and bloodshed in the Middle East since Camp David than before it. It is now time for Britain and the rest of Western Europe to act boldly and publicly, on the basis of their own policy as set out in the Venice Declaration, in an initiative to try to bring all parties together in an international conference. Above all and most urgently, the current view of the Middle East as an area for confrontation between the superpowers must be challenged.

### *28 November 1985*

Just a year ago, after many setbacks and against intense Syrian opposition, the Palestine National Council was finally able to meet in an historic session in Amman, which I was able to attend as an observer on behalf of CAABU(2). It was at that session that King Hussein made the proposal for a joint Jordanian-PLO initiative for peace. The PNC authorized the Executive Committee to discuss the scope for joint action and from that arose the working papers of February 1985 for what became known as the Hussein-Arafat initiative. The ultimate objective was a UN peace conference, to include the permanent members of the Security Council, including thereby the USA and the USSR as well as Britain and France, together with all parties to the Arab-Israeli conflict including naturally, the PLO. The first objective was to secure American involvement in a dialogue with a joint delegation of Jordanians and representative Palestinians. As everyone knows who understands the Middle East conflict, such Palestinians can only be found among members and supporters of the PLO.

From the start, the Israeli government was opposed to the Hussein-Arafat peace process and, as was made abundantly clear by Mr Yitshak Shamir during his visit to London in June, they had no intention of negotiating with any Palestinians, whether PLO or otherwise. What we have seen has been the 1985 manifestation of Mrs Golda Meir's infamous claim in 1969 that "There was no such thing as the Palestinians ..... They did not exist." Opposition to the Hussein-Arafat initiative was conducted through the long-established practice of delay and prevarication. Every single Palestinian who was suggested as a participant in the joint dialogue was objected to on some pretext or other. Meanwhile, of course, the colonization of the West Bank and the Gaza Strip, together with the repression and terrorization of the rightful population there, continued apace. In August, the United States Assistant Secretary of State, Mr Richard Murphy, visited Amman for what had been heralded as a first meeting with a joint Jordanian-Palestinian delegation. In the event, no such meeting took place. The Zionist

---

(2) My presence in Amman was the reason for the exceptional postponement of the 1984 CAABU annual general meeting from late November to early December.

lobby in Washington had organized a campaign to ensure that it would not take place. All the signs were that, once again, an Israeli government had succeeded in destroying yet another initiative for peace.

Meanwhile, starting in June with the visits to London in a single week by Mr Shamir, King Hussein and Mr George Shultz, there were, at last, welcome signs of a British initiative showing some signs of independence of the United States. This culminated in the invitation given by our own Prime Minister in Jordan in September to the Deputy Prime Minister and the Foreign Minister of that country, together with Mayor Mohammed Milhem and Bishop Elia Khoury, to visit London for official talks with the Foreign Secretary. There was at least a faint hope that the peace process might have been revived by that invitation and, predictably, all the forces of Zionism were mobilized, worldwide, to prevent that from happening.

To the insidious activities of the Israeli agencies in this country, the USA and elsewhere was added, on 1 October the terrorist bombing of Tunis by Israeli aircraft, an operation clearly designed to wreck any hopes of peaceful negotiations, to try to kill the Chairman of the PLO, one of the partners in the peace initiative, and to try to do so while the other partner, King Hussein, was actually in Washington talking with the US government. But, apart from Israeli efforts to destroy the British initiative, it collapsed in the event, ignominiously and disastrously through misunderstandings in Amman and in London [(3)]. Whatever the rights and wrongs of the events of 14 October, they left British standing at an all time low level and they left the Middle East in an ugly and dangerous situation.

As the year, which has seen so many disappointments in the Middle East, comes to its close, it is clear that major realignments are taking place in the region. Foremost among these is the resumption of friendly relations between Jordan and Syria, after a break of four years. No less important is the establishment of diplomatic relations with the Soviet Union by Oman and the United Arab Emirates. It is too early to assess the ultimate effect of the Reagan-Gorbachev summit. So far as the Middle East is concerned, the summit needs to be seen not in any splendid isolation of its own but as a companion to the several important developments in the

(3) For more on this, see pp 82 - 84 below.

region. If the totality adds up to an ending of superpower confrontation and with moves towards an international peace conference under United Nations auspices, to involve all parties to conflict, including the superpowers and the PLO, then a year of discouraging developments could yet end with pointers of a more encouraging nature.

### *27 November 1986*

When a CAABU delegation met Sir Geoffrey Howe, the Secretary of State for Foreign and Commonwealth Affairs, in March, they strongly urged that, with the United Kingdom's chairmanship of the European Community Council of Ministers due to operate in the second half of the year, European moves should be initiated to reach a settlement of the Middle East conflict, based on the Venice Declaration of 1980. One of the key features of the Venice Declaration is that it explicitly recognizes the Palestinian people's right to self determination and affirms that the PLO must be associated with peace initiatives. The CAABU delegation also emphasized that Israel's refusal to recognize the central importance of Palestinian self determination and the central role of the PLO as the only credible representative of the Palestinian people, must not be allowed to kill moves for peace.

Yet, as we approach the end of 1986, the reality remains of European and especially British deference to a United States policy which is of disastrous proportions. Among the foundationless pillars of that policy is complete failure to recognize either the principle of Palestinian self determination or its importance for peace. Also included is rejection of the PLO; support for the colonization of the illegally occupied West Bank and Gaza Strip and the brutal oppression of the people there; support for the Israeli occupation of southern Lebanon and regular military adventures against Lebanon; and full support for all other Israeli moves to kill what the Americans themselves once dubbed "the peace process."

So far as any possibility of British influence existed on moves for peace, it was effectively killed by official support for the United States attack on Libya on 14 April and the use of British bases to launch the attack. CAABU immediately protested to the Prime Minister, pointing out that the attempt to justify the attack by quoting Article 51 of the Charter of the United Nations, which defines the right of self defence against armed attack. was not only to take Article 51 out of context but to misinterpret it into the bargain.

When the CAABU delegation met the Foreign Secretary in March, they emphasized that during the then forthcoming visit of the Prime Minister to Israel, it was essential that she should meet and talk with representative Palestinians. That suggestion was followed up but the outcome was, to say the least, disappointing. The Palestinians who met Mrs Thatcher particularly stressed to her that they and the people for whom they spoke, looked to the PLO as the representative body of their aspirations to self determination. She, however, appeared to believe, immediately after meeting them, that they were an alternative to the PLO, a claim which the group of eminent Palestinians repudiated immediately.

Those events further minimized any prospect that the United Kingdom could exert any influence on the course of events. In the first half of 1986, when Mr Hans Van den Broek, the Netherlands Foreign Minister, was Chairman of the EC Council of Foreign Ministers, he had initiated steps to lay a foundation for European moves for peace in accordance with the provisions of the Venice Declaration. Sadly, no further progress was made in the second half of the year, under British chairmanship. The inability of the British government to secure the support it wished from among other EC countries, after breaking off diplomatic relations with Syria, provided its own measure of British ineffectiveness in the Middle East.

Britain's standing has been further undermined by the campaign of anti-Arab racism in the more scurrilous organs of the media. CAABU itself received many objections in particular to the cartoon in the publication *The Sun* on 15 May, which depicted pigs complaining at being called Arabs. CAABU took the lead in reporting the matter to the Press Council, which ineffective though it is, was the only body to which recourse was possible [(4)]. It is clear, however, that the racist sector in the media is determined to maintain this sort of campaign, irrespective of the damage it does to Britain's reputation. With 1986 coming to its close, the Middle East is in a situation about which there can only be forebodings of more dangers to come. There appears to be no prospect of resolution of

---

(4) See also pp 79 - 82 below

the Arab-Israeli dispute, the most fundamental of all the problems of the region. The Gulf War, after six years of some of the most bloody conflict seen even in this war-torn twentieth century, threatens stability throughout the region and beyond, a situation which the rest of the world seems to regard with equanimity. In the African Arab World, Egypt and The Sudan in particular face daunting problems of mass poverty and unrest.

***26 November 1987***

Throughout 1987, Lebanon has remained an especially tragic symbol of a bitterly divided Middle East, a battlefield for conflicts based in ideologies beyond as well as within its own borders. When the year opened, camps filled with Palestinians driven from their own country by the ideology of militant Zionism, were under the most brutal siege by the forces of AMAL. By 1 January, the siege had already been on for three months, but there was virtually no media coverage at all of the plight of the victims. It was not until the CAABU monthly meeting on 28 January that even CAABU members became fully alerted to their plight through the inspired address of Dr Swee Ang, herself a witness of the earlier Sabra and Shatilla massacres, and whose colleagues Dr Pauline Cutting and Nurse Susan Wighton were among the medical team incarcerated in Bourj El Barajneh. It took two weeks of concentrated pressure on the media before they even started to give adequate coverage. Subsequently, coverage reached near saturation level yet, well before it even started, 1800 people had been killed and 4000 wounded, while tens of thousands were starving. On Saturday, 5 September, in Geneva, under the auspices of the European Co-ordinating Committee of Non-Governmental Organizations (NGO's) a deeply moving and very well attended presentation was given on the siege of the camps. The Israelis chose that very day to launch a terrorist bombing raid on the Ain Al Hilweh camp, killing over forty people and injuring as many as one hundred.

It is salutary to recall that the idea of an international peace conference on the Middle East was first put forward in Security Council Resolution 338 of 1973, which proposed a conference in Geneva under joint United States and Soviet chairmanship. Fourteen years and thousands upon thousands of casualties later, conflict is greater than it was then but prospects for a conference are not good in spite of an international consensus in favour.

The Foreign Ministers of the twelve European Community countries, meeting in Brussels on 23 February with the Middle East as the only item on their agenda, firmly supported the idea of an international conference under United Nations auspices. They pledged their countries to play a part and to make an active contribution to bringing about a conference. However, they made little response to a letter from Mr Gorbachev offering Soviet co-operation in working for a conference. The Israeli Prime Minister, Yitshak Shamir, remains resolutely opposed to a conference while the Foreign Minister, Shimon Peres, supports a conference but one hedged around with conditions which would lead to little more than a pointless and cynical charade, designed to buy time during which to consolidate Israeli power and further to divide the Arab countries, rather than to achieve lasting peace, and certainly not to achieve the absolutely essential element of Palestinian self determination. The United States is supporting the Peres line and that constitutes the greatest of the obstacles in the way of a peace conference. Before very long, American policy may well become paralyzed in the run up to the 1988 presidential election. Time and again in the past, such combinations of events have ensured that opportunities for peace have been allowed to slip away.

Sir Geoffrey Howe, referring to an international peace conference, said in his important speed at Blackpool on 6 October, which went virtually unreported in the British media :-

> I am convinced that it offers the best - indeed the only practical - way forward.

Perhaps I may be forgiven some modest conceit in quoting from my pamphlet *The World and Palestine*, the sentence :-

> Any fresh initiative requires the bringing together through the UN of all interested parties in the Middle East and elsewhere.

That was published seven and a half years ago in March 1980. The point is that there is a long, long record of missed opportunities, with the result that the obstacles to peace have multiplied steadily. That is the background which has created the international consensus which is now so strong for a conference. It will be a tragedy of the first order if yet another peace initiative is allowed to go the way of so many in the past.

The prolonged war between Iran and Iraq is another classic example of how, when the world at large is happy to allow a regional conflict to continue indefinitely, the conflict comes eventually to be a threat to peace and stability worldwide. The situation was scathingly summed up by the Kuwaiti Foreign Minister, Sheikh Sabah al Ahmad al Jaber al Sabah when, speaking at the Arab-British Chamber of Commerce annual dinner on 15 September, he expressed his country's astonishment to find that instead of taking action towards the stopping of this war, certain western countries saw in the expansion of the war only an opportunity which sharpened their appetites for quick material profit. So they began to pour fuel on this fire through their desperate eagerness to sell instruments of destruction.

After nearly seven years of war, the Security Council of the United Nations finally got round, in July, to adopting Resolution 598, calling for a ceasefire. It is a singular irony that the net result has been an escalation of threats to international shipping in the Gulf. The international community seems incapable of concerted action to counter these threats and incapable of either agreeing to or enforcing an arms embargo or any other form of sanctions against combatants refusing to accept a ceasefire. Not least among the reasons for this international paralysis is that the Middle East is a zone for confrontation between the superpowers, President Reagan having declared openly that his policy is as much to keep the Soveit Union out of the Gulf as to protect shipping. As 1987 moves towards its close, superpower rivalry where there should be co-operation remains a major factor in ensuring the continuation of conflict and in ensuring that the Middle East remains a dangerous world flashpoint,.

Among its many other features, 1987 has also been a year of exceptional anniversaries:- the seventieth anniversary of the Balfour Declaration, the fortieth anniversary of the UN resolution to partition Palestine, the twentieth anniversary of the 1967 war, and the fifth anniversary of the invasion of Lebanon and the massacres of Sabra and Shatilla. A great deal of CAABU activity has been related to that tragic series of anniversaries - in the year which has also marked the twentieth anniversary of the founding of CAABU. Over those twenty years, CAABU priorities and approaches have changed, not always without controversy, to meet the challenge of changing events and circumstances. Against a background of continuing Middle East conflict, CAABU has accomplished great things. It can go forward with confidence to face the new challenges of the present and of the future.

### *24 November 1988*

By any standards, 1988 has been a momentous year, one in which a basic pattern of events which has lasted over many years in the Middle East has changed dramatically. The change has been created by two outstanding developments; the cease fire in the Iran-Iraq war after eight years of hostilities, and the heroic uprising of the Palestinian people which has put the word "Intifada" into the vocabulary of every language on earth. Nor should the developments in the Mahgreb be overlooked, with the constitutional changes in progress in Algeria and Tunisia; the new steps for long sought after unity among the Mahgreb countries; and the moves under United Nations auspices to try to resolve the Morocco-Western Sahara dispute. It is though a matter for great sadness that offset against all that is the seriously deteriorating situation in Lebanon.

The Iranian decision, in the summer, to accept a ceasefire within the terms of Security Council Resolution 598, a year after the adoption of the resolution, finally brought the Iran-Iraq war to an end, but it is clear that negotiations for a mutually acceptable settlement are likely to be long and difficult. Meanwhile, some of the side effects of the ceasefire are alarming. Syria's support for Iran against an Arab country was deplorable but it will be a tragedy if Iraq now seeks to support, as appears to be the case, anti-Syrian forces in Lebanon simply because they are anti-Syrian. It is a particular tragedy that Iraq and Syria, each claiming the same basic political philosophy and with the two best tried armies in the whole Arab World, should be so much at odds. In alliance, and with less authoritarianism, they could constitute an immense force for peace and progress.

As we meet, it is two weeks short of one year since the start of the Intifada, in which the courage, endurance and solidarity of the brave people of the occupied territories has done more to focus attention on the injustices suffered by the Palestinians than the entire world community has done in the previous forty years. It is most important to appreciate that they are not merely protesting against the illegal occupation of their country, brutal and horrific though that has been for so long. What they are campaigning for is the self determination and independence which is their inalienable right in accordance with the fundamental principles of the Charter of the United Nations and which has now been enshrined in the historic Declaration of Independence made in Algiers by the Palestine National Council on 15 November.

The international legality of that Declaration cannot be doubted. The withdrawal of all claims of sovereignty over the West Bank on 31 July by King Hussein of Jordan left the West Bank without any internationally recognized legal sovereignty. So the legal sovereignty became that of the indigenous inhabitants, the Palestinian people. The situation in the Gaza Strip differs only in minor matters of international legality and is identical in principle. The Palestinians have made absolutely clear that they accept only the PLO as their representative organization. So there can be no doubt but that the Declaration of Independence is legal and should be recognized by member states of the United Nations Organization, and that Palestine should be represented by the PLO in an international peace conference.

It is a pity that the response of our own government should have been less than positive. There has been only a lukewarm response to the Declaration of Independence while, on 3 November, the same day upon which the Prime Minister, speaking in Warsaw, called for human rights in Poland, Britain abstained on a General Assembly Resolution condemning Israel's violations of human rights in the occupied territories, which was supported by one hundred and thirty countries, with only the USA and Israel voting against. It remains clear that, with so much momentum elsewhere, we still need to generate a great deal more of it at home, especially since events in the Middle East have now moved the conflicts and causes in that vital region of the world into a new dimension which will bring new challenges and new opportunities in 1989.

### *30 November 1989*

In last year's report it was possible to point out that 1988 had been a momentous year in which the Palestinian Intifada in particular had dramatically changed the basic pattern of events which had prevailed for many years in the Middle East. Yet as 1989 draws to a close, it is clear that another dangerous stalemate is being deliberately created, as of old, for the specific purpose of delaying progress towards a negotiated settlement.

To start with, the United States dialogue with the PLO, with which the year opened and upon which so much hope was pinned, has clearly run into the sand. Partly in order to ensure that such would happen, the Israeli government, with American support, proposed in May that elections should be held in selected parts of the occupied territories under Israeli military supervision. The purpose would be to elect an Israeli approved group to negotiate the permanent subjugation of the Palestinians. This is obviously unacceptable, not only because it is immoral in concept but still more so because the Palestinians have made clear beyond all doubt that the PLO alone can represent them in negotiations and that the purpose of the negotiations must be to achieve self determination in a two state solution.

In an effort to break the deadlock, President Mubarak of Egypt put forward proposals in September which were basically no more than talks about talks, but whose main effect proved to be to cause serious divisions within the Israeli government. Whereupon the United States put forward a proposal that Egypt, Israel and the USA should decide the composition of a Palestinian delegation to negotiate with the Israelis about negotiations. That proposal showed that, for all the so called dialogue with the PLO, the USA was still firmly committed to keeping the PLO out of negotiations. The proposal tried to create an impression of furthering the search for peace while in reality it prevented progress. The purpose was to save the Israeli government from breaking apart, not to provide justice in Palestine. Even then, the proposal, like that of President Mubarak, was rejected by the Israeli government.

Meanwhile,. although there is less media coverage, Israeli repression of the Palestinians has accelerated to reach new depths of depravity. To the daily killing, maiming and imprisonment without trial has now been added South African style pass laws and a penal system of taxation, designed to be beyond the victims' means to pay, whereupon their property is confiscated. Starvation, too, is now used on a major scale. The town of Beit Sahour, for example has been under siege, starvation, confiscation and looting because of the refusal of its brave inhabitants to pay these taxes which are, in any case, wholly illegal in international law. In addition, with the advent of this year's harvest, there has been large scale uprooting of fruit trees, together with chemical warfare to destroy crops.

It is not surprising that the people of Palestine are demanding with growing urgency to know why it is that, while they suffer so much in the cause of peace and justice, the rest of the world does nothing. If the international community does not move soon, frustration will inevitably turn peaceful protest towards violence. That would be exactly what the Israelis would want, giving them an excuse for the most violent measures. There is no shortage of voices in Israel calling for the Palestinians to be terrorized into fleeing their homeland in the way they were in the nineteen forties. If such a situation were to develop, the consequences would be incalculable. The world community has to ask itself - and urgently - for how much longer it is prepared to allow the government of Israel,. with the connivance of the government of the United States, to continue encouraging the drift towards such a situation in defiance of a worldwide consensus for a two state solution, which alone can meet not only the requirement of justice for the Palestinians, but ultimately the survival of the state of Israel itself.

None of this is to overlook or underestimate the importance of other great issues in the Middle East. For instance, although the Iran-Iraq war ended nearly a year and a half ago, there is no sign of negotiations for a permanent peace settlement, and that must remain a matter for serious international concern.

Of no less concern is the situation in Lebanon, where both the causes and the effects of continuing conflict extend far beyond the borders of that country. A very important development was in the effort of the Arab League, through the Committee of the Heads of State of Saudi Arabia, Algeria and Morocco, to end conflict and create a new constitution in Lebanon. That was a development of fundamental importance, not only for Lebanon but for the whole Arab World in seeking to demonstrate its own capability to apply itself in unity to its own most difficult problems.

The negotiations which resulted in the agreement reached at Taif in Saudi Arabia, which were endorsed by the Security Council of the United Nations and which quickly led to the constitutional election of the new Lebanese President, were conducted on behalf of the Arab League with immense skill by Ambassador Lakhdar

Brahimi. Many of us recall Ambassador Brahimi with high regard from his days as Algerian Ambassador in London and CAABU has sent him a message of congratulations and good wishes in his continuing endeavours. But those endeavours received a huge setback with the assassination of President Muawad after only seventeen days in office, a tragedy showing that there are those who will stop at nothing to prevent both a united Lebanon and unity in the whole Arab World.

It is of course not only the year but also the decade which is drawing to its close. It has been a decade of the most profound developments. Among the most outstanding have been the lessening in the later years of tension between the United States and the Soviet Union and, in the final months, the dramatic and far reaching changes in Europe. For the two superpowers, in the cold war period, the Middle East was the most dangerous of all the points of their confrontation. Today, there is an urgent requirement for the Middle East to become the major point for their co-operation.

With the changed world situation and the now rapidly changing European situation, there is also the opportunity and, indeed, the requirement for a stronger European role. In 1980, the member countries of the European Community stated in the Venice Declaration that they were obliged by traditional ties and common interests with the Middle East to work towards peace. Yet they have done little to activate the Declaration they made as the decade opened. Now, as the decade closes amid intense changes in all Europe, they are much more strongly placed to act and they are under considerable obligation to do so.

Since Venice, European policy has been subordinated to American policy and based in trying to persuade the USA to take a more even handed attitude in the Middle East. That policy has clearly not worked and with the cold war circumstances which helped to create it now so much changed and continuing to change, the policy too needs to be changed. Europe is a major market for Israeli exports and those exports have a privileged, tariff free access to the European Community. Yet, the Israeli government has deliberately set out to wreck the Community's decision to give equality of access to Palestinian produce, even though that access is only on a very small scale. It is in the power of the European Community to make clear to the Israeli government that it is not prepared to tolerate such conduct and that, furthermore, Israel cannot expect to maintain its highly privileged trading status with the Community if it continues so brutally to repress the Palestinians and to refuse to come to the negotiating table. Does the European Community have the will to exert its economic power to implement its declared intention to work towards peace in the Middle East? That is the question for the nineteen-nineties.

### *29 November 1990*

Since the Iraqi invasion of Kuwait on 2 August, not only the Middle East but the whole world has been dominated by the developing crisis. Yet, long before 2 August, the situation in relation to Palestine was also in a state of crisis which, right from the start of the year, had been continuously getting worse. As the year draws to its close, both crises continue to escalate and the linkage between the two is becoming more evident and more undeniable in spite of all the assertions to the contrary from predictable sources. We are meeting on the United Nations International Day of Solidarity with the Palestinian People and, in observing that solemn occasion, it is particularly appropriate to call attention to the link between these two grave crises.

The Iraqi aggression is entirely contrary to the basic principle of the inadmissibility of the acquisition of territory by force, and the brutal repression and looting which have accompanied it are contrary to all principles of civilized conduct. These things cannot be justified in any circumstances. The Security Council, in Resolutions 660 and 661, rightly and with commendable speed, condemned the invasion, following upon which there has been the massive, USA-led, military build up to enforce the resolutions. What a contrast with the reaction to Resolutions 242 of 1967 and 338 of 1973! - which specifically condemned the Israeli acquisition of the occupied territories of Palestine by force and called for withdrawal.

No steps have ever been taken to enforce those resolutions. On the contrary, throughout the twenty three years since Resolution 242, United States policy in particular has actively encouraged Israeli occupation, annexation and murderous brutality towards the Palestinians. Not only has the USA repeatedly used its veto in the Security Council to prevent criticism and investigation of such conduct, but, throughout all those years, it has poured billions of dollars into Israel to support its aggression. These double standards can only be condemned. They make nonsense of claims that there is no link between Palestine and the Gulf. They have done immense damage to the already tarnished reputation of the United States and also to the reputation of our own country because we are seen to be so closely tied to American policy.

The fact is that all Middle East issues require to be dealt with on an equal basis and in accordance with international law. Equal effort requires to be exerted to enforce all United Nations resolutions on the acquisition of territory by force. Equal effort requires to be exerted in support of the fundamental principle of the self determination of peoples. The self determination of the Kuwaiti people is linked inseparably with the self determination of the Palestinian people. All this goes to constitute the linkage between the crisis in the Gulf and that in Palestine.

# 2

# INDOMITABLE PEOPLE

Among those people of the twentieth century who qualify for the description "indomitable" the Palestinians count very highly. As well as being the victims of oppression, they have been the scapegoats in a worldwide campaign of unscrupulous and untruthful propaganda. Yet, throughout the long campaign to obliterate them, they never lost their sense of identity, they became strengthened, not weakened, and their sense of nationhood developed. This chapter seeks to illustrate something of what they have suffered in their homeland and at the hands of their detractors outside.

In 1985, I was invited to present a paper on the condition of the Palestinians in Palestine to the Dutch-Arab Circle in The Hague and that paper, with minor editing, constitutes this chapter. 1985 was the thirtieth anniversary of the Circle and, to mark the occasion, they published a book containing this paper and six others delivered during the anniversary year [(1)]. At the meeting, there was a lively discussion. All the audience had some knowledge of English and many were fluent. How many people, one wonders, in a British audience, could respond similarly to a paper presented, say, in French, which is taught in the United Kingdom as the main second language. In continental Europe, a reasonable knowledge of a

(1) Herman Beck, Fred Ros (editors) *De Arabische wereld en haar minderheden* Nederlands-Arabische Kring, The Hague, 1985..

second language, usually English, is considered both essential and normal in an educated person. In Britain, and especially in England, people are proud that they do not know any language other than their own.

How, one wonders, will the Palestinian people handle the power which, despite all current difficulties, could become theirs in the future and what will they learn from the experience of other indomitable people, including their own persecutors? In 1918, the victorious allied powers imposed on Germany a humiliating peace which paved the way for the rise of Nazism and made the second world war inevitable. The final outcome (to adapt the infamous Nazi phrase "the final solution") of the genocide against the Jews was to show that an indomitable people cannot be obliterated. One of the greatest Jews of the twentieth century, Moshe Menuhin, whom I had the privilege of knowing, pointed out that there was, and is, a centuries old conflict between the prophetic Judaism of Moses and the aggressive nationalism of Joshua [(2)]. The leaders of Israel chose to apply the latter to the Palestinians. The net result has been to prove again that an indomitable people cannot be obliterated. The Moses-Joshua conflict is, of course, present in all peoples and, in the future, the Palestinians could well be given a unique opportunity to lead the world by eschewing the crimes of others and showing that they can treat the Israelis with compassion and humanity.

---

(2) *Zionism Reassessed*, article in *Arab Perspectives*, Vol. 1, No. 1, New York, April 1980.

## THE PALESTINIANS: AN EXPLOITED MINORITY IN THEIR OWN COUNTRY

*Paper presented to the Dutch Arab Circle, at The Hague, 9 May 1985*

When the state of Israel was established by force of arms in 1948, within what we now call the "pre-1967" borders, hundreds of thousands of Palestinians were driven out for the precise purpose of reducing them to a minority. Today, in the remainder of Palestine, that is in the occupied West Bank and the Gaza Strip, they still constitute, as yet, a large majority, but they are a majority subjected to oppression and to a particular form of colonization, of which the ultimate purpose is to force sufficient numbers of them to leave so that, there too, they will become a minority. So, it has first to be recognized that where the Palestinians are not already a subjugated minority in their own country, there is a deliberate and sustained policy to make them such in the whole of the country. Let me first establish that point with two references, both from Israeli sources. One of these is in reference to Israel within the 1967 borders and the other is in reference to the occupied territories.

Inside Israel, it has long been the practice for the Prime Minister to appoint someone to advise him on Arab affairs. When the present government took office, Knesset Members from the opposition parties, Mapam and the Progressive List for Peace, tried to persuade the government that instead of having a single adviser to the Prime Minister they should set up a committee with both Jewish and Arab representatives, to formulate a clear policy towards the Palestinians in Israel. Their proposal was not accepted and the Prime Minister, Shimon Peres, again appointed a single adviser. The significant point is that the person appointed was the head of the Labour Party's department on minorities (3), a clear indication that the longstanding policy of discrimination against the Palestinians was to continue unchanged.

With reference to the occupied territories, the official policy can be well gauged from the report on human rights in the territories which has been produced, after extensive research, by the Israeli non-governmental organization the International Centre for Peace in

---

(3) Reported, *Ha'aretz*, Israel, 26 September 1984.

the Middle East. In the foreword to the report, Knesset Member Ms Shulamit Aloni wrote:

> The ruling authorities have ignored the principles of international pacts concerning the rights of a civilian population in occupied territory, undermined people's freedom and their basic rights, used collective punishment and punishment of the surroundings, and transformed humiliation into a system of rule. (4)

When Mrs Golda Meir was Prime Minister, she proclaimed that "There was no such thing as the Palestinians...They did not exist".(5) In the international uproar which ensued, some of her apologists tried to smooth over those infamous remarks with the explanation that what was really meant was that the Palestinians had no separate identity but that they were "just Arabs like any other Arabs." The profoundly racist nature of that explanation provides much of the rationale for the treatment to which official Israeli policy subjects the Palestinians.

We must not ever forget that there is a brave band of enlightened Israelis who are wholly opposed to such policies. I have quoted deliberately from some of their work, as much to demonstrate that fact as to show the position of the Palestinians. Sadly though, those Israelis are also a minority and we must recognize that there is overwhelming populist support for the official policy.

In dealing with a subject of such magnitude, constraints are obviously imposed on the amount of material which can be presented in a paper of this length. So I propose to deal first with the position of the Palestinians as employees and then to deal with the expropriation of their land. These are not only aspects of the treatment of the Palestinians which are of especial significance but also, as I shall hope to show, the second is closely linked with the attainment of the first. That is to say that the expropriation of the land is closely linked with the accomplishment of a policy of turning such

Palestinians as remain in their own country into a source of cheap and exploited labour. There is, though, another aspect, a

---

(4) *Human Rights in the Occupied Territories*, International Centre for Peace in the Middle East, Tel Aviv, 1983.

(5) Interview, *Sunday Times*, London, 15 June 1969.

more positive and a more inspiring aspect, which will run throughout. That is the continuing struggle of the indomitable Palestinian people, in the face of the most discouraging circumstances and at no matter what the odds, to retain their dignity and to assert their identity and their right to self determination.

The Palestinians in Israel have little choice except to work as cheap labour in Jewish enterprises. In former times, they made their living from the land and, contrary to the often repeated piece of mythology about Palestine being a desert which was made to bloom by the Israelis, it was, in reality, a fertile country which the Palestinians farmed successfully. Now, more than ninety per cent of their land has been taken from them. That has served not only its primary purpose of establishing the Israeli state, but it has also ensured that those Palestinians who did not flee the country have been turned into an easily exploited source of cheap labour.

A few of them now work in the kibbutz settlements established on their own land. They are, however, only allowed to work as employees doing the menial work and they are totally denied any voice or share in the running of those so-called co-operatives. It is worth adding, to put the much publicized kibbutzim into perspective, that they only constitute a very small proportion of the Israeli economy, accounting for less than two per cent of the total employed labour force of the country. In every sector of the economy, Palestinians are confined overwhelmingly to the menial jobs and, even in those, they receive much lower wages than Jewish workers. Their wages are generally only between a half and two thirds of Jewish wages and are becoming even less with the growing economic crisis in Israel. On those lower wages, they pay proportionately more in taxes, mainly because they pay the same amount for social security as Israelis although they receive only a fraction of the social services.

A good example of discrimination in social services is in family allowances. When the government introduced family allowances, they were alarmed to discover that, in accordance with the principles of the constitution, they would have to pay the allowances to both Jews and Palestinians. So, taking pride both in their patriotism and in their loyalty to the constitutional principle that Israel does not have any laws of racial discrimination, they drafted the law to make the allowances payable only to the families of those liable for military service. Palestinians, of course, are not liable for military service and so their families are excluded from benefit. The Israeli legal code observes that the state:

> Will ensure complete equality of social and political rights to all its inhabitants irrespective of religion, race or sex.

All are equal but, very clearly, in the immortal words of George Orwell, "some are more equal than others."

It is a deep irony that the whole Israeli economy has now become heavily dependent on exploited Palestinian labour. In addition, while the Palestinians have been reduced to a minority inside the 1967 borders, the Israeli economy has also become heavily dependent on employing large numbers of them drawn from the occupied territories outside those borders. More than a third of the Palestinian workers who live in the occupied territories travel to work in Israel. Their conditions of employment are even worse than those of the Palestinians living there. Their wages are only a half, or even a third, of those paid to Jewish workers and they have to pay proportionately more tax. Over thirty per cent of their incomes go on taxes, but only a fraction of what they pay is used in the occupied territories where they live. Many of these workers have to make long bus journeys to get to work, which makes it impossible for them to travel daily. So they have to stay overnight. In Israeli law, it is illegal for Palestinians from the occupied territories to remain overnight in Israel but, in practice, many do stay, locked inside huts, warehouses and places of work, while the police turn a blind eye.

Palestinians have no trade union protection. It is only since 1966 that those in Israel have been allowed to join the Histadrut, the so called "trade union" movement. Even so, they are only allowed into a Jewish controlled section of inferior status, in which they have neither a voice in policy nor protection against exploitation. Those from the occupied territories are debarred from joining even that. Those who can join find themselves far from acquiring any sort of protection in their conditions of employment. On the contrary, they actually find themselves subjected to an additional form of discrimination. It is most important to understand that the Histadrut is not in any way a trade union movement as such is understood in the western world. In reality, it is a business empire which employs one quarter of the national workforce of Israel. Trade unionism constitutes a mere fraction of its activities and is actually handled by a sub department called "The Department for Labour Unions." It is only a sub department of that sub department which admits Palestinians.

The Histadrut is not officially a part of the structure of the state but, in practice, it is not only a big business organization, but also an agency which is responsible for important state responsibilities. There is no state run national health service in Israel and the main health fund, called "Kupat Holim" which owns most of the hospitals and clinics, is administered by the Histadrut. To be eligible to receive sick pay, you not only have to belong to the Histadrut, but you also have to be in regular employment. Almost all Palestinians are not employed on a regular basis but only as casual day labourers and therefore they do not receive any sick pay when they are ill.

In the occupied territories, the Histadrut operates solely as a major employer and a contractor to the government. A large part of its operations is in the construction of the illegal West Bank settlements. In the territories, no trade union activity of any sort is tolerated, not even on the spurious Histadrut model. The 1983 report of the International Labour Office showed that, in the occupied territories, in less than one year alone, thirty-six trade union activists were arrested and detained and that the deportation of leading trade unionists was a regular occurrence. The actual number of trade union members in the West Bank is, not surprisingly very small and so those victimized constitute a deliberately crippling proportion of the active membership. Last year, a paper prepared in the office of the distinguished Israeli advocate, Ms Lea Tsemel, named eighteen trade unionists who, at the time of writing, were either in prison or on trial for trade union activities and another ten who were subjected to town arrest. [6] That is, they were restricted to their town of residence by day and to their homes by night.

Prior to 1967, there were about thirty-five trade unions in the West Bank. Many were simply closed down by the military authorities and such as remain are subjected to harassment which makes it impossible for them to operate as organizations and which constantly threatens the freedom of every individual who is bold enough to be a member. The main basis for the fully legalized harassment is Military order 825, made in 1980, which gives the

(6) *Harassment of Palestinian Trades Unions*, CAABU, London, 1984.

Military Governor the authority to approve candidates for trade union office and to remove from the election lists candidates of whom he does not approve. If that still does not produce the desired result, he can declare the election results null and void.

In the Gaza Strip, the situation is even more repressive. All trade unions, there, were dissolved in 1967. After a visit from the International Labour Organization in 1978, the Israelis were forced to go through the motions of permitting them to re-organize. But it was a propaganda exercise only. Today, with a workforce of over one hundred thousand in Gaza, there are only about three hundred union members. The only workers allowed to join are those who were members before the 1967 dissolution and so there are no young members at all and an inevitable wastage towards zero membership. The head of this so called trade union movement was appointed by the military. He is a major employer of labour, who owns a factory and a fleet of taxis. Lea Tsemel states in her paper, in a masterpiece of understatement that "He is not trusted by union activists."

So, the lot of the Palestinians at work, both in Israel and in the occupied territories, is one of exploitation and oppression. They are a source of cheap labour upon which the Israeli economy is heavily dependent and the reason for which they are discriminated against is none other than that they are Palestinians in Palestine. Those in the occupied territories also face the expropriation of their land, homes and possessions on the scale, and for exactly the same purpose, as has already been accomplished inside the 1967 borders.

When the British Mandate over Palestine ended in 1948, Zionist organizations owned or leased about seven per cent of the land in that part of Palestine which then became the state of Israel. The remaining ninety three per cent was in Palestinian ownership or control. Today, less than ten per cent is in Palestinian hands. Or, to put it another way, in Israel today, eighteen per cent of the population are denied the right to live or work on ninety per cent of the land of their own country [(7)]. As soon as the Israeli state was proclaimed, military government was declared. The military government had the power to interfere in every aspect of people's lives, including the power to confiscate or destroy property. In theory, its power extended over the lives of Jews and Palestinians

---

(7) Figures taken from the official 1984 *Statistical Abstract of Israel*, published

alike. In practice, it used its power solely to persecute Palestinians. In the early months of the Israeli state, some 750,000 Palestinians were driven from their homes and from the land upon which they depended for their livelihood. By 1967, no less than three hundred and eighty five Palestinian villages and settlements had been destroyed [(8)]. The most famous (or more correctly the most infamous) was Deir Yassin, where some two hundred and fifty men, women and children were massacred by forces under the leadership of Menachem Begin.

Among all the other infamies, there is one other in particular which I single out for mention - a village called Aqrat, in Galilee. Aqrat was occupied by Israeli forces in 1948 and its inhabitants were ordered to leave, supposedly temporarily and for their own safety. They were never allowed to return. As the Israeli state became established, supposedly as a democracy under the rule of law, the people of Aqrat resorted to every peaceful and legal means they could think of, including two appeals to the Israeli Supreme Court, to regain their property and their rights. While the second appeal was proceeding, the military destroyed every house in the village by explosives. It is not unworthy of note, as a measure of the mentality of the Israeli military, that Aqrat was inhabited entirely by Roman Catholic Christians and that it was destroyed on Christmas Day 1951.

But it is for legal rather than religious reasons that I single out Aqrat, for it is a classic demonstration of how the rule of law in Israel is structured quite specifically to deny justice to the Palestinians. The numerous laws related to land are designed for two basic purposes - first, to legalize the initial seizure of land by force and second, to institutionalize a permanent system for expropriation. What is happening today, in 1985, in the occupied territories, where, already, the Palestinians have been deprived of control over more than half the land, is an exact repeat of what was done within the 1967 borders in the 1950's and onwards.

First, in 1950, came the law on the Aquisition of Absentees' Property. The basic feature of that law was in its definition of absentees. The definition was that any citizen of Israel who was not in his ordinary place of residence at any time after 1 September

---

(8) M R Mehdi, *A Palestine Chronicle*, Alpha, London 1973. Dr Mehdi listed the villages and settlements by name.

1948 and until the end of military government (which was not until 1966) was an absentee. What that meant was that all those Palestinians who were terrorized out of their homes, both in 1948 and later, were declared to be "absentees." The property of all such absentees - land, animals, buildings and their contents, was transferred to an official of the state who was called "The Custodian of Absentees' Property." The effect of the law was to legalize and make permanent the theft by armed robbery of the property of those Palestinians who had been terrorized out of their homes by the Haganah, the Irgun Zvai Leumi and the Stern Gang, as well as by the successor to those three organizations, the Israeli Defence Force. Since the enactment of 1950, there has been a whole series of subsequent and consolidating laws, all designed primarily to deprive the Palestinians of their birthright in the country where they were born and where their ancestors lived before them for many generations. (9)

The persecution continues unabated. As well as being confined to the menial jobs, the Palestinians continue to be subject to constant, legalized persecution over their land and their homes. In Galilee, there is a place called Jabel Kamaaneh. In the days when Palestine was a part of the Ottoman Empire, a number of Bedouin gave up the nomadic life and settled at Jabel Kamaaneh. They held proper title deeds to the land and they were not so-called "absentees" as defined in the 1950 and subsequent laws. Nevertheless, in 1963, their deeds were declared null and void and the land was transferred to the state. Last November, the following appeared in a report in the Israeli paper Hadashot on the situation:

> For the last nine months, five Bedouin have been sitting in Damoun jail. They have not been convicted of any crime but are merely 'in contempt of court.' This contempt consists of having refused to carry out the ruling handed down by Acre's Justice of the Peace, who ordered them to demolish their homes with their own hands. Not the housing authorities or the police but they themselves must destroy the roof over their children's heads! They are refusing to do so, and so they remain in jail. (10)

That does not seem to require any comment.

---

(9) For a full and documented account, see Sabri Jiryis, *The Arabs in Israel*, Institute for Palestine Studies, Beirut, 1968. (Reprint, IPS, Washington DC, 1984).

(10) *Hadashot*, 16 November 1984, article by B Michael.

Every year, on 30 March, the Palestinian people celebrate what is called "The Day of the Land." The significance of the celebration is little known or understood in the western world, but it is an important annual event which ought to be better known. The Day of the Land commemorates events which occurred inside Israel on 30 March 1976 and which were the culmination of two months of mounting protest over the confiscation of Palestinian land. More than two thousand hectares were taken in Galilee and, on 30 March, there was an eruption of demonstrations. Israeli police and military reacted brutally. Six Palestinians were killed, one of them a fifteen year old boy in the ancient biblical village of Canaan. The demonstrations were not confined to the Galilee area where the confiscation took place. There were also organized protests in other parts of the country, including demonstrations in Jerusalem outside the Knesset.

Those demonstrations were the first large scale, organized public protests by Palestinians inside Israel. They came from those who had not been driven out and who had endured - and survived - constant persecution, repression and theft. The demonstrations proved to mark the starting point for a general and widespread revival of spirit among the Palestinians inside Israel. The revival continues, but now using a more sophisticated approach. That approach is well demonstrated in the cases of the two villages of Taiyiba and Deir Al Assad.

At Taiyiba, in the northern area, a group of Palestinians have founded a charity, which is legally registered under Israeli law, to build an Arab Heritage Centre. The Arab municipality has made a grant from such land as does remain under its control for the building of the centre. Such a grant of land is subject to approval by the Minister of the Interior. Successive ministers have delayed a decision for what is now the better part of two years and it seems near certain that the application will eventually be rejected. If that is the case, the trustees, all of whom hold Israeli citizenship and who have the support of enlightened Jewish Israeli citizens, propose to challenge the minister in the courts, on the grounds of his making an unconstitutional decision outside the due process of law. The minister might of course claim that a negative decision was for policy reasons and not illegal but, either way, he will have some awkward explaining to do.

At the other village, Deir Al Assad, in Galilee, another long struggle ensued after land was confiscated in the early 1960's. Yet, in May 1983, the foundation stone was laid for a Palestinian cultural and social centre. The construction has proceeded to the extent that, today, the ground floor of the two-storey building is completed and furnished. That project has the active support of Christian based charities in Western and Northern Europe, including of course considerable help from the International Christian Committee for Development Projects (ICCO), here in The Netherlands. Such international support cannot easily be ignored by the Israeli authorities and it is a fine example of how people of conscience in the West can give practical as well as moral support to the Palestinians.

The projects at Taiyiba and Deir Al Assad exemplify the resurgence of the Palestinians in Israel which started in the first Day of the Land in 1976. The full significance of the events of that day was that they sent a message of unity to all other Palestinians from those who were already resisting their treatment as an exploited minority in their own country. The annual celebration is no mere academic marking of a date in history, but the celebration of a living, growing reality by an indomitable people.

This paper has touched upon two aspects of its subject. The first aspect is that of the Palestinians as employees - underpaid and oppressed in menial jobs; the second aspect is their position as a people forcibly and unjustly dispossessed of their land, homes and property. There is a powerful link between the two, because the first has been created by the second.

The systematic seizure of their land took away from the Palestinians what was - and remains - dear to them above all other material things. But it was also the deliberate taking away of their means of livelihood. Before the forcible establishment of the Israeli state, the Palestinians were successful farmers in a fertile country. The seizure of their land turned a proud, independent people, accustomed and able to provide for themselves, into an easily exploited proletariat, dependent in obtaining a living on the dictates of others who saw themselves as their masters.

Ever sine that deliberately demoralizing process was embarked upon, the Israelis have additionally subjected the Palestinians to a systematic deprivation in education, to try to turn them into what Sarah Graham-Brown has referred to in her recent book as "a minority with a devalued culture."(11) It is the measure of the educational discrimination against the Palestinians in Israel that while they produce one of the lowest ratios of university students in the world. their compatriots in the West Bank and elsewhere, throughout the world, produce one of the highest. If any further proof were required that they are an exploited minority in their own country, that is it.

Yet, there is a profound irony in that the shaky Israeli economy has now become heavily dependent on the labour of that exploited minority. Furthermore, it is dependent not only on the labour of the minority within the pre-1967 borders, but also upon the labour of large numbers drawn from the occupied territories outside those borders. In Israel's growing economic crisis and mounting unemployment, there is powerful agitation for the Palestinians to be put out of work altogether. That in no way alters the fact of Israeli dependence on their labour and it does not alter the fact that an organized withdrawal of their labour could inflict far more damage on the Zionist state than could any feasible application of armed struggle. And it cannot be beyond the Palestinian people, who have proved to be so indomitable in the face of so much, to organize towards such an effective, peaceful use of their strength in their fight for self determination.

The self determination of peoples is one of the most fundamental principles of the Charter of the United Nations, to which, supposedly, all nations subscribe. Yet, in Israel and in the territories which have now been illegally occupied for the past eighteen years, the subjugation of the Palestinians continues with a cold blooded ruthlessness which the world community is only too prepared to countenance, but which is an affront to all humanity.

I conclude with a reference to the inspiring words of Rabbi Elmer Berger of the USA at the International Conference of Non-Governmental Organizations, at Geneva, in August last (12). Dr Berger, that lifelong advocate of peace and justice, said that beyond what he called "microscopic examination of the deliberate ambiguities of diplomacies (and) the still frustrating shrouds of ignorance woven of either Zionist wilfulness or neglect of those who could supply information" he sensed "something of a soaring

---

(11) Sarah Graham- Brown, *Education, Repression and Liberation: Palestinians*, World University Press (UK), London 1984, p. 37.

(12) Speech delivered to the conference, 21 August 1984.

human spirit which will not be denied." Dr Berger showed that, if justice and dignity are to be achieved in Palestine, for all the peoples there, irrespective of race or religion, then there is a clear duty upon all "we who have known for so long so much about these problems (to) continue to hold the standard high."

It is beyond argument that there is an inescapable duty upon all of us to do exactly that.

# 3

## MEDIA AND POLITICS IN BRITAIN:

# PUTTING DOWN THE ARABS

This chapter is a slightly edited version of an article published originally in *Arab Affairs* Autumn-Winter 1986 (League of Arab States, London) to discuss the realities of trying to present the Arab case in Britain. It mentions *inter alia* an infamously racist cartoon which was published in one of the main organs of the British trash press, The *Sun*, in May 1986. That was well before the Palestinian Intifada, although British cartoonists continued by and large to fail the nation throughout that heroic episode. In December 1988, to mark the first anniversary of the Intifada, the American-Arab Anti-Discrimination Committee (ADC) published a booklet *The Uprising in Cartoons,* in which was reproduced a selection of cartoons from North American newspapers. Many of these cartoons were brilliant and, for all the immense power of the Zionist lobby in North America, it was striking how sympathetic they were to the Palestinians and how bitingly critical they were of the Israelis. Nothing remotely comparable appeared in the British press. In those stirring times, the successors to such geniuses of the cartoon as Low and Vicky sadly failed the British people in the columns of the monopoly-capitalist British press.

The current campaign of anti-Arab racism in sections of the British media, is to some extent, a reaction to the hard won and less biased coverage of the Middle East which came to be achieved in the nineteen-seventies and early nineteen-eighties. It may be compared with the backlash swing to right wing politics in the eighties which was a reaction to what the conventional wisdom likes to refer to as the more liberal mood of the sixties. It is not uniform and on the whole the standards of the broadcasting media are less debased than those of the press.

For example, the television feature *Courage Along the Divide* which was nationally networked on the commercial television channels in September 1986, fairly portrayed Israeli colonization and oppression in the occupied territories and provided opportunities for the expression of both Arab and progressive Israeli viewpoints. On the other hand, the programme was shown late in the evening, after peak viewing time. Even so, the usual, strenuous objection was raised by the Israeli lobby. Every radio and television station is invariably subjected to a campaign of pressure, sometimes public but more usually, the British tradition, private, whenever any such programme is broadcast or even when the news does not depict events wholly as seen from a pro-Israeli and pro-Zionist standpoint.

One consequence of that constant pressure is a relentless campaign in the news and current affairs programmes playing up acts of terrorism committed or alleged to be committed by Arabs, as for example in the bombing campaign in Paris in September 1986. The daily acts of terrorism against the population of southern Lebanon or occupied Palestine by Israelis are as relentlessly played down or presented as if justified. It is an interesting exercise to count up, in any given week, the number of favourable references to Israel on radio and television and to compare them with the number of unfavourable references to Arabs.

The expression "Arab terrorists" is used repeatedly. Even where outrages are committed of which the perpetrators are not know, the expression "Arab terrorists are suspected" is a regular standby for news editors. Resistance fighters in occupied Lebanon and Palestine, even when conducting operations against the occupying military forces in self defence, which are recognized as legitimate in international law, are invariably described as "terrorists" in obedience to Israeli requirements. The overall effect is a calculated implanting into much of the collective public mind of the idea that all Arabs are terrorists without any right on their side.

It is salutary to contrast the reporting of events in South Africa with the coverage of events in Palestine. The Palestinians are the victims of an apartheid system as rigorous as that enforced in South Africa, while the Israeli state which subjects them to that regime is the closest of all South Africa's military allies and trading partners. There is wide coverage of the iniquities of apartheid in South Africa and spokespersons for the black people are regularly seen and heard presenting the case against apartheid. By contrast, the case against the apartheid practised by the Israelis is rarely featured, while there is something strongly resembling a conspiracy of silence over Israel's close links with South Africa.

Britain is the only major country which permits the ownership and control of its media to be in foreign hands and a majority section of the British press is foreign owned and controlled. It is mainly, although by no means exclusively, in the American owned sections of the British press that the lowest depths have been plumbed in the hostile depiction of Arabs. It is one aspect of the current British subservience to the policies and demands of the Reagan administration in the United States. The bombing of Tripoli and Benghazi in April 1986, with the use of British bases, was justified on the grounds that it was a counter to an international conspiracy aimed at subverting "the free world" which was being masterminded from Libya. The lack of any convincing evidence for such a ludicrous claim was finally revealed when, on 8 October 1986, Bernard Kalb, one of the Reagan administration's leading spokesmen, resigned because, in his own words, he could no longer stomach being expected to tell deliberate lies about Libya. It is in the absence of any credible evidence that the anti-Arab campaign has been deployed instead.

The most notorious although by no means the only example of the depths plumbed in the hostile depiction of Arabs has been in the *Sun* newspaper, an American owned mass circulation publication specializing in the crudest right wing politics, soft pornography and racism. The Times has passed into the same ownership, since when more than one hundred journalists have left it and the deteriorated standards of a paper once held in worldwide renown have become a matter of international comment.

On 23 July 1986, the *Sun* devoted much space to the return to the United Kingdom of a Libyan resident who had an English wife. He had been deported from the country following the murder of a policewoman, WPC Yvonne Fletcher, by shots fired from the Libyan "people's bureau" in London. There was no evidence of any complicity by this particular Libyan in the murder. An abusive *Sun* front page article was headed "Arab Pig Sneaks Back In" and was accompanied by an abusive editorial article. A complaint was lodged with the Press Council that the headline was racist and that the editorial was unfair and "inflaming and aggravating existing bigotry and prejudice." (1)

The Press Council rejected the complaint on the grounds that it accepted the paper's legal manager's explanation that "There was no remote suggestion that all Arabs were being compared with pigs", but only that the metaphor was applicable in the newspaper's judgement to this particular Arab and perhaps to the group of which he formed part."(2)

There is no right of reply in the British press and there have been no less than four Royal Commissions of inquiry into the press since 1947 - an indication of constant and continuing public concern over the standards of the press. The Press Council was set up in 1953 on the recommendation of the first Royal Commission. Included in the Council's definition of its principal objects is "To preserve the established freedom of the British press" and "To maintain the character of the British press in accordance with the highest professional and commercial standards." (3) The Council has no statutory authority, it is financed by newspaper proprietors and it is largely ignored by editors.

On 14 May 1986, the *Sun* reported the Press Council's rejection of the complaint with the headline "The *Sun* right to call Arab a pig." The following day it published a cartoon depicting a mob of pigs demonstrating outside the paper's heavily guarded plant, before a placard proclaiming, with carefully calculated ambiguity "The Sun's right to call Arab a pig." (4) The cartoon showed a security guard speaking into a handset radio telephone and it was captioned

---

(1) Press Council statement, *United Kingdom Press Gazette,* 19 May 1986.
(2) Ibid.
(3) Press Council leaflet 109 (revised January 1984), 5798.6.
(4) Can be taken to mean either "The *Sun* has a right to call Arab a pig" or "The *Sun* is right to call Arab a pig" (that is "Arabs are pigs.")

"Trouble, now the pigs object to being called Arabs." The cartoon was strongly condemned in the London Jewish Chronicle[(5)] and the Prime Minister, Margaret Thatcher, wrote to the author of this article:

> ..... I have seen the headline and cartoon in the Sun newspaper and find them most distasteful. I fully understand that they cause real offence. I attached great importance to our relations with Arab countries and share your wish to promote further understanding between us. The Press Council was established to handle complaints against the press and an approach was quite rightly made to them about this matter. Although the Press Council did not agree that the items were racist, they described them as "intemperate" and "abusive." I am sure that very many people in this country would be equally critical of such reporting....[(6)]

There did seem to be some confusion in Mrs Thatcher's letter over the first and second subjects of complaint. However, the cartoon proved to have wider political repercussions. The Arab League office in London took legal advice on the matter and lodged a complaint with the Attorney-General - the principal law officer of the British government - with a view to securing a prosecution under the law which makes an offence of incitement to racial hatred. The response of the Attorney-General, Sir Michael Havers, QC, MP, was interesting.

On 30 July, one of his legal secretaries communicated to the Arab League's solicitors that the Attorney-General had decided to institute proceedings for incitement to racial hatred in view of the cartoon. Twelve days later, another secretary in the Attorney's office informed the solicitors that the first communication "did not accurately set out the position" but that the police would be making inquiries. A senior police office was appointed to collect evidence for the Director of Public Prosecutions, whose function is to decide if there is sufficient evidence in cases referred to him to justify a prosecution. Among the potential witnesses from whom a statement was taken was the author of this article, who gave a statement on 13 August. But, before the police inquiries were completed, the Director of Public Prosecutions abruptly ordered

---

(5) Jewish Chronicle, 23 May 1986, article by Philip Kleinman.
(6) Letter from 10 Downing Street, 3 June 1986.

their termination [7]. No reason was given by either the Director of Public Prosecutions or the Attorney-General for the sudden change of policy. The Arab League then considered bringing a private prosecution. For that course of action, it was necessary to have the approval of the Attorney-General who replied, again without explanation, that he refused to give his consent.

These disturbing events raise questions which go even wider than suppression of the Arab viewpoint and open anti-Arab racism in the media. The *Sun* is a strong supporter of the Thatcher government. There has been open speculation that pressure was exerted on the government to cause the withdrawal of any legal action against the newspaper. The government predictably denied being subjected to any pressure and also denied any political motivation in changing its course of action and in denying the right of a private prosecution. The combination of the highly secretive nature of the British government process and the overwhelmingly pro-Establishment slant of the British media ensured that a curtain of silence was drawn over the issue.

If the practices of the British media in relations with the Arab World are questionable, the policies of the British government in the same area are also a matter of concern to those involved with fostering Arab-British relations. British power in the world is, of course, greatly reduced and successive British governments have responded by opting out of active involvement in efforts to resolve the problems and conflicts in the Middle East. The classic examples are the Arab-Israeli conflict, which Britain played such a historical role in creating in the earlier age of British Imperialism, and the Iran-Iraq War, the ending of which could be of major commercial significance for Britain in the post-war reconstruction of both Iraq and Iran. Although it must be added in fairness that the ending of the war through any sort of mediation is made impossible by the absolute refusal of the Iranian side to respond to any efforts from any quarter.

The Camp David Conference in 1978 and the Egyptian-Israeli Treaty brought a major reduction of British, and indeed of other Western European effort in the Middle East. The official line was that with a greater United States involvement in what the Americans euphemistically called "the peace process." It was a masterly

---

(7) Reports, *The Guardian*, 4, 12, 13 September 1986.

rationalization of growing feelings of European helplessness and a desire to wash official hands of the whole messy business (although of course at the same time seeking the maximum commercial advantage in the region). The British Foreign Secretary at the time was Dr David Owen, Minister in a Labour government, and it was his policy and that of the then government to subordinate British policy to that of the United States. Dr Owen subsequently left the Labour Party and later became leader of the Social Democratic Party. Unfortunately, even as it became clear, with the invasion of Lebanon and with the events since then, that the net result of "the peace process" was to create more war and bloodshed than had existed before, the subordination of British policy to that of the United States remained the policy of British governments and it is under the present government that the process has been carried to its current extent.

The difficulties of gaining practical support for the Arab viewpoint within the British government can be illustrated by the three episodes of : (1) the visit to London in October 1985 of Bishop Elia Khoury and Mayor Mohammed Milhem, for talks which in the event did not take place; (2) the British government's support for the American bombing of Tripoli and Benghazi in April 1986 and (3) Mrs Thatcher's visit to Israel in May 1986. None of those was an isolated incident and, together, they indicated a pattern in government policy.

Bishop Khoury's and Mayor Milhem's visit was supposed to be an important breakthrough in creating contact between the West and representatives of the Palestinians who were acceptable to the PLO. The Hussein-Arafat initiative was already in trouble and it was hoped that joint British-Jordanian-Palestinian talks might be a means to revive it. In the event, the handling of the visit did as much as anything towards destroying the initiative. Before the Mayor and the Bishop came to London, a document had been drawn up in Amman by the British and Jordanian governments which was supposed to be a draft for a final statement after the London talks. The statement was drawn up in Mohammed Milhem's absence and, it can be suspected, without Elia Khoury really being given the time or the encouragement to consider all its implications.

In London, the statement, which was more in accord with American and Israeli demands than with Arab aspirations, proved not to be an amendable draft for a final declaration but a ticket of admission which the two distinguished Palestinians were expected to sign in advance in order even to be allowed into the talks. When they not surprisingly refused to submit to such treatment, the talks were immediately cancelled by the British and Jordanian governments. The rally which the British Zionist lobby had organized for the same evening to protest against any talks between the British government and representative Palestinians, was turned instead into a celebration of the latest failure in "the peace process."

Little comment is required on the second episode, the collusion of the British government in the bombing of Libya, since the subordination of British interests to American requirements is self evident. However, the episode of Mrs Thatcher's visit to Israel, only a few weeks later, in May 1986, illustrated the confusion and divisions in British policy.

Representatives had been made to the government in advance by concerned British people, in and out of Parliament, that while the Prime Minister was in the Middle East, it was essential for her not just to meet with Israelis and with Israeli approved persons but with representative and responsible Palestinians. The upshot was her meeting with a group of eight eminent Palestinians in the British Consulate in Jerusalem. The events which ensued were remarkable. The eminent Palestinians impressed upon Mrs Thatcher that it was to the PLO alone that Palestinians looked as the only body to represent them in negotiations for peace and self determination and that they. the eminent persons. upheld that viewpoint. Mrs Thatcher emerged from the meeting immediately to attack the PLO and to announce that there were alternative negotiators. Apparently, in her view, these were comprised of such as those whom she had met. The eminent Palestinians were forced to issue an immediate repudiation of that and to restate what it was that they had really said and, as they thought, made clear.

What the episode illustrated was the British Prime Minister's dilemma. She had taken a minor initiative the previous year. in inviting Bishop Khoury and Mayor Milhem to go to London and then she found that, when it came to the crunch, she was stepping outside what was acceptable to the Israeli Prime Minister Shimon Peres and to Ronald Reagan. She found herself in the same dilemma in Jerusalem, with similarly unproductive results.

However, if the British attitude was a low profile one, it was no more than in step with that of the twelve member European Community. Between July and December 1986, Britain was holding the chairmanship of the Council of Ministers, effectively the policy making body of the EC. Speaking for the EC at the General Assembly of the United Nations in New York on 23 September, Sir Geoffrey Howe, the British Foreign Secretary, merely said in the Middle East section of his speech that the EC appealed to parties concerned, the Arab states, Israel and the Palestinian people, to open the door to peace by recognizing each other's rights. Referring to the Gulf War, he said merely that the EC "urged Iraq and Iran to agree to an immediate ceasefire and to seek a peaceful, honourable solution to their difficulties, co-operating fully with the Secretary-General of the UN in his exercise of good offices."(8)

Those pious sentiments contrasted somewhat with the more specific EC views on South Africa, concerning which Sir Geoffrey said that the twelve member countries forcefully condemned South Africa's armed incursions against neighbouring countries and that they had repeatedly called on the South African government to release Nelson Mandela and other political prisoners. He said that the South African government also bore a heavy responsibility in Namibia and that the EC countries called upon the South African government to implement the United Nations plan (that is, to withdraw) without further delay(9). The similarity between the South African and Israeli armed incursions against other countries, unjustifiable imprisonment of political prisoners and illegal occupation of territory is inescapable, as is the oppression of the Blacks in the one case and the Palestinians in the other. Yet, while the EC could speak out specifically and with relative force in relation to the persecution of Black Africans, it could speak only with vague generalizations on the persecution of Arabs.

In a multi-party parliamentary democracy like Britain, the attitudes and policies of the opposition are as important as those of the government. For many decades, the Labour Party was overwhelmingly pro-Zionist and pro-Israeli, a situation which was at its height during the Labour governments of the nineteen-sixties and nineteen-seventies, under the premiership of Harold Wilson. In retrospect, it can be seen that the Israeli lobby in Britain reached the

---

(8) UN News Summary, No. WS/86/26, 25 September 1986
(9) Ibid.

zenith of its power at and around the time of the 1967 war in the Middle East. The current campaign of anti-Arab racism in the media, as well as a campaign of both public and private Zionist pressure in the media and within the political parties, is part of an attempt to restore that power.

At the time of the 1967 war, anyone who dared publicly to express Arab sympathies, especially in the Labour Party, was attacked venomously. Will Griffiths, a senior and respected Member of Parliament, who had served in the army in the Middle East in World War II, who knew the region well and who had just returned from a visit to Egypt, was subjected to continuous barracking and outright attempts to shout him down in the House of Commons when he spoke in defence of the Arab position(10). Another Labour MP, Mrs Margaret McKay, retired at the next election, after being subjected to a particularly scurrilous campaign.

Yet, and probably inevitably, the very excesses of that period brought a reaction. The formation of the Labour Middle East Council in 1969 (which was followed by the formation of Conservative and Liberal Middle East Councils in 1980) for the specific purpose of working within the party to challenge the then all-pervading power of the Zionist lobby and to bring the party to a more balanced view of conflict in the Middle East, was an important milestone. Today, the Labour Party has undergone the most dramatic change of attitude of any of the British parties. The annual party conference, a representative assembly which defines the broad principles of party policy, debated and carried in 1982 a resolution condemning "the continuing pattern of Israeli aggression", calling for the recognition of the PLO and declaring support for the inalienable right of the Palestinian people to self determination within an independent sovereign state(11). Continuing support for that position and yet, at the same time, the continuing hangover of attitudes fashioned in earlier years, was demonstrated in a minor and unpublicized but significant incident connected with the party conference in 1986.

For the first time, in 1986, the National Executive Committee, which is elected annually by the conference delegates, decided to invite Palestinian visitors to attend the conference as official guests

---

(10) House of Commons Official Report (Hansard) Fifth Series, Vol.747, Cols. 142-153, 31 May 1967.

(11) Annual Conference Report 1982, The Labour Party, pp. 131-138, 146, 281-282.

of the party and it was proposed to invite Hanna Siniora, editor of the *Al-Fajr* newspaper and Fayez Abu Rahmeh, the lawyer from Gaza, both of whom had been in the group who had met Mrs Thatcher in Jerusalem. The party secretariat, which is subject to constant behind-the-scenes Zionist pressure, described these two, in its report to the Executive as being "acceptable to the Israelis." A prominent member of the Executive, who had formerly taken an ambivalent attitude on the Palestinian cause but who had recently become a strong supporter, objected because, he said, "We want Palestinians acceptable to the PLO, not to the Israelis." Whereupon the Committee, not well informed on the subtleties of the situation, decided not to invite them - which was very acceptable to the Israeli lobby. However, better informed party members took the matter to the top level in the parliamentary leadership, where it was seen to that the invitation was re-instated.[12]

One thing which is clear is that a Labour government would seek to be more independent of American influence than the Conservative government, something which has already brought upon the party the wrath of Messrs. Caspar Weinberger and Richard Perle, as well as the more diplomatically expressed concern of Mr. Charles Price, the United States Ambassador in London. If a Labour government should be elected, it can still be only a matter for speculation as to what extent its Middle East policy, in practise, would be able to reflect the sympathy for the Arab position which is now strong within the party. American political and economic power over Britain, as well as the internal power of the Israeli lobby in Britain, which would receive massive backing from the much more effective Israeli lobby in the USA and which would also receive strong support in the overwhelmingly anti-Labour British media, would be powerful factors against a more progressive British approach.

(12) In the event, Fayez Abu Rahmeh's arrival at the conference was delayed through Israeli obstruction of his departure from Gaza.

# 4

# THE SOUTH AFRICAN CONNECTION

By the mid nineteen-eighties, the longstanding relationship between Israel and South Africa was finally starting to become more widely known. Informed people had known about it for years but there were too many in influential positions who, while prepared to campaign against violations of black human rights in South Africa, were either unaware of or aware of but only too willing to turn a blind eye to. the close parallel with Israel's treatment of the Palestinians and the close alliance between the two countries. The trigger to wider appreciation of the situation came with the declaration of the state of emergency in South Africa in 1985 and the sickening brutality practised in consequence against (and also, it must be said, among) the black people. The killing and beating was seen daily on the world's television screens until the South African government imposed censorship and restricted media access - a policy to be followed later by the Israelis in response to worldwide media coverage of their own, identical response to the Palestinian Intifada.

In response to growing calls for more information on the Israeli-South African relationship, CAABU organized in October 1986 a one day seminar in London on the theme *Israel and South Africa: Zionism and Apartheid.* It was a pioneering effort which proved a huge success and when the proceedings were published, they sold out. The participation was invited of both the Palestine Liberation Organization and the African National Congress, and both accepted. Faisal Aouidha, the London Representative of the PLO, and Solly Smith, the Chief Representative in London of the ANC, were among the speakers. I was amazed to discover that it was the first time they had met each other. Even had CAABU accomplished nothing else, it performed a major public service that day in bringing them together and in inaugurating an important co-operation in London between the two liberation movements. It was noticeable afterwards that Solly Smith became a regular guest at Arab Embassy receptions. The seminar also heard an outstanding address from Jane Hunter, the best informed expert in the world on the Israeli-South African connection, whom CAABU brought from California to speak and also to carry out a number of other engagements in the United Kingdom and other western European countries.

Amid a strongly continuing demand for information, CAABU held another very successful seminar in May 1989 on *Israel and South Africa: A Strategic Alliance* (1). Jane Hunter was again among the speakers, as also was Denis Goldberg, the Jewish campaigner against apartheid who was imprisoned for many years in South Africa and who was released as a result of direct intervention, of which he did not approve, by the Israeli government.

What follows in this chapter is, first, a revised version of an article I wrote in 1985 for the newspaper *Al Khaleej* (The Gulf), which is published in Sharjah in the United Arab Emirates. This is followed by a speech I was invited to deliver to a conference on the Middle East which was sponsored by Liberation (formerly The Movement for Colonial Freedom) when I shared the platform, under the chairmanship of an old friend from parliamentary days, Stan Newens MEP, with among others, Felicia Langer, the distinguished Israeli lawyer who devoted her career to defending Palestinians. Felicia Langer is the author of two books on the treatment of the Palestinians. The first is *With My Own Eyes*, originally published in Hebrew in Tel Aviv in 1974 and in English in 1975 by Ithaca Press, London. The sequel. *These Are My Brothers,* was published by Ithaca in 1979. Mrs Langer was born in Poland and her husband was a survivor of Buchenwald, the Nazi death camp. After a lifetime defending Palestinians in the Israeli courts, she finally left

(1) Proceedings published, CAABU, London, 1989.

the country in disgust and emigrated to Germany.

Only the tip of the vast iceberg of the Israeli-South African connection is touched upon in this short chapter. Reference here is of course to the nineteen-eighties and earlier. By the nineties, an important contrast was developing between the two states. By then, South Africa was moving away from apartheid. Certainly, it was doing so painfully, slowly and against strong resistance, especially from its pro-apartheid fascist movement, but the government was opposing the fascists. In Israel, by contrast, apartheid was intensifying and fascist groups seeking its intensification were being encouraged by the government. The changes in South Africa came about because measures were taken by the international community to support the black people's struggle for justice. Comparable international measures are clearly necessary to support the Palestinians' struggle for justice.

# APARTHEID IN THE MIDDLE EAST

**Article in *Al Khaleej*, September 1985**

Just three weeks after the South African government declared a state of emergency to enforce apartheid, a visitor from South Africa to Israel met Prime Minister Shimon Peres in Jerusalem. The visitor was Chief Gatsha Buthelezi, chief of the Zulu people and president of the Zulu Inkatha movement. The Chief was told by Mr Peres that Israel deplored apartheid and would express its views "in ways that are open to us, to the South African authorities." Now, that raises at least three interesting questions. First, from what moral standpoint does Israel deplore apartheid? Second, what exactly are the special ways which are open to it to approach the South African authorities which are not open to others? Third, what is the standing of Chief Buthelezi in South Africa and why was he given a top level reception in Israel?

The first question can be answered quickly. Israel has no moral authority to deplore apartheid, because it practices a similar system against the Palestinian people in Israel and in the occupied territories. Within the 1967 borders, the vast majority of the Palestinians have been driven out by force of arms and dispossessed from more than ninety per cent of the land. They depended on that land for their living. Driving them out both established the state of Israel on the land of Palestine and ensured that those Palestinians who did not flee their country could be exploited as cheap labour by their new masters.

The treatment of the people in the occupied territories is designed to achieve the same ultimate result. Under a brutal military occupation, the West Bank and Gaza, like the Arab villages within the 1967 borders, have been turned into a Middle Eastern version of the South African bantustans, from which Palestinian workers travel to work for very low wages in menial jobs in Israel. Many of them are kept there overnight, illegally locked away in the places where they work. The Israeli newspaper *Ha'aretz* reported recently that several such places had been entered by security guards who beat up a large number of the Palestinians.

Plenty of other evidence exists of the growing racism of Israeli society and it is proving deeply disturbing to enlightened Jewish people. The London *Jewish Chronicle* recently reported that on at least three occasions in a single week, Arabs who were Israeli citizens were, in the Chronicle's own words "driven off public beaches by Jewish thugs or public facilities administrators, simply because they were Arabs." When the Palestinians asked why they were being asked to leave, they were told "Because we say so. And because you are Arabs." The *Jewish Chronicle* commented that those incidents indicated that "an evil spirit is creeping into Israeli society" and that there are disturbing signs that a de facto apartheid system is being implemented." In fact, of course, it is not a new thing but another manifestation of the longstanding apartheid character of Israeli society. But it is especially illuminating that an important pro-Israeli publication in Britain finds itself obliged to speak so critically.

To turn to the second question, just what are the special channels of communication which the Israelis have to the South African authorities? The answer is that they have unique channels, for Israel is closer to South Africa than is any other country in the world. Only in February of this year [1985], in the closest secrecy, Israel and South Africa signed an agreement for joint development in science and technology. That secret agreement was no new departure. On the contrary, it was merely the latest move in years of highly secretive joint development, including military co-operation and the developing and testing of nuclear weapons.

Near Tel Aviv is the Iskoor steel processing plant, which is jointly owned by a South African company and the Israeli Histadrut, and which is especially important for both Israeli and South African trade with the countries of the European Community. Since the beginning of this year, the tariffs which the European Community previously levied on imports from Israel have all been removed. Before that, manufactured products which had value added to them by processing in Israel, no matter where they originated from, were relieved of tariffs. Since well before the abolition of the tariffs, crude steel made in South Africa was being sent to Israel, from where, after being processed into high grade steel at Iskoor, it was re-exported to the European Community, thereby obtaining access there for South African products which would not otherwise be accepted. So the apartheid state of South Africa, universally despised except by Israel, is well placed to bypass any sanctions to which it might be subjected. It can and no doubt will do so by trading through the similar but more widely accepted apartheid state of Israel. No wonder Mr Peres could tell Chief Buthelezi that Israel had special access to the South African authorities.

So what is the Chief's standing in South Africa? He is widely quoted in the international media and at a first glance his position appears impressive. However, he is far from universally accepted by opponents of apartheid and his Inkatha movement is in open conflict with the multi-racial United Democratic Front (UDF), the principal organization against apartheid. The destruction of the UDF is a primary objective of the state of emergency imposed in South Africa and, while Chief Buthelezi has been free to visit Israel, leading members of the UDF have been arrested and imprisoned. The government's policy is also to destroy the African National Congress (ANC), which they declared illegal many years ago. Mr Nelson Mandela of the ANC, the universally recognized leader of South Africa's black people, has been imprisoned for well over twenty years and the South African President, in a much heralded speech made on 15 August, once again rejected the strong international calls for the release of Mr Mandela.

The apartheid government has ambitions to negotiate some sort of so called "settlement" with Chief Buthelezi, and the Chief was interviewed, from Jerusalem, on British television for his comments on President Botha's speech. The Chief expressed disappointment and said that he would not negotiate unless those held in prison, including Mr Mandela, were released. On his return to South Africa, he made a widely reported speech, again criticizing the apartheid regime but also making a strong attack on the UDF and ANC. His acceptability in Israel and his speech on his return home did not improve his standing among those resisting apartheid.

In the USA, in the early eighteen fifties, in the days of slavery, Mrs Harriet Beecher Stowe wrote her famous novel *Uncle Tom's Cabin.* The book made a great impact on public opinion and played a large part in bringing about the eventual abolition of slavery. Even so, it needs to be noted that it was not until the southern states which practised slavery were defeated in the American Civil War in the eighteen-sixties that slavery actually was abolished, The hero of the book "Uncle Tom" was an elderly Negro slave of impeccable character and fortitude who endured passively the evil and ill-treatment of slavery without active protest. For exploited people in general, the name "Uncle Tom" has since become a term of contempt for those among their number who accept an oppressive status quo without effective protest. "Uncle Tom" was what is now called, in one of the most overworked jargon words of the established order in the Western World, a "moderate" - someone who is amenable to whatever the establishment does, however immoderate the establishment is itself.

Now that is how the western establishment, as well as that in Israel, would like to see Chief Buthelezi, the former to protect its commercial interests in South Africa, the latter to further its political interests. For the Israelis, the chief has two special qualities. First, he is the sort of leader they would like to find if they could among the Palestinians. Second, he is acceptable as a necessary tool to be used in their policy of currying favour with the black African countries which Israel wants as outlets for its exports and, of course, in the case of Nigeria, as a source of oil.

The government of Israel has no more intention of making any effective protests about apartheid to its close friends in the government of South Africa than it has of talking with the Arabs. How could it? In the nineteen-seventies, the Arab League countries and the black African countries in the Organization of African Unity established the Afro-Arab Dialogue, in mutual defence against South Africa and Israel. In the grim situation of 1985, an active and effective Afro-Arab Dialogue is more needed than ever.

## ISRAEL AND SOUTH AFRICA

**Address to Liberation Conference,**
**13 December 1986 at Conway Hall, London.**

On 24 September, an advertisement appeared in the *Jerusalem Post* inviting people to join a "dream holiday on board the luxurious cruise ship Achille Lauro to South Africa, from only US $999 including return flight via South African Airways." (2) That is just a glimpse at the surface of the very deep Israeli alliance with South Africa. There is a worldwide consensus against South Africa but, at the very time when many countries are weakening their links with that country, Israel is actually strengthening its links.

Only in August, a high level Israeli delegation visited South Africa, headed by the Director of the Ministry of Finance, Dr Emmanuel Sharon. The *Jerusalem Post* reported on 23 August that they had discussed new agreements between the two countries which are to operate from 1987 onwards. Those agreements include credits for South African exports to Israel, South African investments in Israel and Israeli fishing rights in South African waters. What is even more important is what was not reported, for there is every reason to believe that the real subject on the agenda was Israel's role in breaking sanctions which the rest of the world might seek to impose against the apartheid state. It requires to be well noted, as a measure of how long has been the association between the two countries, that the agreements reported did not constitute any entry into new arrangements but were a renewal of existing agreements. The fact is that there is a very longstanding commercial and military alliance between the two states.

It was back in 1978 when the then Israeli Finance Minister, Simha Ehrlich, speaking in Johannesburg, inaugurated the joint policy whereby South African manufactured goods could be completed in Israel and then re-exported to countries of the European Community where, he said "They would benefit from advantages enjoyed by Israel." Israel, even then, had a very favourable trading relationship with the European Community, which has become even more advantageous since. Indeed, since

(2) The Achille Lauro was the ship on board which a dissident Palestinian group murdered an elderly, disabled American passenger, Leon Klinghoffer, in October 1985 and threw his body into the sea, precipitating a major crisis.

1 January 1985, all exports of manufactured goods from Israel to the EC have been completely free of tariffs. Israel also enjoys much the same advantages with the USA, as a result of the free trade agreement concluded with that country and which came into operation on 1 September 1985. The published trade figures between Israel and South Africa omit two vital factors and give an impression of relatively modest trade which is a complete misrepresentation of the real situation. The first omission is the export of rough diamonds from South Africa to Israel which is conducted secretly via London and other European centres of the diamond trade and which may well amount to as much as US $1 billion per year. The second omission is in the export of Israeli arms and military technology to South Africa.

Israeli arms exports are kept quiet because they breach both the 1963 and 1977 United Nations mandatory embargo on arms exports to South Africa. Those exports have been going on for a very long time. Israeli arms are used to enforce apartheid and also for aggression against neighbouring countries. But the Israeli-South African military alliance goes much further than that. There have been many years of co-operation to produce nuclear weapons. It was as long ago as September 1979 when the two countries carried out their first joint nuclear explosion over the southern Indian Ocean. If you add up the years of work required to reach that stage, you start to get an idea of how long and how deep the alliance is between the two apartheid regimes and how serious a threat it is to the world at large.

There is a fundamental similarity between the two which accounts for their close alliance. The similarity is demonstrated, first, in South Africa's treatment of its black citizens and Israel's treatment of the Palestinians. It is demonstrated in their common policies of constant threats against other countries, military incursions into and occupation of the territory of other countries, and in their common contempt for the international community and for international law. South Africa disregards all UN resolutions calling upon it to leave Namibia, Israel disregards all UN resolutions calling upon it to leave Lebanon and the occupied territories of Palestine. What an irony it is that the Israeli state, which was created out of the Nazi genocide against the Jewish people, is today the closest ally of a state governed by a nationalist party which openly supported Nazism in the second world war and which now also has its own openly resurgent Nazi Party which even uses a swastika-type symbol.

The similarity between Israel and South Africa has never been more clearly demonstrated than in the report of the Commonwealth Eminent Persons Group on South Africa [(3)]. With nothing more than certain changes of nomenclature, it could be a report on Israel and the Middle East. The Eminent Persons defined their terms of reference as follows :-

> Our mandate was to foster a process of negotiations across lines of colour, politics and religion, with a view to establishing a non-racial and representative government. It is our considered view that, despite appearances and statements to the contrary, the South African government is not yet ready to negotiate such a future- except on its own terms.

In that passage you only have to replace "process of negotiations" with "international peace conference" and to replace "South African government" with " Israeli government" and you have a remarkable parallel with the Middle East. The Eminent Persons also observed "The black people of South Africa can no longer stomach being treated as aliens in their own country." Exactly like the Palestinians!

It is also stated in the report that "There can be no negotiated settlement without the ANC; the breadth of its support is incontestable and this support is growing." You have only to replace ANC with PLO and you have an exact parallel with the Middle East. In Palestine, the huge strength of support for the PLO was well measured in July and August of this year in a scientifically conducted public opinion poll in the occupied territories. The poll indicated that no less than 93.5 per cent of the Palestinian people supported the PLO.

No less interesting than the poll itself was the official Israeli reaction. The poll was conducted by Mohammed Shadin, a distinguished academic who is an American citizen working at the An-Najah University at Nablus. A few weeks ago, he was summoned by the Israeli authorities who demanded that he should announce either that the poll was faked or else that it was not

---

(3) Mission to South Africa, Penguin Books, London, 1986, report by seven eminent citizens appointed by the 1985 Commonwealth Conference to visit and report on South Africa.

accurate. He refused angrily to compromise his professional integrity in such a way. The Israelis did not dare to arrest him as they would any Palestinian inhabitant because he is an American, so what they have done is to withdraw his work permit to prevent him from earning his living. They told him that they had received complaints about the poll from the Jordanian government. That might or might not be true but it is an allegation which raises interesting possibilities and is worth thinking about, not least against the background of the current detention in Jordan of Dr Rafiq Husseini, the Director of the British registered charity Medical Aid for Palestinians.(4)

In the Eminent Persons' report, there is another reference which makes yet another devastating comparison between South Africa and Israel:-

> Even while we were in discussion with senior ministers in the South African government it carried out bombing attacks on the three neighbouring Commonwealth countries of Zambia, Zimbabwe and Botswana.

The parallel with the Israeli attack on Tunis in 1985 is overwhelming. At that time, the Hussein-Arafat initiative for peace was very much on the world agenda. King Hussein was in Washington, talking with President Reagan and senior officials. One of the objects of the attack was actually to try to kill Yasser Arafat, the other partner in the peace initiative, at the very time when the king was engaged in the work of the initiative.

The parallels between Israel and South Africa are overwhelming. They exist in the similarities between the two systems of government, in the treatment of the Palestinians by the one and the treatment of the black people by the other; in the similarities of their policies towards other countries and in their common contempt for the world community. No wonder there is longstanding collusion and a close alliance between them. Separately, each is an affront to democracy. Together, they represent a major danger to peace.

---

(4) Dr Husseini, a microbiologist, resided in Britain. His wife was British. He held a Jordanian passport and, on visiting Jordan in 1986, he was refused permission to leave for about two years, on allegations of association with the PLO.

# 5

# AN INTERNATIONAL PEACE CONFERENCE

Pressure for an international peace conference on the Middle East grew throughout the nineteen-eighties. By late 1987, even Sir Geoffrey Howe, the British Secretary of State for Foreign and Commonwealth Affairs, who was not renowned for his innovative approach, was saying that an international conference offered "the best - indeed the only practical - way forward" (see page 54 above). Yet the decade ended without a conference being convened.

The start of the nineteen eighties campaign can be traced to a conference in Geneva in September 1983 to which governments and also non-governmental organizations (NGO's) were invited by the General Assembly of the United Nations "to seek effective ways and means to enable the Palestinian people to attain and to exercise their inalienable rights." [(1)] The governments of Israel and the USA made a determined effort to organize a boycott but in the event a substantial number of governments were present or represented by observers, while 104 NGO's attended from countries worldwide,. including the USA and Israel. Yasser Arafat was among those who addressed the conference. In the Geneva Declaration the gathering called for an international peace conference under UN auspices with the participation of all parties to the Arab-Israeli conflict, including

---

(1) Conference Report, document A/CONF 114/41, 16 September 1983.

the PLO, as well as the USA, the USSR and other concerned states "on an equal footing." The purpose would be "a comprehensive, just and lasting solution to the Arab-Israeli conflict, an essential element of which would be the establishment of an independent Palestinian state in Palestine." The General Assembly endorsed the Declaration by 124 votes to 4, the four against being Israel, the United States, Canada and Australia. There were seventeen abstentions, including Britain. American hostility ensured that if any attempt were to be made to bring the Declaration before the Security Council, it would be vetoed.

The Geneva Declaration expressed what was by then already a very widely held international consensus which had been developing for a long time. Its roots could be traced as far back as Security Council Resolution 242 of 1967 and it had developed via Resolution 338 of 1973, which first proposed negotiations among all parties to the conflict, including the two superpowers. The consensus had further developed via the USA-USSR co-operation which resulted, however briefly, after Resolution 338, and via the European Community's Venice Declaration of 1980. It was a consensus commanding support among most Arab governments, among the people of the occupied territories as well as among enlightened Israelis, by the Soviet Union and its allies, and by the countries of Western Europe. It was rejected only by the Israeli government, by the USA due to Israeli power over American policy and by a few governments which America was able to influence. Israel and America, and their ability to muddy the international waters, proved to be the main obstacles which were able to frustrate the international consensus throughout the decade. However, in the aftermath of the Gulf war in early 1991, American policy started to move towards the consensus and the outcome was the conference held in Madrid later the same year.

What follows are three analyses, made in 1987-88, of the problems of convening a peace conference under United Nations auspices, and then an analysis of the Madrid conference, written shortly after it took place. In April 1987, I was invited to speak in Washington DC, on the subject of a peace conference, at the annual convention of the American-Arab Anti-Discrimination Committee (ADC), as one of a four-member panel on "Palestine Occupied; Where Now?" The overall theme of the convention was "Arab America: A Strong New Voice." it was a time when American citizens of Arab origin, estimated variously to number from two and a half to three million, were finally getting organized and standing up to be counted in opposition to the Zionist-Israeli lobby which had for so long exercised such powerful influence in the United States. Next, is an article from the London *Palestine Post* and then an address to a Wilton Park conference. The Wilton Park Conferences are held under the aegis of the Foreign and Commonwealth Office at Wilton Park Conference Centre, a country house near Steyning, in the heart of the lovely West Sussex countryside. The conferences, which last for the greater part of a week, deal with various aspects of international affairs and those attending are drawn from a wide and high level international background, mostly diplomats, academics and journalists, sometimes with a sprinkling of legislators. That was the third occasion, over a period of several years, upon which I was honoured with an invitation to address this prestigious gathering, each time on a Middle Eastern topic.

# A VIEW FROM EUROPE

**Address to ADC National Convention, Washington DC, 4 April 1987**

It has been my very great pleasure to cross the Atlantic and to take part in this Convention. It is my especial pleasure to respond to ADC's invitation to give a view from Europe on the subject of an international peace conference on the Middle East. The idea of such a conference has been around for several years but it has recently been given fresh impetus when the twelve member governments of the European Community, following the meeting of their Foreign Ministers in Brussels, Belgium, on 23 February, declared for such a conference. That was an important step forward by the European Community countries. First, though, I want to make the point that it is especially appropriate that we should consider the subject at this convention of a major NGO, that is a non-governmental organization, because it was at an international conference on Palestine involving NGO's as well as governments that the idea of an international peace conference originated. That conference was held in Geneva, Switzerland, in 1983 by the United Nations and it was from that conference that there arose the General Assembly Resolution 38/58C of December 1983 which called for an international conference. Dr Cheryl Rubenberg [previous speaker] outlined the terms of reference of that resolution in her address. Since the passing of the resolution, NGO's worldwide have consistently shown themselves to be ahead of governments in their support for an international conference.

Now, I want to remind you of the reasons why such a conference is urgently necessary. Again it is especially appropriate that we should be considering the subject within a panel on "Palestine Occupied - Where Now?" because let no-one be under any illusion - the injustice suffered by the people of Palestine over many years is the very core of the whole conflict in the Middle East. I realize that there are very few people in this audience who are likely to be under any illusion about that, but the point needs to be hammered home on every possible occasion to every possible audience which can be reached. The Palestinians live under an apartheid regime and their situation is very comparable with the sufferings of the Black People in South Africa. There is worldwide appreciation that justice in South Africa can only be obtained by worldwide international action. Exactly the same applies in the case of the Palestinians and in the first place an international peace conference is necessary for that reason.

Another telling reason for international action is provided in the Israeli invasion of Lebanon in 1982. That was proof positive that bilateral action like Camp David and the Israel-Egypt peace treaty, however well intentioned, cannot bring peace. The government of Israel saw the Egyptian treaty essentially as a means to neutralize Egypt so that it could invade Lebanon in the north without having to fight a defensive war in the south. The sad fact is that since the Camp David so called "peace process", bypassing the fundamental Palestinian issue, there has been more war and bloodshed in the Middle East than there was before. The events of 1982 and since make the case for a full international approach to peace involving all the parties to the conflict.

The final reason for an international peace conference is that the Middle East is the most dangerous flashpoint on earth for a potential East-West superpower conflict which would destroy all civilization. So however you look at it, whether from the point of view of the situation of the Palestinians, from the point of view of the failure of bilateral action or from the point of view of the Middle East as a flashpoint for world conflict, there is an unanswerable case for an international peace conference.

Let me come back now to the latest move to advance a conference - that is to the Brussels Declaration by the twelve European Community governments on 23 February, and I quote two sentences from that declaration:-

> The Twelve would like to state that they are in favour of an international peace conference to be held under the auspices of the United Nations with the participation of the parties concerned and of any party able to make a direct and positive contribution to the restoration and maintenance of peace and to the region's economic and social development .... The Twelve would be prepared to play their part with respect to such a conference and will endeavour to make an active contribution.

Nearly seven years ago, in the Venice Declaration of June 1980, the European Community countries made a number of important points. Among these were that the Palestinians must have the right to self determination and that the Palestine Liberation Organization must be involved in negotiations. Today, the involvement of the PLO is clearly and unmistakably predicated in the new Brussels Declaration. Anyone who knows the Middle East knows that the PLO is overwhelmingly the representative body of the Palestinian people, that it must be recognized as such and must be involved in negotiations and in an international conference.

Those who oppose the national liberation of oppressed people always describe national liberation movements as "terrorist organizations" because that automatically stops most people from thinking about the real issues of national liberation. Those who describe the PLO as "terrorist" are those who are opposed to the liberation and self determination of the Palestinians. Above all, the technique is used by the Israelis. Yet they themselves, every day, are terrorizing the civilian population of the occupied territories. Nor is their terrorism confined to distant Palestine. It does not really need me to remind you that you here in ADC have also had your own experience of their terrorism and of the terrorism of their agents [(2)]. The forces which are responsible for that sort of terrorism must not be allowed to obstruct the international peace conference.

And it must be a real peace conference. I very much underline Cheryl Rubenberg's analysis of the situation and of the problems, and state that it must be a real peace conference designed to bring about peace and not just another example of endless argument about semantics, designed to avoid peace rather than to bring it nearer, and it must be a conference involving the PLO and both the superpowers.

I must say a further word about the superpowers because the Brussels Declaration of 23 February also clearly envisages both USA and USSR involvement and I have to tell you that there is growing disillusion in Europe with those aspects of United States policy which see the Middle East as a region for confrontation with the Soviet Union. The disillusion arises because the Middle East is a region where the problems cry out not for confrontation but for co-operation between the superpowers.

Noam Chomsky pointed out in 1983 in that outstanding book

(2) A reference to Alex Odeh, ADC's Southern California Regional Director, who was murdered by a bomb in his office in 1985.

*The Fateful Triangle* that there was then already an international consensus in favour of peace with justice for the Palestinians. It was a consensus which existed already in Europe, both East and West, throughout the Third World and among thinking people everywhere, including in Israel. Now, in 1987, I suggest to you that the consensus has progressed to recognizing the role of the PLO and to recognizing the need for an international peace conference with both superpowers taking part together with all parties to the Arab-Israeli conflict. It will be a terrible tragedy if the USA remains isolated from the world consensus because its Middle East policy continues to be manipulated by Israel, and manipulated in a manner which is absolutely against Israel's own real, long-term interests and which is certainly against America's real interests.

Now I must be careful not to get involved in internal American politics, but I am aware that those who favour that sort of manipulation of American policy try to justify it by saying that "Israel is America's only friend in the Middle East." The real fact is that if it were not for Israel, America would have many friends in the Middle East. They would be real friends. They would not have their networks of spies operating here in Washington (3). And they would be a hell of a lot less expensive for the American taxpayers.

In conclusion, I return to my opening theme, which is that non-governmental organizations worldwide have played a special part in putting an international peace conference onto the world agenda and that they have also consistently shown themselves to be ahead of governments, and governments of all complexions, on the subject. I suggest that now more than ever, American NGO's in particular have a uniquely important part to play in the search for peace with justice in the Middle East by impressing upon the United States government, by all the means at their command, the need for an international peace conference. There indeed is a role for a strong new voice.

---

(3) Reference to Jonathan Pollard, an American found guilty as a long term Israeli spy and who attempted to take refuge in the Israeli Embassy to avoid arrest.

# THE INTERNATIONAL COMMUNITY MUST ACT

**Article in Palestine Post, June 1987**

Conflict in the Middle East threatens peace and stability worldwide. It follows that measures to resolve the conflict can be effective only through worldwide co-operation. Lesser measures, like Camp David and the Egypt-Israel treaty, have not produced peace in the past. There has been more war and bloodshed in the Middle East since Camp David than there was before. Such measures, bypassing the issue of justice for the Palestinians which is the basic cause of the whole conflict, will fail similarly if tried again in the future. So the need for an international peace conference is clearly demonstrated.

The idea of such a conference originated in the UN Security Council Resolution 338 of 1973, which proposed a conference under joint USA and USSR chairmanship. That conference was destroyed by Israeli opposition and the power of the Zionist lobby in America. But the idea was strongly taken up again at a conference called in Geneva in the late summer of 1983 by the General Assembly of the United Nations. Non-governmental organizations (NGO's) as well as governments were invited. The object was "to seek effective ways and means to enable the Palestinian people to attain and exercise their inalienable rights." Israel and the United States government made a determined effort to organize a boycott but in the event no less than one hundred and thirty representatives of governments attended, together with one hundred and four NGO's from countries worldwide, including the USA and Israel. The PLO attended and Yasser Arafat was among those who addressed the conference.

In the Geneva Declaration on Palestine, the conference called for an international conference under United Nations auspices with the participation of all parties to the Arab-Israeli conflict, including the PLO as well as the USA, the USSR and other concerned states "on an equal footing." The General Assembly endorsed the recommendation by 124 votes to 4, with 17 abstentions, in Resolution 38/58C of December 1983. That resolution is fast becoming as famous as the Security Council Resolutions 242 and 338. Leaving aside all other considerations, that in itself demonstrates how UN resolutions on the Middle East require to be taken together and not separately and with false interpretations of their meanings. Taken together and interpreted accurately, they reflect the ever growing world consensus on the Middle East.

Since that first conference, the United Nations has called an annual meeting of NGO's which every year, with growing authority, has reiterated the call for an international peace conference. Each year, too, the international meetings of NGO's have elected an International Co-ordinating Committee which meets regularly and has, through its own fund raising, established a small office in Geneva. A series of regional conferences of NGO's has also taken place and it is significant, as an indication of how NGO thinking is frequently ahead of government thinking, that the North American NGO's were the first to hold a regional conference. Because 1987 includes a number of notable anniversaries, the NGO's International Co-ordinating Committee has designated it "The Year of the Palestinians."

Nineteen eight-seven is the ninetieth anniversary of the first Zionist Congress, the seventieth anniversary of the Balfour Declaration, the fortieth anniversary of the UN Partition Resolution, the twentieth anniversary of the 1967 war and occupation, and the fifth anniversary of the invasion of Lebanon and the massacres at Sabra and Shatilla. In their historical order, those anniversaries vividly trace the conflict, from misconceived political theory in the eighteen-nineties, through international intrigue, to war and massacre. No year could be more appropriate than 1987 to initiate an international peace conference to bring the whole tragic epoch to a close. Fortunately, 1987 is a year in which a number of factors are in existence to show that a world grown weary of the endless conflict has a growing will to do something.

A significant step forward was when the Foreign Ministers of the twelve member countries of the European Community, meeting in Brussels on 23 February, called for an international peace conference, in terms clearly in line with those of Resolution 38/58C. Nearly seven years earlier, in the Venice Declaration, the EC countries had called for Palestinian self-determination and declared that the PLO must be a party to negotiations. The Venice Declaration was heavily attacked by the Israelis and the USA as an obstacle to the Camp David so-called "peace process" and nothing was done about it by the EC powers until the 1987 Brussels

Declaration. In the meantime, the terrible events in Lebanon and the iron fist policy for terrorizing the Palestinian people have all been perpetrated. The Brussels Declaration was a significant indication of growing European impatience with the failure of American policy.

Even in Washington itself, realization has dawned that US policy has failed. There was no opposition, this time, to the European initiative and Mr George Shultz has even made noises, even if very vague ones, in favour of an international peace conference. Another important development was the letter sent from Mr Mikhail Gorbachev to the EC countries in advance of the Foreign Ministers' meeting, in which he declared the Soviet Union's willingness to co-operate with the EC to bring about a Middle East peace conference. It was the first time that a Soviet government had recognized the EC as an entity in its own right instead of as a mere collection of states to be dealt with separately and, if possible, divided from each other.

Meanwhile, important developments in the Arab World also fitted into the growing will to do something. The Palestine National Council in Algiers restored a huge measure of unity which even Syria cannot ignore and negotiations to restore PLO-Syrian relations are clearly on the agenda. No less remarkable was the recent meeting in Jordan between those bitter enemies Presidents Hafez Al Assad and Saddam Hussein. All these events point to a realization of the crucial need for Arab unity, to be realized, hopefully, in the near future. The fact is that, if such unity is not brought about, and quickly, then we might all just as well forget about a peace conference.

Not least among the new 1987 portents is the reaction in Israel, where the Foreign Minister, Shimon Peres, is openly defying the Prime Minister, Yitshak Shamir, by declaring for a peace conference. Peres' motives are very dubious but he has created the situation where Shamir is the only head of any government in the world who is openly opposed to the principle of a peace conference. So it is demonstrably established that there is a world consensus in favour of an international peace conference on the Middle East. But a great stumbling block remains as to what sort of conference, because many of the advocates of such a step have different ideas about it. And some of those ideas are far removed from and, in fact, a negation of the proposals of Resolution 38/58C.

The Peres version is founded in the traditional Israeli policy of consolidating and retaining the supremacy of the Zionist state as a regional superpower in the Middle East. Recognizing that the world consensus is growing irresistible, the concept is of an international conference without the PLO which would then dissolve into individual negotiations between Israel and Jordan over the future of the occupied territories, almost certainly without Jerusalem and the Golan Heights being discussed. The USSR, even to be admitted to the conference, would have to resume diplomatic relations with Israel on Israel's terms, with agreements for the enforced large-scale emigration of Soviet Jews to the Zionist state. Palestinian self determination would continue to be bypassed. Israel would retain effective power over the West Bank and Gaza which, after protracted negotiations, would be subjected to some sort of quasi-autonomy in association with the rule of the King of Jordan.

None of this is any more than the classic position adopted ever since the self proclamation of the Israeli state and its establishment by force of arms in 1948 - to retain and colonize territory occupied through war and to play for time until further expansion becomes possible. The hope is that any actual peace conference can be delayed as long as possible and that even if it does convene, there can then be the usual delaying tactics and endless arguments about semantics, dragging on for years on end without any real settlement ever being reached. During that period, the power of the American Zionist lobby which, following the Jonathan Pollard spy case, is being more critically scrutinized in the USA than hitherto, will be fully re-established. With American backing, the Zionist state will then once again be in a position for another war if such should be thought to be necessary - against a divided Arab World. Between Shamir and Peres there is no real difference in objectives. It is simply that Peres is much the cleverer political tactician and knows that he must at least give the appearance of being in line with world opinion. His objective, no less than Shamir's, is to ensure that a peace conference does not take place. Peres seeks to achieve that by laying down impossible conditions for its agenda.

When the American Secretary of State, George Shultz, makes noises favourable to an international conference, he has ideas in mind very similar to those of Peres, with the additional belief that Israel will continue to be the policeman of Reaganite imperial purposes in the Middle East. What the rest (and by far the greater part) of the world now has to ensure is that there are moves for a real peace conference, with the objective of establishing real peace - with Palestinian self determination in an independent state. The Israeli state's military and expansionist aims must be contained by an international peace force under UN control on behalf of the entire world community. A first necessity is an Arab League summit to follow up the unity of the Palestine National Council and to determine the Arab component of the international peace conference. That could possibly be a pan-Arab delegation with PLO representation as part of its make-up. But whatever the Arab component, the PLO must be there to represent the Palestinian people for, by whatever standards are used to judge the situation, there is clearly nobody else who can do so.

If the Israelis persist in their usual wrecking tactics,. then international measures must be taken to ensure peace. For example, the European Community, which has declared its support for an international peace conference, must look seriously at the extent to which it can continue the highly privileged trading status which Israel enjoys with the EC. In this notable year of anniversaries - the Year of the Palestinians - the international community must act to right the grievous wrongs it has allowed to accumulate over so many decades. Consensus of words requires to be turned urgently into consensus of deeds.

# AN INTERNATIONAL PEACE CONFERENCE ON THE MIDDLE EAST

**Address to Wilton Park Conference, 13 April 1988**

The Arab-Israeli conflict is the longest running dispute of the twentieth century. Throughout, there has been an international unwillingness to face the basic issue of the rights of the Palestinians and that has ensured the continuing escalation of the conflict to the point where there has been created in the Middle East a flashpoint, potent with danger for the peace of the entire world. Yet, at least, today, there is a worldwide consensus in favour of an international peace conference. Such a conference is not a new idea, it is not a "gimmick" which has suddenly emerged from nowhere. On the contrary, it is an idea which has matured and developed over many years. There is now really only one voice on the world stage which is against the whole principle of such a conference - that of Yitshak Shamir, the Prime Minister of Israel - although others in his own government, notably Shimon Peres, the Foreign Minister, is in favour, together with many others in Israel. Yet, for all the wide consensus in favour, the prospects of such a conference taking place are not good. I want to trace how the present consensus has developed and why, despite all the support, the prospects for a conference are not good.

In examining the development of the consensus it is salutary to recall that it was as long as nearly fifteen years ago when the idea was first put forward - in Security Council Resolution 338, which followed the 1973 war. Resolution 338 called for immediate negotiations between the parties concerned to establish a just and durable peace. A conference was duly convened in Geneva under the joint chairmanship of the USA and the USSR but it soon broke down because Israel rejected any negotiations with any Palestinians. It should be heeded that it was not a question of refusing to negotiate with the PLO, but of refusing to negotiate with any Palestinians. In October 1977, there was an important example of international co-operation, when the United States and the Soviet Union acted together to try to save the Geneva Conference. They issued a joint statement in which they sought an early resumption of the conference, with representatives there of all parties and specifically including those of the Palestinian people. In the statement, the two superpowers also offered their joint participation to guarantee the borders of all states in the region through the setting up of demilitarized zones under full international supervision.

My purpose in referring to that particular episode is to illustrate that there has been a period when, however briefly and despite all that has happened since, there has been superpower co-operation in pursuit of peace in the Middle East. The initiative broke down, mainly because the Israeli lobby in the USA, reflecting Israel's traditional rejectionist policy, forced the United States Administration to back away from joint action with the Soviet Union. It was frustration with the breakdown of the Geneva Conference that was in no small measure responsible for President Sadat's famous visit to Jerusalem in November 1977.

Taking into account all that has happened subsequently, it must be noted that in his speech in the Israeli Knesset, he did not depart from the principles of the then already developing world consensus on Palestine or from the principles of pan-Arab policy, which was closely in line with the world consensus. He said that Israel must end the occupation of the territories taken in 1967, as called for in Security Council Resolution 242 of 1967, and that the rights of all countries to live in peace within secure borders must be observed - a very clear reference to the rights of Arab countries to be protected from Israeli aggression. He also said that the rights of the Palestinians, which he described as "the core and crux of the conflict" must be realized, including the Palestinians' right to self determination and to establish their own state.

His visit led, of course, to the Camp David Conference and to the Israel-Egypt Treaty of 1979. Unfortunately that treaty was regarded by the then and subsequent Israeli governments as giving them permanent control over the West Bank and the Gaza Strip, with the large-scale theft of Palestinian land and the overwhelming theft of the West Bank water resources, all accompanied by the repression of the population which has led ultimately to the great uprising which is now taking place and which is currently being witnessed on the world's television screens. With Egypt neutralized, the treaty also led to the invasion of Lebanon in 1982 and to the continuing occupation of Lebanese territory and the regular air attacks on targets in Lebanon.

Now I want to return to the question of superpower involvement, which is self evidently crucial to the region and to prospects for peace and for an international conference. One aspect of Camp David which is not appreciated in the West as it should be, is that Camp David and the developments which flowed from it were regarded by the Soviet Union as a unilateral breach of Resolution 338 and of the joint approach embodied in the Geneva Conference. Then, in 1982, United States support for the Israeli invasion of Lebanon and the development of a US policy of seeing the Middle East as an area for confrontation with the Soviet Union, with Israel as a forward post, led to a highly dangerous situation which negated prospects of peace for several years. Fortunately, now, in 1988, there are signs that we are all moving forward from that. If anything at all is to be learned from the events of the early and middle nineteen-eighties it is that, beyond doubt, there is a fundamental need for United States-Soviet co-operation if there is to be a peace conference and a settlement.

Let me now repeat that among the problems of the Middle East is that the world as a whole has been prepared to turn its back on the Palestinians for forty years. The Palestinians were deliberately bypassed at Camp David and afterwards. It is a sad commentary that it has taken the Palestinian uprising, with its loss of life and limb, to focus international attention on the brutal Israeli treatment of the Palestinians. But the uprising has also set in motion moves for a peace conference, for example, Secretary of State Shultz's current visits to the Middle East.

Of growing importance is the Western European approach. In 1980, the countries of the European Community issued the Venice Declaration. They called for the security and peaceful existence of all states within recognized and guaranteed borders, to be guaranteed by the United Nations, and they declared that the European Community would participate in maintaining such guarantees. They called for Israeli withdrawal from the occupied territories in accordance with Resolution 242 and they described the Israeli settlements in the occupied territories as illegal in international law and as "an obstacle to peace." They declared that the Palestinians must have the right to self determination, that the achievement of a comprehensive settlement requires the support and the involvement of all parties and that the PLO must be a party to negotiations. However, the pressure of Israeli rejectionism, deployed both in Europe and in North America, prevented any implementation of the Venice Declaration.

In 1983, the General Assembly of the United Nations carried Resolution 38/58C, which calls for an international peace conference with all parties represented on an equal basis, including the PLO, which the resolution specifically recognizes as the legitimate representative organization of the Palestinian people. The resolution was carried by 124 to 4, with 17 abstentions. Those against were Israel, USA, Canada and Australia. The United Kingdom and most of Western Europe abstained but, in February 1987, the Foreign Ministers of the European Community, meeting in Brussels with the Middle East as the only item on their agenda, issued what might be termed the "Brussels Declaration" in which they reiterated the Venice Declaration and called for an international peace conference. They clearly implied that the PLO should participate. In February 1988, just a few weeks ago, again from Brussels, they repeated their call. The present proposals put forward by George Shultz also envisage a peace conference in principle, although with limitations in practice to which I will come back.

So, the present situation [April 1988] is that the principle of an international peace conference is supported in the USA; by Shimon Peres although not by Yitshak Shamir in Israel; by the PLO and by the leadership of the Palestinian uprising - which also supports the PLO and its participation in the conference; by the whole Arab World; by the Third World; and by the USSR and its allies. Yet, for all that, the prospects for a conference are not good. And they are not good because different supporters put different interpretations on what they mean by an international peace conference.

There is general support for a conference under United Nations auspices with the five Permanent Members of the Security Council to be included in the participants, and there is widespread support for the inclusion of all parties to the conflict, including the PLO. The Arabs and the Third World support that. The Soviet Union and its allies support that. The European Community supports it with some reservations. But Shimon Peres, although nominally supporting a conference, does not support a conference with any power for negotiations, neither does he support the inclusion of the PLO. What he wants is an International Meeting, rather than a conference, where world leaders would, presumably, do little more than express the usual platitudes about peace. The meeting would then be followed by negotiations between Israel and individual Arab countries, with negotiations about the Palestinians to be between Israel and Jordan. The Palestinians would have no self determining role in their own future. This, of course, is an attempted perpetuation of the Camp David formula, in which the future of the Palestinians was to be settled over their heads. It is a formula which is entirely unacceptable to the Arab World and it is, in fact, entirely unrealistic because self determination and independence is the rallying call of the uprising.

So there remains an impasse, and a great gap which George Shultz is trying to bridge with his current proposals. These proposals are based in bilateral negotiations between Israel and its neighbours. He proposes that, two weeks before the start of such negotiations, there should be an international "conference" but one without any powers. The major emphasis is on negotiations between Israel and what is termed a "Jordanian-Palestinian delegation" with United States participation, which would proceed independently of all other negotiations. The essential objective would be to settle the position of the occupied territories under some sort of joint Israeli-Jordanian control.

These proposals have several flaws. They are a perpetuation of the Camp David approach. They envisage the future of the Palestinians being settled over their heads and without the participation of representatives acceptable to them. The occupied territories would be put under some sort of joint Israeli-Jordanian control. This is designed to avoid, not to achieve Palestinian self determination and independence. But what the Palestinians in the occupied territories have made absolutely clear, and what they are making ever more clear with every day that passes, is that they will no more accept Jordanian rule than Israeli rule. Neither will they accept the exclusion of the PLO from negotiations. Neither is the exclusion of the PLO acceptable to the Arab World as a whole. Proposals for separate Israeli-Jordanian and Israeli-other Arab negotiations are seen in the Arab World as a stratagem to keep the Arabs divided without solving the basic problem, in order to maintain Israel as a regional superpower backed by the USA for its own strategic reasons rather than for a real commitment to peace. This is, of course, the Kissinger strategy. Incidentally, I was astonished to see that, just a few days ago, former President Richard Nixon actually suggested that Henry Kissinger should be recalled to office and put in charge of America's Middle East policy. It was a great relief that President Reagan rejected the idea - surely one of his wiser decisions. There is a third, serious flaw in that even these proposals are not acceptable to the Israeli Prime Minister, who is resolutely opposed to any loss of control over the occupied territories, who still thinks that he can maintain control there by brutal military repression and who wants ultimately to annex the territories.

To sum up, there is worldwide support for an international peace conference. It is support which has been built up over and by a long and painful series of events. There is a general consensus for Palestinian self determination, for independence and for a role for the PLO. But Israeli rejectionism rejects that. In doing so, it has deeply divided Israel itself. Currently, the USA is trying to reconcile Israeli rejectionism with Palestinian rights and we do not know as yet what effect their efforts will have [(4)]. Until Israel gets in step with the world consensus, the prospects for an international peace conference are not good. The key question, to which you might like to give some attention, as we meet here this morning with so much happening around us, is how can Israel be influenced to get in step?

---

(4) The Shultz plan collapsed shortly after this address was delivered.

## MADRID 1991

As mentioned in the preamble to this chapter, American policy started to move towards the international consensus in the aftermath of the war against Iraq. By then, the USA was the only superpower, the USSR being faced with the break-up of the union. Nominally, there was a Middle East partnership for peace between the two as there had been in the past but, in reality, the US was virtually the sole driving force behind the peace conference which opened in Madrid on 30 October 1991. Many of the proposals for the shape of the conference had their origins in ideas canvassed in the Reagan-Shultz era but among the factors for change in policy was the presence of George Bush in the White House instead of Ronald Reagan and the replacement of George Shultz as Secretary of State by James Baker. Changes in policy, though, were impelled far more by events outside the USA than by domestic changes in leadership.

In order to make allies of Arab countries against Iraq, the Bush administration had to give them assurances that it would turn its attention to the Arab-Israeli conflict once Kuwait had been released from Iraqi occupation. During the war, under pressure from its powerful Zionist lobby, the administration adopted the Israeli claim that there was no linkage between the Iraqi occupation of Kuwait in defiance of United Nations Resolutions, following a war of conquest, and the Israeli occupation of Arab territory, also in defiance of UN resolutions and following a war of conquest. After the war against Iraq, the administration was forced to recognize that there was linkage, and that there would never be stability as long as the Palestinian question remained unresolved. With the cold war over and the gravely weakened Soviet Union virtually withdrawn from international involvement, the American perception of the Middle East as a cold-war, front-line area where Israel was its only reliable ally, was no longer tenable - an important circumstance which had the side effect of diminishing Israeli power over American policy. All these were key factors for a President whose Gulf policy had drawn him irrevocably into the ongoing turmoil of the Middle East. Then, having announced his "New World Order," he had to do something about the region in his assumed role as a President seeking to enforce a pax Americana. And so, after so many years of Israeli-controlled American resistance to an international peace conference, it was to that idea that he finally turned.

The Israeli government led by Yitshak Shamir was wholly opposed to the idea and used every possible tactic and stratagem to obstruct and, if possible, destroy the initiative. As momentum gathered towards the conference, they supplemented diplomatic obstruction by deploying a worldwide, diversionary campaign to rescind the 1975 UN General Assembly Resolution 3379, which had determined that Zionist ideology as practised in Israel was "a form of racism and racial discrimination." The resolution had arisen directly from the similarities between Israel and South Africa and the campaign against it was singularly hypocritical in view of what was actually happening at the time in both countries. In South Africa, apartheid was crumbling. Major laws of racial discrimination had been repealed. Nelson Mandela and other leaders of the African National Congress had been released from their long imprisonment. The ANC had been made legal and black South Africans were negotiating their future with whites. In direct contrast, while the campaign was being waged against the UN resolution, discrimination against Palestinians in Israel and especially the repression in the occupied territories was being intensified and official Israeli racism was exceeding anything then prevailing in South Africa.

However, it was not only Israeli opposition which had to be dealt with in setting up a peace conference. In view of the past record, there was strong Arab suspicion of American intentions. Syria proved especially obdurate. President Hafez Al Assad, most wily and most able of all Arab heads of state, recognizing the demise of his Soviet ally in the Middle East and consumed with hatred for his fellow dictator Saddam Hussein in Iraq, had taken the opportunity of the war to switch to the American side, to which he was welcomed after years of being denounced as a friend of terrorists. He remained the most implacable enemy of Israel, the enemy most feared by the Israelis, and a particularly difficult leader with whom to deal. To deal with the many complexities and cross currents, James Baker had to make no less than eight visits to the region in as many months before sufficient acceptance was secured among all the parties to make possible the historic conference which finally convened in Madrid. The very fact that the conference took place at all was an immense tribute to the political and diplomatic skill of the American Secretary of State. It was a step forward of lasting significance, even though, due mainly to American deference to Israeli demands, it bore little relationship to the sort of conference so repeatedly called for by the United Nations and by so many individual countries, groupings of countries and non-governmental organizations.

In deference to Israeli demands, the United Nations was excluded, as was the European Community, both being granted only observer status. The PLO was to be rigidly excluded. The fact was that the Israeli government did not want to negotiate with any Palestinians, PLO or otherwise. Negotiations involving Jordan and the PLO achieved the setting up of a joint Jordanian-Palestinian delegation. Having pressured the Americans into excluding the PLO, the Israelis then demanded the right to decide the composition of the Palestinian part of the joint delegation - a demand as arrogant as any in the history of diplomacy. They succeeded in pressuring the Americans into excluding any Palestinians from occupied Arab Jerusalem or from the Palestinian diaspora. That left only Palestinians from the occupied Gaza Strip and the West Bank outside the considerable area of occupied Jerusalem. The Israelis then demanded that the names of all proposed delegates, even from that restricted background, should be submitted for their approval. An important objective of that stratagem was to provoke Arab governments and even more importantly, the PLO, into refusing to accept and withdrawing from the preliminary negotiations, so that they could then be blamed for obstructing "the peace process."

Back in the USA, the President faced an onslaught from the Israeli lobby. The Israeli government was demanding guaranteed loans of $10 billion for the resettlement of Jews from the USSR, who were at that time being taken into Israel at a rate in excess of ten thousand a month. In September, President Bush asked the Congress to delay a decision on the loans for four months - that was to say until after the peace conference. The Israeli lobby, confident in its long-standing stranglehold on Senators and Congressmen, waged a furious campaign to persuade them to reject the President's request. If the campaign succeeded, it would be a humiliation for the administration which, it was calculated, would not only lead to another huge increase in American aid but would also kill the peace conference. The President opposed the Israeli lobby and defeated them. He was the first President to do so since Eisenhower at the time of Suez in 1956. It proved what Eisenhower had demonstrated all those years earlier, that the only way to deal with the lobby was to refuse to be intimidated and to challenge it head-on. It spoke volumes for the power of the lobby in the American media that the campaign against the President's request received huge coverage but that its defeat went virtually unreported. The American people could be informed about a campaign to use their money to support a foreign country trying to undermine their country's policy. They could not be informed of the defeat of such a campaign by their own elected representatives. The setback for the Israeli lobby was an important development in relations between the government and the lobby and therefore for the independence and effectiveness of US policy.

With all that behind him, James Baker went once again to Jerusalem, this time jointly with the Soviet Foreign Minister. Diplomatic relations between the USSR and Israel, which had been broken off in 1967, were resumed and, on 18 October 1991, the USA and the USSR issued joint invitations for the conference to be held under their joint chairmanship, starting in Madrid on 30 October. The US Consul General in Jerusalem handed Faisal Husseini, the prominent Palestinian spokesman, an invitation to attend which was addressed, significantly, to the "Palestinian Delegation." The invitation, which had previously been a subject of much Palestinian heart searching and consultation, was accepted immediately and the Consul was given a list of fourteen from the West Bank and the Gaza Strip who would constitute the delegation. To the fury of Shamir, this list was not disclosed to him until after the Israeli government had decided to accept its own invitation, so that he was deprived of the opportunity of refusing to accept the list.

The Israeli government was divided over the conference. The most extreme members of the far right wing cabinet rejected the invitation. Shamir, who shared their views, announced that he, not the Foreign Minister, David Levy, would be leading the Israeli delegation. The delegation was entirely composed of hard line reactionaries and Levy was excluded because he was in favour of negotiating instead of simply obstructing. Angered by his exclusion, he at once announced that in due course he would be challenging Shamir for the leadership of the Likud Party and the premiership.

Invitations to the Madrid conference were issued to Israel, Syria, Jordan, Egypt, Lebanon and the Palestinians. It was proposed that direct negotiations would take place between the Arab states and Israel and also between Israel and the Palestinians. The negotiations would be based on Security Council Resolutions 242 of 1967 and 338 of 1973. That was to say that the negotiations would be based in Israeli withdrawal from territory occupied in 1967 in exchange for peace and recognition by its Arab neighbours. The form of the conference was to be that each of the invited parties would be given forty-five minutes to state its position and that each would be given fifteen minutes to reply to the opening statements. Within four days of the opening, bilateral negotiations were to start. Additionally, such parties as wished would attend multinational negotiations two weeks after the opening in order to discuss arms control, regional security, water resources, the environment and economic development. The conference would have no power to impose solutions and no power to veto any agreements made between the parties. It would not have any authority to make decisions for the parties and it would not be able to vote on issues or results. The conference could only convene with the consent of all the parties.

The Israeli-Palestinian negotiations would start with talks on arrangements for self government although the invitation deliberately omitted specifying to which territories these arrangements should apply. That was done to defer the issue of East Jerusalem which Israel had illegally annexed and claimed as part of its "eternal capital." The negotiations on self government were to be completed within one year and once agreed, they were to be interim, to last for five years. During the third year, negotiations were to open on permanent status and this was to be on the basis of Resolutions 242 and 338. Like East Jerusalem, the Golan Heights, which Israel had illegally annexed from Syria, were not referred to, nor was the occupied, so called "security zone" in southern Lebanon. From the start, though, it was clear that none of those issues could be avoided, whatever the terms set down for the agenda of the conference.

Even before the participants gathered, the Israeli government objected to the Palestinians being allocated time to address the conference and tried, without success, to prevent their participation other than as silent witnesses. Yitshak Shamir made the first statement. It was largely devoted to an account of the distorted view of history held by extreme Zionists and to a categorical refusal to exchange land for peace. Before the conference, he had already made clear that the expansion of the settlements in the occupied territories would continue. At the conference, he said that territory was not the issue - a statement which caused the Jordanian Foreign Minister to ask what they were supposed to be there for at all if not to talk about territory. The only concrete proposal in Shamir's speech was that the proposed bilateral negotiations should take place in the Middle East. He invited the participants to start in Israel, after which, he said, he would be prepared to go to Jordan, Lebanon and Syria. That was a restatement of the long standing Israeli desire to exclude the full international community so that it could try to control all negotiations as a regional superpower.

Throughout the proceedings, the Israeli armed forces subjected Lebanese territory to continuous bombing and shelling. It was hardly surprising that when the Lebanese Foreign Minister spoke, he concentrated on his country's requirement for Israeli withdrawal from the south of the country. The most bitter exchanges were between Israel and Syria, with the Syrian Foreign Minister demanding Israeli withdrawal from all occupied territory as a necessary starting point for all negotiations. That brought a vituperative attack on Syria from Shamir when he made his reply, after which he immediately left the conference without waiting to hear anybody else's reply.

There could be little doubt but that the Palestinians were the "stars" of the conference. Prior to Madrid, they had handled skilfully the attempts to exclude them and then to restrict their participation. They had put together an outstanding delegation. The fourteen official delegates from the occupied territories who formed the negotiating team were led by Dr Haidar Abd al-Shafi, a medical doctor from Gaza with long experience in the Palestinian cause - he had been at the meeting in Jerusalem in 1964 at which the PLO was founded. At seventy-two, he was the oldest of the delegation, the large majority of whom were in their thirties and forties, the youngest being thirty-six. The average age, as well as the level of ability of the delegation provided its own evidence of the resourcefulness of the new generation coming up in Palestine and demanding their rights. To support the negotiating team there was an "advisory panel" consisting of seven who were precluded from the conference but who, installed in a nearby hotel, provided a remarkably effective back-up. They included three from the diaspora - one each from Britain, France and the USA - and four from the Jerusalem area, including Faisal Husseini, who was appointed "co-ordinator" (in effect overall leader), and Hanan Ashrawi, who was appointed spokeswoman, a part she played with an outstanding grasp of public relations. In addition, Nabil Shaath, one of Yasser Arafat's closest advisers, and other senior PLO officials, maintained constant liaison between Madrid and Tunis.

PLO headquarters in Tunis, under intense pressure, both international and from their various constituencies, which included those pressing for outright rejection of the conference, had avoided, unusually and to everyone's surprise, all the traps and pitfalls set for them. The outcome left no doubt whatever that in reality, it was the PLO speaking at the conference and that it alone could claim the right to represent the Palestinian people.

Dr al-Shafi, in his opening statement, declared that the Palestinians neither sought from the Israelis an admission of guilt after the fact nor vengeance for past iniquities, but rather an act of will that would make a just peace a reality. He pointed out that the invitation to discuss the peace which both peoples desired and needed had come to only a portion of the Palestinian people, who had been denied the opportunity publicly to acknowledge their loyalty to their leadership [the PLO]. Jerusalem, he said, the city of peace, had been barred from a peace conference. The Palestinians had been asked to negotiate with their occupiers, while thousands of their people were in Israeli prisons and detention camps, most of them incarcerated without evidence, charge or trial. Territory for peace was a travesty when official Israeli policy and practice was territory for illegal settlement. Even so, he expressed the Palestinians' willingness to accept the proposal for the five years transitional stage, provided of course that interim arrangements were not to be turned into permanent status. Ultimately, they were determined to exercise their right to self determination and to establish an independent state alongside Israel.

It was a masterly performance, delivered with great skill and great dignity, keeping within all the complicated conditions set down to restrict it, yet making absolutely clear that it was in the name of the PLO that he was speaking and that the PLO was the representative body of the Palestinian people. It was a compelling message to the whole world for the recognition of the PLO as well as for the righting of the massive injustice inflicted on their people. Perhaps most effective of all was that, in contrast to Shamir's rejectionist approach, it was constructive, forward looking and practical.

When the parties reassembled after the plenary sessions in order to start the bilateral negotiations, no progress was made because the

Israelis refused to discuss anything except the venue. The proceedings were adjourned and the Israelis had achieved their first objective. The intention that bilateral negotiations should start within four days was killed and the proposal for multinational negotiations on regional issues within two weeks was effectively a non starter.

Little attempt was made to disguise official Israeli attitudes to the conference. On the date after the proceedings were adjourned, a new settlement for immigrants from the Soviet Union was inaugurated with great ceremony in the occupied Golan Heights. As soon as Mrs Ashrawi returned home from Madrid, the Israeli police demanded her arrest and prosecution on the grounds that she had met members of the PLO. It was an indication of the threat of personal intimidation hanging over every member of the delegation and brought a strong protest from the USA. Further proceedings against Mrs Ashrawi were prevented only by the US government's intervention and by the general pressure of international opinion. The threat to the delegation members, which was no more than an extension of the long established practice of imprisoning and deporting articulate Palestinians, showed the impossibility of acceding to the Israeli demand for negotiations to be transferred to the Middle East. But the implications went much wider. For what was really being demonstrated was that international pressure was necessary not only for the protection of the Palestinian delegates but for a number of other reasons. The real issue was the very long standing one that neither peace nor justice could be achieved by negotiations between parties in the Middle East without the widest international involvement.

There was a need for involvement to influence Israeli public opinion, which was always sensitive to international opinion. There was evidence that among Israeli people, there was a growing questioning of the government's rejectionist line. For any settlement, much depended on turning the questioning minority into a voting majority who would elect a more progressive government. Those opposed to the rejectionist line were far more in touch with the tide of international opinion than the government, showing the scope for pressure in their support, above all from the USA, where, whatever the machinations of the Israeli lobby, it was becoming clear that a majority of the large Jewish population was increasingly sceptical of the hard line rejectionizm of the Likud government.

Like the Israeli government, the PLO was faced with internal challenge. Control was moving away from an old guard in exile and towards the new, dynamic generation in Palestine itself. Yasser Arafat and his advisers had shown themselves well aware of that and had accommodated to it in spite of strong opposition from their rejectionists. Ironically, the new, Palestine based approach was very much along the lines of the pragmatic, gradualist approach adopted almost a century earlier by the Zionists and by which they had achieved their objectives. They, though, had been foreigners seeking to establish a settler state on the soil of an indigenous people. Now, it was the indigenous victims who were negotiating pragmatically to regain lost rights. It was going to be a long drawn out process with no guaranteed outcome which would put severe strains on all Palestinians, especially since there were opponents of the gradualist approach within Palestine as well as in the diaspora. The PLO faced a many sided challenge. Its policy as enunciated at Madrid was clearly acceptable to the world at large and likely to increase its standing, but that policy needed the world at large to help the PLO to sustain it. What remained to be seen was if a world supposedly dedicated to the self determination of peoples would be prepared to uphold the Palestinians' chosen representative body in their struggle for self determination.

Above all, though, there was a need for pressure from the international community on the USA. Like Eisenhower in 1956, Bush had successfully defied the intimidation of the Israeli lobby, but it was precisely because of its 1956 defeat that the lobby had reorganized to create the large political machine that had come to infiltrate every aspect of decision making on the Middle East within the US government. In 1991, the lobby quickly set about reorganizing again to reassert its power, helped by the fact that President Bush, with the next presidential election just a year away, was deeply unpopular at home because of the failure of his economic policy. It was exactly the situation for the lobby to exploit, with its usual mixture of election largesse and intimidation among the entire Congress and the third of the Senate who would also be up for election.

There were early and ominous signs that Israeli prevarication and obstruction were starting to be appeased instead of further challenged, as when the President repeated the call he had made some months earlier, for the United Nations to rescind the 1975 resolution on Zionism and racism. There was no guarantee that the more balanced US policy which had taken so long to achieve could be maintained through negotiations likely to be protracted over years, unless there was international pressure for it. Therein lay an especial challenge for the European Community, the most effective source from which such pressure could be applied.

When the US government invited the participants to resume the adjourned bilateral negotiations in Washington, the Israeli government objected instantly and launched into new attempts to delay and obstruct the proceedings. Another factor to help them arose from the break-up of the Soviet Union. That not only finished such influence as the former union had exerted but also ensured that, with the American government heavily preoccupied with the new situation, it downgraded the Middle East as a priority. As Israeli tactics frustrated progress in Washington, it soon became clear that the US government was withdrawing from its commitment to exert pressure to advance progress. The Israeli strategy was to delay and obstruct the proceedings until such time as they might collapse, meanwhile persisting in the colonization and eventual annexation of the West Bank and Gaza Strip. It was a repeat of the strategy they had successfully applied in 1973-1974 to the Geneva Conference which had been called under the terms of Resolution 338, also under joint Soviet-American chairmanship.

Repression and racism in the occupied territories was actively stepped up and maintained throughout as the proceedings in Washington ground to a standstill. Even as that was proceeding, the United Nations General Assembly, under American pressure, rescinded the Zionism and racism resolution by 111 votes to 25 with 13 abstentions and 17 nations absenting themselves. It was an act of appeasement which predictably brought no improvement in the actions or the policy of the Zionist state.

Madrid was a step on the long road to the justice without which there could never be peace in the Middle East but, from the start, it was clear that its capacity to achieve progress was limited. The overwhelming lesson from the proceedings in Madrid and then in Washington was that which had in reality existed for so long already. That was that no settlement could be achieved from within the Middle East. It could only be achieved by strong pressure from outside the region, exercised through the machinery of the world community. The possible nature of such pressure is discussed in later chapters in this book.

# 6

# NON-GOVERNMENTAL ORGANIZATIONS

Reference has been made in previous pages to the International Meeting of NGO's on the Question of Palestine, which has been convened annually by the United Nations since 1984, either in Geneva or in Vienna. These meetings grew out of the conference of governments and NGO's held in Geneva in 1983, which issued the call for an international peace conference which became embodied in the General Assembly Resolution 38/58C. The convening of the original 1983 conference arose in large measure from frustration over the continuing failure of governments effectively to apply themselves to the Palestine situation. The purpose was to try to create an instrument to enable the growing number of pro-Palestinian NGO's worldwide, to influence governments.

At the 1983 conference, the NGO's elected an "Interim Co-ordinating Committee" whose purpose was to liaise with the UN Division for Palestinian Rights and with the Committee on the Exercise of the Inalienable Rights of the Palestinian People. The Co-ordinating Committee had a British chairman, Ernie Ross MP, Labour Member for Dundee West but, unfortunately, he succumbed not long afterwards to an illness which incapacitated him for a full year and he was not available when the Interim Committee was reconstituted on a permanent basis in 1985, with the title International Co-ordinating Committee. He was succeeded by an

American, Dr Donald Betz, formerly a UN civil servant at the New York headquarters, who had returned to the academic world at the Northeastern State University of Oklahoma. In due course, the Committee came to call itself the ICCP (International Co-ordinating Committee on Palestine), which was self evidently an improvement on its official, jargonesque designation as the International Co-ordinating Committee of the United Nations Annual Meeting of Non-Governmental Organizations on the Question of Palestine.

My first international NGO meeting was the one in 1985, at which the ICCP, to which I was elected, was reconstituted on a permanent basis. By that time, I had acquired some reputation as the Director who had saved CAABU from bankruptcy and who was restoring its reputation in the forefront of NGO's and, on the strength of that, the ICCP appointed me as its Treasurer-Rapporteur. The Treasurer half of that position arose because, if the committee was to function to any effect, it had to acquire an office and a secretariat. The United Nations Organization had no resources to make any such provision and so the ICCP had to raise its own funds. At the next international meeting, in July 1986, an Executive Director was appointed. He was Jean-Marie Lambert, who had a long and distinguished record in working for Palestinian and other human rights. He was an ordained minister of the Reformed Church in France although, by choice, he had not been employed in Holy Orders for a number of years. He took only a modest salary and at once set about establishing a small office in Geneva. Due to his standing and integrity, he proved to be a valuable fund raiser but, for all our combined efforts, the secretariat only existed on a very precarious basis. The large majority of NGO's were themselves very short of money and few of them could make or be expected to make much financial contribution. It was well into 1989 before the ICCP finances were put onto any reasonably sound basis and before the forward planning of activities became possible.

The Rapporteur half of my title arose through English being the primary language used by the Committee as well as by the International Meetings of NGO's, and from the requirement thereby for someone whose first language was English and who had at least some facility in it to record proceedings and express ideas in a manner acceptable to participants from many languages and cultures. In this far from easy task, I also found myself consistently nominated and approved as Chairman of the Drafting Committee of the International NGO Meeting, with responsibility for distilling the essence of the proceedings to produce the Declaration,

Membership of the ICCP was determined by consensus in a system weighted to try to make it as representative as possible of the UN world regions plus the areas and peoples most directly involved in the cause it existed to promote. The system of election was often, understandably, a matter for heated debate but, in my experience, it was almost always friendly and tolerant debate. The constitution evolved through experience and by the end of the decade, the agreed membership was three from the UN region of North America (two from USA, one from Canada), three from the European region (two Western, one Eastern), with one each from the African, Asian and Latin American regions. There were three from Israel, four from Palestine and one from the wider Arab World. There were places for four members from international NGO's, such as the Parliamentary Association for Euro-Arab Co-operation and the International Jewish Peace Union. Finally, there were three who were designated as "Members de facto." They were the representatives of the Palestine NGO Committee, which was associated with the PLO, and the Chairpersons of the North American and European Co-ordinating Committees. From 1989, the Chairman was elected independently in his or her own right rather than as a representative from any particular NGO. The whole committee was elected for a two years term of office. When the committee met, there were as often as not vacant seats in the Palestine section due to the Israelis preventing representatives from attending.

The official function of the ICCP was to meet once a year to plan the agenda of the International Meeting of NGO's and the UN paid travel expenses and subsistence for that meeting. From its inception, though, the committee decided to hold two additional meetings each year and since the members had to find their own costs for those meetings, it was greatly to their credit that they attended consistently. By common agreement, there were three officers, Chairman, Vice-Chairman and Treasurer-Rapporteur and we three constituted the "Bureau" with responsibility for urgent matters between meetings. The Vice-Chairman was Bahig Nasser of the World Peace Council, who was originally based in Helsinki but who subsequently moved to Cairo.

It was a fascinating committee. In the early days it was frequently chaotic, with certain strong willed and articulate persons expressing themselves forcefully and articulately, more from an egotistical than a co-operative standpoint. There was also and there remains a related problem in the international meetings, where there is often a strong desire to make statements designed for consumption back home rather than as a contribution to international resolution of the problem (by no means a unique situation in international conferences!). Gradually, though, and not without some changes in membership, the ICCP resolved its early problems and came to act in a more responsible and corporate manner. Not least among the reasons for its progress was the skill and patience with which Don Betz presided.

NGO thinking in the nineteen-eighties was more progressive and creative than any official governmental thinking - a point to which I drew attention in drafting the Declaration of the fifth (1988) international meeting (paragraph 13). I had wanted to include a phrase urging governments to catch up with NGO thinking, but that proved too strong for the international consensus and we ended up with "We urge all Governments, in the interest of peace and justice, to consider seriously the options defined by NGO's" Then in 1989. I wanted to relate the theme of the conference to the Palestinian Declaration of Independence of 15 November 1988 by making the theme "Independence: from Declaration to Reality" but we ended up with the more pedestrian "Intifada: the Continuing Struggle of the Palestinian People for Independence." Those two examples were perhaps demonstrations of the limitations of consensus but, like the agreed procedure for electing the ICCP, they also demonstrated that deadlock could not be broken and progress could not be made without consensus. They also served in debunking the assertion which became fashionable among right wing politicians in the eighties that consensus required to be replaced by "conviction" politics, a dangerous theory, lineally descended from Adolf Hitler, the most dedicated of all conviction politicians.

From the international meetings, there evolved a series of regional meetings or "Symposia" as they were officially designated and these, in turn, created their own regional co-ordinating committees. First off the mark were the North Americans who had to contend, in the USA, with the most powerful indigenous Zionist lobby and the most intransigent government. They were soon followed by the Europeans and later by the Asians and Latin Americans. Strong efforts were also made in Africa but these had not really born fruit by the end of the decade.

I have vivid memories of the first European Symposium, which was held in Vienna in 1986. It took place immediately prior to the Third International Meeting, establishing what was to become the regular practice that, since the International Meeting was invariably held in Europe, it should be preceded immediately by the European Symposium. For the European event, I found myself totally involved, conscripted by the consensus into being Chairman, Drafter of the Declaration and Spokesman to the UN Officials at the formal opening and closing sessions. I was just as fully involved in the immediately following International Meeting, where onerous duties also included presenting a paper to one of the plenary sessions. It was as exhausting a week as any I have lived through and I was happy to decline membership of the newly created European Co-ordinating Committee

That committee went on to do a remarkable job. The UN made no provision for a European Symposium the following year but the committee organized and financed its own, with Jean-Marie Lambert working day and night on the administration, assisted only by his wife, Martine, and with myself much exercised over paying for it. The unofficial European Symposium was a huge success, in striking contrast with the official, UN organized International Meeting which immediately followed it and which came near to being a disaster.

All these conferences and of course the ICCP were constantly exercised by what they could do towards the convening of an international peace conference, which was hardly surprising since international NGO co-ordination arose directly out of the gathering in 1983 which called specifically for such a conference. The NGO's certainly played a not inconsiderable role as the call for a peace conference strengthened and became worldwide as the eighties progressed. Another theme which stayed strong in their deliberations was how to mobilize public opinion and, in pursuit of that, I was invited to submit a paper to the International Meeting in 1986 and a further one to a workshop at the 1987 meeting. For that conference, I was also invited to present a paper to a plenary session on planning co-ordinated activities. The latter was never delivered because of the chaotic mess into which the conference degenerated.

When the ICCP met in the Spring to formulate the agenda for that International Meeting, it was decided to press for Yasser Arafat to be invited. Those were the doldrum years before the Intifada changed the course of events with such dramatic effect. It was a time of great frustration, when there was no progress and seemingly little hope of any. It was therefore deemed important to provide a world platform for Arafat. He accepted the invitation and, although he said nothing new, his speech was widely acclaimed. He also stayed several days at the conference and a number of important liaison meetings were held with him and with his staff. Unfortunately, between the ICCP meeting in the Spring and the full conference in the Autumn, pressure was exerted on the Committee on the Exercise of the Inalienable Rights of the Palestinian People, which resulted in the carefully drawn up agenda of the ICCP being altered out of recognition in what appeared to be an attempt to turn the meeting into something resembling a PLO rally rather than an international conference of NGO's.

An infuriated ICCP assembled on the eve of the conference to be told what had happened. One factor which the ICCP had taken into account in drawing up the agenda was that, ever since the commencement of the NGO meetings, there had been a growing demand from participants for less time to be devoted to the plenary sessions which provided the main platform for expert panellists to present papers and for more time to be devoted to workshops on specific subjects at which NGO representatives, themselves, could participate more fully and contribute more effectively. The ICCP had also been told that the number of expert panellists who could be invited had to be limited to an absolute maximum of six and preferably less, even to as few as four, because of the cost. Having taken both those seemingly complementary factors into account in drawing up the agenda, the ICCP discovered that there was to be an excess of plenary sessions with no less than eighteen panellists.

That year, there was a greatly increased participation of NGO's, including a large contingent from Israel and, with Arafat present, there was a tremendous atmosphere of enthusiasm. A number of the Israeli delegates made a special point of being photographed with Arafat, in gestures of open defiance of the Israeli law forbidding contact between Israeli citizens and members of the PLO. But the atmosphere became soured almost immediately by the ill-judged attempt to stage manage the proceedings and there was a remarkable development in the creation of what amounted to an alternative conference, running parallel with the official one, with the ICCP enthusiastically leading the delegates in organizing a mass of ad hoc workshops and "special interest groups."

Professor James Graff, of the Near East Cultural and Educational Foundation of Canada, a member of the ICCP, was the major inspiration and driving force behind the alternative conference, which received huge support from the delegates. The workshop on mobilizing public opinion, which was actually part of the official proceedings, and was addressed by Jim Graff, Don Betz and myself, was packed to the doors. So also were the many ad hoc and unofficial meetings and study groups. Behind the scenes, incarcerated for much of the time in a private room, but with constant interruptions, I was engaged in drafting the Declaration. By the time of the workshop, I had completed most of the first draft and leaving it in the back room, I left to speak at the workshop, to return an hour and a half later to find that the draft had disappeared. We never discovered who had stolen it, for what reason or what good it did the thief. There was no alternative to starting all over again, which meant sitting up most of that night.

A number of important lessons were learned from that 1987 International Meeting. A personal lesson was never, ever to let important papers out of sight. But, on the wider and more important scale, there was a huge row over the way the ICCP and the conference had been treated, the ICCP expressing itself in no uncertain terms to the UN hierarchy, confident in the knowledge that it had worldwide NGO backing. The ICCP is only an advisory body to the UN but the point was taken, as was the weight of opinion behind it and the ICCP's standing was enhanced and its influence increased as a result.

Even so, the NGO's continued to feel dissatisfied with the conduct of the conferences. The UN was bound by protocol tied to meetings of representatives of governments rather than to meetings of representatives of NGO's. This was irksome for the NGO's, who were not addicted to protocol and who continued to complain that they were denied effective participation. The complaints became stronger as the NGO's grew in strength and in confidence. But the very spread of the NGO movement, itself, also contributed to making the situation more complex.

Nowhere was that better demonstrated than in the African region. No genuine NGO's existed there because of the lack of popular, participatory democracy and the authoritarian nature of governments while, in a continent containing some of the most impoverished countries of the world, where the very struggle for existence itself surpassed all other problems, there were other priorities. However, there was no lack of support for the Palestinian cause. The African Regional Symposium was the last to come into existence, in April 1990. Held in Freetown, it was a combined NGO Symposium and Seminar (the UN term for a gathering involving government representatives and invited individuals). With the lack of NGO's in the region, it was in reality a gathering of government representatives and government front persons. Even so, it was an important step forward, an attempt in a difficult situation to develop NGO's to participate in a movement developing on a worldwide scale. It was made possible largely through the indefatigable efforts of Dr Mourad Ghaleb of the Afro-Asian People's Solidarity Organization (AAPSO). Dr Ghaleb was an able and dedicated former Egyptian Foreign Minister who understood the limitations of the African situation and who also had the vision to see the need to bring the continent into the orbit of the worldwide NGO movement.

The Arab World itself was not easy. There, too, the very concept of organized groups, fully independent of and critical of governments was at best not understood and at worst not tolerated. Two incidents, one in London in the nineteen-eighties and one in Cairo in the nineteen-fifties, may be quoted to illustrate the situation.

In London, shortly after Neil Kinnock was elected Leader of the Labour Party in 1983, the Arab Ambassadors discussed whether they should seek an early meeting with him. One Ambassador opposed the idea on the grounds that "We only talk with governments, not with oppositions." As an Arab friend said, with whom I discussed the incident "In his country, all the opposition are in prison!" In his book *The Arab Military Option* (American Mideast Research, San Francisco 1986), General Saad El-Shazly described (p. 174) an incident at a seminar on Arab poetry, held in Cairo in the nineteen-fifties and attended by poets from all over the Arab World. A poet from North Yemen stated that in Yemen "Poetry has only two themes. The first is to praise the Imam. The second is to ask his forgiveness." Shazly commented :-

> Thinking he was being ironic, the audience broke into laughter. The poet was shocked. Not merely was he serious, it had not occurred to him that this state of affairs might be regarded as strange.

The two incidents give fascinating insights into deeply entrenched attitudes. These are attitudes, too, which have produced the ambivalent pan-Arab approach to Palestine. The Palestinian cause provides a rallying point for practically all Arabs, but among those who govern in Arabia, there is a fear of the democracy of the dynamic Palestinians, among whom power comes up from the people rather than being paternalistically handed down from above. Such attitudes are self evidently inimical to the development of NGO's and the paucity of Arab NGO's other than Palestinian ones was a feature of International meetings.

Another aspect of the complexities of worldwide developments was unfolding in Europe. In the nineteen-eighties, in the one-party dictatorships of Eastern and Central Europe, the so called NGO's were in practice front organizations for governments. With the overthrow of the dictatorships at the end of the decade and the moves to multi-party systems, the NGO's were faced with new and bewildering challenges in becoming independent. There was no less a challenge for the PLO. It had been officially recognized by all the former governments and, in the various capitals, its ambassadors had enjoyed cosy relationships with governments and "NGO's" alike. With the tumultuous changes in Europe and the sudden realization that the old governments had represented only a small section of the public, the PLO too found itself in a new situation.

All this illustrated some of the problems facing the NGO movement at the start of the nineteen nineties. Among NGO's, there was a unanimity of support for the Palestinians. There was dissatisfaction with limits placed on NGO self expression within the framework devised by the United Nations for the actual purpose of NGO self expression. There were deep and challenging problems about the nature of NGO's. Yet the very fact that the problems were recognized and that there was a ferment of agitation to try to resolve them was an indication of a self aware and strengthening movement with a growing role for the nineteen-nineties. The lusty child of the eighties was growing through a stormy adolescence towards an adulthood of much potential.

# THE MOBILIZATION OF PUBLIC OPINION AND THE QUESTION OF PALESTINE

**Paper presented to the International Meeting of NGO's, Vienna, 3 July 1986**

To mobilize public opinion effectively in any country or world region, the methods employed must be adapted to match national and regional conditions. Methods in the developed world require to be different from those in the developing world and, within the developed world, methods in the West require to be different from those in the East. On that basic premise, this paper is related to the urgent requirement to mobilize public opinion in the developed countries of the Western World. First, it is necessary to establish exactly what it is in the western context that constitutes an NGO. In the United Kingdom there is an acronym "QUANGO" which stands for Quasi Autonomous Non-Governmental Organization. The NGO's so described are agencies of the government which are wholly or partly financed by the government. But there is not a single NGO in the UK, whose sole concern is to advance the question of Palestine, which comes in that category and there are none, or at most, very few such in any of the other developed western countries.

There are important NGO's in Britain, as in other developed western countries, whose purpose is the relief of suffering in underdeveloped regions and which do receive some government subsidy because of the humanitarian nature of their work. By the nature of that work, such NGO's have acquired important experience of the suffering of the Palestinian people, because they often send members to work in the Middle East. Invariably, those members find themselves so outraged by the treatment of the Palestinians that they become strong upholders of the Palestinian cause and anxious to mobilize public opinion in its support. But the NGO's concerned have to proceed with great caution and not to advocate any cause which is deemed by established authority to be so-called "politically partisan" - which, in practice, means unacceptable to established authority.

There is keen interest in and advocacy of the Palestinian cause within the Christian Churches. The number of Christian based NGO's represented in this meeting is its own eloquent testimony to that. Their interest and advocacy also arises in large measure from humanitarian concern and from experience and witness by western Church members among the Palestinian people. For those members, there is an especial task to mobilize opinion among fellow Christians and that is of particular importance because the impact of the view of the Churches and Church people upon other public opinion is of significant importance.

Moving on from humanitarian and Church based NGO's, we come to those whose sole purpose or major concern is to advocate the Palestinian cause and its central importance to peace and justice. Such NGO's in the developed western countries are invariably created and maintained by groups of dedicated individuals and, almost invariably, they have to devote much time and effort to raising funds to perform their task. A major point which must be made is that, contrary to views sometimes held elsewhere, the great majority of NGO's in the West have to work on strictly limited financial resources. Which brings up a point which is of paramount importance, namely, that in seeking funds, they must never accept any finance which can compromise them. They must be seen as independent and dedicated to principle and conscience. In no way must they appear to be lobbyists for particular vested interests more concerned with their own objectives than with the cause of justice. It is one thing to press a great cause. It is something quite different to lobby for vested interests. The need for NGO's to have integrity and credibility in the eyes of the public whose views they seek to mobilize is nowhere better demonstrated than by the Israeli lobby in the United States of America. One of the most powerful weapons now in the hands of the NGO's in the USA is that the immensely powerful and wealthy Israeli lobby in that country is starting to be recognized, however belatedly, to lack credibility in that it exists solely to sustain the interests of a foreign power, at high financial and political cost to the citizens of the United States.

Basic to the problem of mobilizing public opinion in the Western World is that the Zionist and Israeli lobby has worked for not less than seven decades to create a picture of the Middle East which is widely at variance with the facts. It is little more than one decade since a more balanced and accurate view has come to be perceived, except within a small minority of informed public opinion. A world renowned American authority, Dr John H Davis, who was for five years the Commissioner-General of UNRWA, wrote in his book *The Evasive Peace*, published in London in 1968:

> As Commissioner-General of UNRWA, the writer found that the world's understanding of the Palestine refugee problem was at variance with the truth; in several important aspects even the opposite of the truth. Then as he began to study the broader aspects of Arab-Israeli relations, he found the same thing to be true - particularly in regard to the cause of the conflict.(1)

It is just one measure of the power of the Israeli lobby in the USA that, at that time, 1968, it was not possible to find an American publisher for the book and that such a distinguished American authority on the Middle East had to find a British publisher. Similarly, in 1965, Moshe Menuhin had to go to the Institute for Palestine Studies in Beirut to secure the publication of his monumental work *The Decadence of Judaism in Our Time*. More immediately, Paul Findley, another distinguished American and a Congressman for twenty-two years, had great difficulty in finding a publisher for his book *They Dare To Speak Out*, (2) another monumental testimony, in this case to the power of the Israeli lobby in the USA.

This brings us to the very core of the problem of mobilizing public opinion in the developed western countries - that there is an immensely powerful and deeply entrenched Zionist lobby. In Western Europe it is less powerful than formerly, but in the USA it remains far more powerful than can possibly be justified by the cause it promotes and, as Paul Findley demonstrates in his book, it is quite unscrupulous. Yet, even in the USA, the sales of Paul Findley's book show that the situation is changing. The book was published only in 1985 by a small publisher at some risk. The latest figures I have show that sales have already run to fifty -two thousand copies in hardback and that is even before the forthcoming paperback edition (3) . So the signs are that, for all the problem in the western countries, the work of the pioneers in the mobilization of public opinion has already created a foundation from which NGO's can take encouragement and upon which they can build.

To turn to the practicalities of how they can do so, the first priority has to be to mobilize opinion among those who decide the

---

(1) John H Davis, *The Evasive Peace* (John Murray, London, 1968) p. IX (Introduction).
(2) Paul Findley, *They Dare to Speak Out* (Lawrence Hill & Co., Westport, Connecticut, 1985). Information given to the acknowledgements.
(3) Conversation with Paul Findley, London, 23 May 1986.

policies of governments and among others who are opinion formers. A high priority is for NGO's to seek face to face meetings with government ministers and party leaders. In so doing, it must not ever be forgotten that in multi-party parliamentary systems, the opposition is as important as the government, since it may well form the next government. As well as meetings with ministers, there should be regular exchanges with members of legislatures, while efforts should be made to encourage sympathetic constituents to write to, telephone or meet their elected representatives. With further reference to such contacts, communication with officials in ministries are no less important than with elected members of governments and legislatures. Such officials have their own important role, not only in carrying out the policy decisions of governments but also in advising the elected members who decide policy. It cannot be too strongly emphasized that all representations made must be most meticulously based in accurate, up-to-date information and must be capable of being argued successfully against indifferent or hostile viewpoints.

Members of legislatures should, themselves, be involved in NGO's. In Britain, each major political party has its own NGO in its Middle East Council, with Members of Parliament actively involved. The Council for the Advancement of Arab-British Understanding (CAABU), which is an all party NGO, always has two joint chairmen who are Members of Parliament, one from the government and one from the opposition. The Paris and Brussels based Parliamentary Association for Euro-Arab Co-operation is an NGO consisting, apart from its small staff, of Members of Parliaments from a substantial number of Western European countries.

Meetings and demonstrations organized by NGO's have an important role, but a word of caution is necessary for there is always a danger that they will only appeal to those who already agree. That is not to belittle the importance of such activities - after all, this very gathering is of that nature - but, if public opinion is to be mobilized, it is absolutely necessary to carry the message beyond those who already accept it. In doing so, a vital part of the work is in providing experienced speakers, as well as videos, films and information packs for meetings among other groups and especially to address the opinion formers of the future in schools and universities. Success for this form of activity will depend on NGO's themselves being sufficiently widely known and sufficiently credible to receive invitations from other groups and organizations.

I would like to quote a recent personal experience. On Sunday evening, 11 May last, I spoke, as Director of CAABU, together with two others of differing views, in a London synagogue, in response to an invitation, to an audience of about two hundred Jewish people. At the end of the meeting, the audience voted on a show of hands, by something between two and three to one, in favour of Shimon Peres opening negotiations immediately with Yasser Arafat, and that was duly reported in the London *Jewish Chronicle* (4). That cannot be claimed as other than a quite exceptional event and I have to confess that I was as surprised a person as any in the meeting. That, however, is not the main point. The main point is that it is one among a number of indications that there is a growing body of Jewish opinion, certainly in Britain and in other European countries, as there is in Israel, which is gravely concerned over the Question of Palestine. That is an especially important sector of public opinion to which the Palestinian side of the case must be taken.

Worldwide, the media is obviously basic in mobilizing public opinion. In the Western World, the media is overwhelmingly capitalist and, with honourable but relatively few exceptions, tends to be pro-Zionist and anti-Palestinian. The more scurrilous elements engage openly in anti-Arab racism. For example, The *Sun* newspaper of London recently published a cartoon depicting a gathering of pigs complaining at being called Arabs (5). Even though protests by decent people against such conduct may well be ignored by those who indulge in it, protests should nevertheless always be made.

Radio and television are probably the most influential media of all for mobilizing public opinion. Radio and television stations should always be telephoned to protest when inaccurate and biased statements are made in news and current affairs programmes, as well as when anti-Arab bias is included in fictional programmes. An "action alert" system of lists of persons who can be alerted with appropriate information to contact members of governments and legislatures, as well as editors, producers and others whenever developments require it, is most useful where the resources of NGO's run to its provision. As part of the effort of countering

(4) *Jewish Chronicle*, London, 16 May 1986. Shimon Peres was then the Prime Minister of Israel.

(5) *The Sun*, London, 15 May 1986

unfavourable coverage and moving towards a more positive situation, it is especially valuable for NGO's to have well-informed speakers available for interview on radio and television, and NGO's should try to build up confidence among producers that they can provide such speakers. In approaching producers and editors, it must always be appreciated, even if it is in certain instances distasteful, that it is they who have the ultimate choice over whom they interview.

To try to create a better informed climate of opinion, CAABU, like other NGO's, publishes a regular Bulletin. Published twice monthly, it is a digest of up-to-date information written by a professional journalist and aimed not only at Middle East experts but also at other opinion formers in the media, in politics, in official quarters and in universities.

Advertising in the media is an expensive form of activity which requires to be used selectively. It may be helpful to refer to two recent CAABU exercises in the field of press advertising. This year, the Palestinian Day of the Land coincided with the Christian Festival of Easter Day and CAABU inserted an appropriate advertisement. The same thing was done for International Prisoners' Day on 17 April, to publicize especially an assembly held in the yard of a central London church, an activity which particularly infuriated elements in the Israeli lobby, which is always a good indication of success.

One of the Israeli lobby's longstanding activities is inviting students and other young people to spend their holidays working on a kibbutz. This year, the London Friends of Palestine produced a leaflet entitled *The Kibbutz: Who Benefits, Who Suffers.* Advertisements were then inserted in appropriate publications inviting anyone thinking of taking such a holiday to write in for a copy. There was a most encouraging response, again to the fury of the Zionist lobby. The disadvantage of media advertising is the cost, which is beyond the reach of many NGO's, while even those who can afford it need to approach it in a strictly cost-effective manner.

This paper has sought to identify some of the problems of mobilizing public opinion in the developed western countries and to suggest some practical means to do so. It is essential that whatever methods are used, they must be truthful, cost effective and not counter productive, so that the maximum effect is produced from the deployment of what are usually limited resources. Above all, the message must not merely be put across to those who already agree with it but must reach out, in convincing terms, to mobilize wider public opinion. Much public opinion is gravely misinformed because Zionist and Israeli organizations have been doing so much for so long to create that situation. For decades, they have been spreading disinformation - the fashionable new jargon name that is now given to plain, old fashioned lying - and they have often been doing so by using the very methods outlined here. The techniques themselves are neither new nor untried. What we have to do is to bring to them a newness and an integrity in deploying them in the causes of truth, justice and peace.

# THE MOBILIZATION OF PUBLIC OPINION (II)

**Shortened version of paper presented to workshop of the International Meeting of NGO's, Geneva, 8 September 1987.**

In 1968, I had a meeting in Cairo with a senior official of the then Egyptian government which I recall vividly. I had said to him in the course of the discussion that you could not speak to the wider world as if you were addressing a crowd in the streets of Cairo. His reply was unforgettable. He said "Mr Watkins, the days have gone when we can solve anything by addressing crowds in the streets of Cairo."

From that I draw a basic first point - that in our efforts to mobilize public opinion in support of the inalienable rights of the Palestinian people, we must recognize that the methods used must be adapted to match national and regional conditions. Of course there is still cause for speakers to address crowds in Cairo and in other great cities in all regions of the world. But we must recognize that in more and more of those cities, as well as in smaller centres of population, the people gather less and less in great crowds to hear speeches. Instead, they read newspapers, listen to radio and watch television. And we require a different approach in the developed world, we require different methods in the East and in the West.

But that does not mean that we must say different things to different people, for our great strength is that we have that most basic essential, a universal message of truth and justice around which to mobilize public opinion. What is different is that we must recognize variations in cultures and we must put the message across by methods which are most effective in those various cultures. This is an area in which every NGO has an especially important role, for they are the best judges of how best to approach the subject in their own cultures, countries and regions.

We have another great strength. That is that there now exists in all cultures and regions an important international consensus. Broadly, that consensus recognizes that the Palestinian people have suffered and continue to suffer one of the greatest injustices of the twentieth century, in the loss of their homeland by force of arms and the suppression of their basic human rights. The consensus upholds the Palestinians' right to self determination in their own independent state, recognizes that the PLO is their representative organization and supports an international peace conference. So, before addressing ourselves to the problems of mobilizing public opinion, let us be aware of the advantages at our disposal, first by the universal nature of our appeal to justice and second by that world consensus which recognizes and responds to that appeal.

Let me now return to that conversation in Cairo in 1968. Please note the date. It was in the aftermath of the disastrous war of 1967 and well before the war of 1973. By 1973, the Arab armies were far better armed, trained and led. The result made 1973 a turning point. The war itself was a decisive event in mobilizing public opinion in the Middle East and worldwide. But all war is terrible and ultimately futile, and no sensible person can advocate war and bloodshed in any form as a means of mobilizing public opinion. Our purpose is to mobilize public opinion by peaceful means for the express purpose of avoiding war and bloodshed. Let me remind you of the old saying "Beneath the rule of men entirely great, the pen is mightier than the sword." The power of the pen is now greatly supplemented by radio, television and all the other and ever growing aspects of information technology. These are our weapons and these are what we have to use to the greatest effect.

We will do well to ask ourselves "What is public opinion?" Is it the opinion of the public - that is of the mass of the people? Or is it the opinion of a ruling or otherwise influential and, in some cases, self opinionated minority expressed in public for consumption by the public? The answers to these questions are themselves matters for debate and they will vary according to political systems and levels of mass education. They require to be answered in deciding whom to target, for experience shows that we must work with suitably selected target groups if we are to be effective in mobilizing opinion. The answers can only be decided within the experience of NGO's in their own national and regional environments.

Turning first to ruling or otherwise influential minority groups, there is a clear need to mobilize opinion among those who decide the policies of governments and among others who are opinion formers. Another group of great importance is comprised of those who interpret and teach the faiths and theologies of all the great religions. Their impact, not only on their fellow believers in their own faiths, but also upon public opinion in the widest sense, is of major importance. Organized labour is another very major sector of the public, so trade union leaders and other activists constitute another group of major importance. Nor should we ever forget the coming generation and the importance of addressing the opinion formers of the future in schools and universities. Turning, second, to public opinion in the sense of the mass of the people, we have to recognize their dependence on the mass media for information. It comes down again, in practical reality, to influencing those minority groups who control what the media puts out, especially those who control radio and television, probably the most influential media of all.

This year. 1987, the International Co-ordinating Committee has instituted a series of visits to western countries by women from the occupied territories. Already, experience shows that visits like these are an exceptionally effective method of mobilizing opinion. Nothing makes a greater impact on people than seeing, hearing and, especially talking face to face with those whose everyday life is of occupation and oppression.

It cannot be too strongly emphasized that all efforts to mobilize public opinion must be based in truthful, up-to-date information. This information must be put across by articulate, well informed persons who can argue successfully against indifferent or hostile viewpoints. And we must reach beyond the converted, for it is no good merely to talk only with those who agree already. We have a universal message of truth and justice and we know that there is an appreciation of that message within a consensus stretching around the globe. We have to use modern methods of information, adapting them to meet the requirements of all cultures and all regional and national conditions. As we seek to reach out to mobilize public opinion as widely as is humanly possible, every NGO, with its specialized knowledge and experience, has its own important role to play.

## MOBILIZING AND TWINNING

This year 1987 has been notable as the first in which a real attempt has been made to plan co-ordinated NGO activities stretching beyond coming together in international or in regional meetings. The project to organize visits to certain countries by small groups of women from the occupied territories has been especially successful. In looking at planning to co-ordinate activities forward into 1988, this paper will draw on the valuable experience gained from that project and make some further suggestions. First, however, it will touch upon co-ordination in reaching out to and informing public opinion, another subject which is strongly upon our agenda. The very fact that, this year, we have a workshop on the mobilization of public opinion is an indication of the extent to which this important subject is now central to our deliberations and activities and is likely to remain so.

One of the most basic essentials in reaching public opinion is to disseminate accurate information to the wider world about what is actually going on in Palestine. Obviously, the media has a key role and some very able and dedicated media people are working to that end in Palestine and in Israel, as well as elsewhere. There is though a basic problem in that accurate information is often suppressed by the occupation authorities at its source and prevented from being transmitted outside. One very important and welcome move to counter that is the publication and international distribution of the *Al-Fajr* newspaper of Jerusalem from the United States of America. NGO's and, for that matter, individuals, might well consider that subscribing to it might be one valuable co-ordinating effort.

Worldwide, the name of Bir Zeir University is synonymous with the ferment of ideas under occupation and also with resistance to the determined, brutal and frequently bloody efforts of the occupation authorities to try to suppress that ferment of ideas. Some universities and colleges elsewhere have twinning arrangements with Bir Zeit. One example, but by no means the only one, is the University of Durham in the North East of England. Durham has a Centre of Middle Eastern and Islamic Studies which is one of the foremost in Europe and which is very active in reciprocal exchanges. The Durham Students' Union is twinned with the Bir Zeit Students' Council. There are regular academic exchanges, both of students and lecturers, between the two universities. What a marvellous example that is of planned co-ordination!

At Bir Zeit, the university public relations office, operating, as it is forced to, under great difficulties, regularly sends out information on what is happening. On the positive side there is information on the university's work but the negative side - the oppression under which the university is forced to operate - comes through just as clearly and in the same, clinically accurate style. But there is no certainty that the information can reach its destination and there is plenty of evidence that frequently it does not. A valuable piece of NGO co-ordination would be to establish regional centres in countries in Europe, America, Asia and Australasia, to ensure the receipt of information, not only from Bir Zeit University, but also from other reliable sources in Palestine and in Israel, so that the information could then be disseminated as widely as possible from the regional centres. Our own NGO office, here in Geneva, already performs a most valuable service as a distribution centre for information but its resources are already stretched to the limit and such a worldwide regional network would be a valuable addition.

Bir Zeit is of course by no means the only Palestinian university to suffer constant harassment. On 6 April 1987, Professor Saeb Erakat of An-Najah University was convicted by a military court on a charge of so-called "incitement." He had published an article in the university newsletter entitled *Nineteen Years of Israeli Occupation*. The article included the sentence that "the Palestinians have to suffer, refuse and resist until we get back our freedom." For expressing that self evident truth Professor Erakat was convicted in the kangaroo court system of the military occupation. News of that outrage reached the outside world largely through efforts from within Israel, using regional contacts to inform people and to arouse international protest.

Before leaving the subject of informing and mobilizing public opinion, there is another point to be considered, and that is in making the exercise a two-way process. We are all only too well aware that what appears in the media outside Palestine frequently bears little relationship to what is actually happening in Palestine. Very often, the media portrayal stretches from the muddled and mistaken to the deliberately untruthful. The point of a two-way process would be in a co-ordinated effort to ensure that Israeli and Zionist propaganda, designed to misrepresent the situation in

Palestine to the outside world, is transmitted back to Palestinian NGO's. Their position would thereby be strengthened in further mobilizing their own public opinion through greater awareness of this misrepresentation. We should not ever forget that, for decades, while the Palestinians thought that their persecution and ill-treatment was so obvious that it must be known worldwide, the reality was that much of the world was convinced of the exact opposite of the truth. Much of it still is and that is what we have to counter.

The idea of visits to certain countries by small groups of women from the occupied territories was first put forward at last year's International Meeting by Dr James Graff of the Toronto-based Near East Cultural and Educational Foundation of Canada. Three visits of the type he envisaged took place in the early summer to the United Kingdom, to Belgium and The Netherlands, and to France and Switzerland. Visits are projected in the near future to Canada and the USA. Meanwhile, delegations were invited to the World Congress of Women in Moscow in June 1987 and further visits and tours of Soviet cities are planned. For all the power of information technology, there is really nothing which makes a greater impact on people than seeing, hearing and talking face to face with those whose everyday life is of occupation and oppression. That was certainly our experience of the visit to Britain by three very able and articulate women. By any standards, their visit was so successful, as I am sure were the other visits, that there can be no hesitation in recommending such visits as a most important area of planning co-ordinated activities forward into 1988. Well before their visit, a co-ordinating committee of British NGO's was set up, which arranged an extensive tour of England, Wales and Scotland. The committee devised a programme which ensured that the visitors met thousands of people, both formally and informally. During their visit, they were interviewed by, among others, the BBC Arabic Service. One outcome of the interview was that telephone calls were received from delighted people in Palestine, indicating that the interview had been heard and appreciated - another indication of the importance of the two-way process in communications, especially in making known to the Palestinians the worldwide support they have.

There is a wide field for co-ordinated activities of this sort in the future but some words of caution are necessary. The forces of occupation will not be slow to react as they too come to appreciate the success of such visits. They will do their best to persecute the participants and to prevent future visits. What we must also face up to is the need for wide international co-ordination in resisting such tactics. Another important activity, both in its own right and as a means of resisting victimization, is in twinning arrangements. For example, these can be between trade unions, as well as between businesses, between women's organizations, between churches and parishes, as well as between cities, towns and villages. For twinning purposes among organizations, it is essential that those outside Palestine have on the spot information as to what groups exist in Palestine with which they might co-ordinate, how those groups function, what are the constraints on them and what are their relations with each other. As an example of the sort of complex situations which exist and of which due account has to be taken, it is known that under the extreme persecution of trade unionism and trade unionists which prevails in the occupied territories, several quarry workers' trade unions exist in Nablus. In twinning initiatives by organizations outside Palestine, one basic thing we must do is to ensure that we do nothing to encourage divisions and everything to encourage solidarity.

In London, within recent months, an organization called "Living Stones" has been established. This is an all-denominational Christian group which aims to establish better relations with Christians in Palestine and, in due course, to establish twinning arrangements between parishes in Britain and parishes in Palestine. "Living Stones" co-ordinates to an important extent with the already established Jerusalem and Peace Service which is in effect an alternative travel agency which has already organized successful travel parties to the Holy Land. These are parties of tourists who stay in Palestinian owned hotels and go specifically to meet Palestinians and to see the real conditions in Palestine. The great majority of tourists do not have such opportunities and the truth is deliberately kept from them. There is important scope for co-ordination in these directions, to which our religious based NGO's in particular might wish to give special attention.

There is great scope for international co-ordination in twinning arrangements between towns and cities in various countries with towns and cities in Palestine. Where that has been tried, it has proved a great step forward in international relations, in improving local knowledge in the places involved and in providing great encouragement for the citizens of the twinned towns in Palestine.

The city of Dundee in Scotland has been officially twinned with Nablus for several years and official exchange visits have taken place. In the past, Bassam Al Shaka'a, the indomitable Mayor of Nablus, himself a victim of Israeli terrorists,[(6)] has visited Dundee and his opposite number, who in Scotland is called the Lord Provost, has visited Nablus. The predictable fury of the Zionist lobby over initiatives of this sort is its own measure of the value of such initiatives. When the twinning was proposed, it was a matter of enormous, vicious and prolonged outcry by the Zionist lobby. The city of Dundee was threatened with withdrawal of trade and other dire consequences, but the citizens stood up to the outcry and they have defeated the massive campaign against their city.

Without digressing into British party politics, but to illustrate an important point, it may be mentioned that it was a Labour Party Council in Dundee which took the decision to twin with Nablus. In the run-up to the recent election in Britain [1987], one of the anti-Labour parties, the Scottish National Party, in a television broadcast, attacked the city of Dundee for flying the Palestinian flag over the Civic Centre. Dundee elects two Members of Parliament. One of them is Ernie Ross MP, who was the first Chairman of the Interim Co-ordinating Committee, the fore-runner of the present ICCP. In the election, he increased his majority from 10,150 to 16,526. The other seat was formerly held by the Scottish National Party. In the election, Labour also decisively won that seat. The point of quoting those facts is not to give any boost to the Labour Party but to illustrate that, especially in western countries where the Israeli lobby is so powerful, it should always be resisted and never surrendered to.

The city of Glasgow in Scotland is now twinned with Hebron and the city of Aberdeen is actively considering a Palestinian twinning arrangement. Twinning between towns worldwide and towns in Palestine presents a major and valuable field for co-ordinated activities. A worldwide drive for such arrangements would be a powerful move to support the struggle to uphold the inalienable rights of the Palestinians. Their struggle for justice is everyone's struggle and worldwide town twinning arrangements would be a most valuable means to emphasize that to the citizens of countries all round the globe.

---

(6) Bassam Al Shaka'a lost both legs through a bomb planted in his car by an Israeli terrorist group.

Mention must be made of the necessity for co-ordination to sustain the recent decision of the European Community in relation to Palestinian imports. Products from the occupied territories now have privileged tariff-free access to the EC in their own right as specifically Palestinian products. This decision was arrived at in the teeth of Israeli opposition. Now, the Israeli government is trying to prevent the implementation of the decision by insisting that the goods which are, so far, only a tiny trickle, should go via Israeli agencies, so that they and not the Palestinians will gain the benefit. There must be a powerful co-ordination to resist these moves and to ensure that, not only does the gain go to the Palestinian people as intended, but also that the trickle of Palestinian exports grows to a flood.

In securing the European Community decision, a powerful force for good was the Parliamentary Association for Euro-Arab Co-operation, one of the major NGO's affiliated to this meeting and represented on the ICCP. Yet in the Spring of this year, the Association was forced to close down its modest office and dismiss its staff in Brussels, the headquarters of the European Community. In the Autumn, it has had to close its other and original office in Paris. These closures were due to lack of finance. For the same reason in March of this year, the ICCP, meeting here in Geneva, was faced with the strong likelihood that our own modest office would have to be closed down and the staff dismissed. We were only able to avoid that by a last minute infusion of finance. We cannot be effective or co-ordinate anything in 1987-88 or further into the future if we have to lurch along like that. We clearly have to look to financial as well as to other planned co-ordination.

This paper has looked at the planning of co-ordinated NGO activities for 1987-88 with a basis in the experience of the remarkable progress made already. Apart from the final point on the absolute need for co-ordination in financial matters, it has dealt mainly with co-ordination in mobilizing public opinion and in the field of twinning arrangements of several sorts. We have already accomplished far more than could have been foreseen when the United Nations called the first International meeting of NGO's. We still have a long way to go. Let us plan and co-ordinate ever more strongly to go there.

# 7

# PEACE DENIED

The mid nineteen-eighties constituted a profoundly depressing period in the Middle East. The ever more urgent but ever more abortive efforts to secure peace and justice through negotiations were epitomized in the ill-starred Hussein-Arafat initiative, which originated on the initiative of King Hussein of Jordan, at the meeting of the Palestine National Council (PNC) in Amman in November 1984.

The PLO invited me to attend the PNC as an observer and I retain two especially abiding memories of the proceedings. The first was King Hussein delivering his set-piece speech to thunderously stage-managed applause. The second was the democratic nature of the PNC, vividly illustrated when one of the Members, a good friend from London, Dr Anis Al-Qasem, a noted international lawyer and Secretary-General of EAFORD (International Organization for the Elimination of All Forms of Racial Discrimination), raised a point of order during Yasser Arafat's presentation of the Executive Committee Report. The point Anis made, to applause, was that the Chairman was presenting his own, personal views rather than those of the Committee. The President of the PNC, after consultations, rebuked the Chairman who, after some mild argument, accepted the point before resuming his speech. It was like being back in the House of Commons.

It would be difficult to imagine such an incident in relation to any other Arab leader. It was the time when President Hafez Al Assad of Syria was trying, with characteristic brutality, to replace the PLO with an organization under his own control. He had prevented a sizeable body of PNC Members who resided in Syria from attending and the Syrian state-controlled radio was screaming abuse at the proceedings every day. Palestinian democracy is far in advance of anything elsewhere in the Arab World and it frightens authoritarian regimes. All Arab regimes pay lip service to the Palestinian cause while in practice, many of them see the Palestinians as a political football to be kicked around to suit their own purposes.

By chance, my attendance at the PNC resulted in an opportunity for me to write regularly on the events of those depressing mid-eighties. While waiting to board the Amman flight at the departure gate at Heathrow Airport, I was approached by a fellow passenger, a young man who introduced himself as Mohammed Maatouk, London correspondent of *Al Khaleej* (The Gulf), the newspaper published in Sharjah in the United Arab Emirates. Rather to my surprise, he came straight out with an invitation for me to write a series of articles for the paper, to comment in an analytical way on current events. He wanted me to write a weekly article. I did not have the time to undertake such a commitment and was not enthusiastic about it. He persisted though and asked what about an article every fortnight and eventually, with some reluctance, I agreed to do one every three weeks.

I did not really take the proposition seriously but be obviously did and he contacted me again shortly after I returned from Amman and, in December, I wrote the first article and then continued providing them on a three-weekly basis until July 1986, when Mohammed Maatouk wrote to tell me that the column was to be discontinued due to a "re-assessment for new plans" for the newspaper, There were five articles outstanding for payment (which had always been irregular) and, as he requested, I notified him of what I was owed. There was no response either then or to subsequent reminders and shortly afterwards, he vanished from London. I never was paid for those last five articles. The selection reproduced in this and the next two chapters is mainly Middle East related although it widens out to some other issue. I have done a fair amount of editing but the articles retain their original character as a contemporary record of events and thoughts on events in that period.

# BRITAIN AND THE MIDDLE EAST

There is a clear feeling in official circles in the Arab World that, among the Western European countries, Britain's current stance is especially negative and unhelpful. During a recent visit to Tunis (1) I had detailed discussions with Mr Chedli Klibi, the Secretary-General of the Arab League, with Ministers of the Tunisian government and with Mr Farouk Kaddoumi of the PLO (2) Concern over the British attitude was very clear from all those talks and it was sufficiently strongly expressed for me to make it a matter of priority to convey my own concern to the British Foreign Office as soon as I returned home. But the message did not come only from Tunis. In London, the same concern was being expressed among the Arab Diplomatic Corps. It was certain actions of the British government and especially of the Prime Minister, Mrs Margaret Thatcher, that had given rise to those feelings. Unfortunately, and to the detriment of British policy, Mrs Thatcher often speaks and acts impulsively without due consideration for the effect she will have.

In 1982, the year of the Israeli invasion of Lebanon, Mrs Thatcher refused to meet the top level delegation appointed by the Fez summit conference because it contained a member of the PLO. At that time, I was myself a Member of Parliament and Chairman of the Labour Middle East Council and I have a very clear recollection of joining with Mr [later Sir] Dennis Walters MP, Chairman of the Conservative Middle East Council, to lead an all-party group of MP's to meet the Prime Minister, to try to persuade her to change her mind. We met her at eleven o'clock on the evening of 29 November, the United Nations Day of International Solidarity with the Palestinian People, after we had both been speakers at a huge public meeting in support of the Palestinians and the Lebanese, organized by CAABU, and we argued with her for an hour, but without persuading her.

Mrs Thatcher had long been a member of the organization called the Conservative Friends of Israel and in May 1984 she had agreed to become President of its North London Area Council. That

---

(1) January 1985.
(2) Head of Political Department, in effect the PLO's "Foreign Minister."

ill-judged action caused grave concern in the Arab World and strong representations were made by MP's and others in Britain to urge her to change her mind. However, she declined to do so and in a letter to myself on 13 June 1984, she strongly denied that either she or the government had followed a partisan policy. She referred to a speech in which she had criticized the Israeli state before the Board of Deputies of British Jews in 1981 and she wrote :-

> I believe that criticism from an acknowledged friend - and one who believes that Israel, like other states in the area, should live in security and peace - is often more telling than it would be from other quarters.

That was, no doubt, well intentioned but, as the old saying has it, "The road to hell is paved with good intentions" and it is very unlikely that there was any impact on the Zionist state. Even Harold Wilson, the most pro-Israeli Prime Minister Britain has ever had, refused to accept any official position in the Labour Friends of Israel throughout all the years during which he was Leader of the Labour Party.

It was against that background that Farouk Kaddoumi, presenting his report to the Palestine National Council at the Amman meeting last November, singled out Britain as the most unhelpful of the European countries and compared Britain unfavourably with France, Italy and Greece. Unfortunately, very shortly after the PNC meeting, British standing was still further lowered at the summit meeting of the heads of governments of the countries of the European Community which took place in Dublin in early December. At Dublin, the British government and the government of the Federal Republic of Germany both went out of their way to stress that "the security of Israel" was the central concern of their policies on the Middle East. There is little that could be more unhelpful to European-Arab relations and there is nothing that could be more unrelated to the facts of the situation. The facts are that it is not Israel, with its huge war machine, whose security is threatened. It is the security of every other state in the region and even the security of the entire world which is threatened by Israel's ambitions.

When I was in Tunis in January, it was Arab concern over the Dublin summit declarations of Britain and West Germany which was especially stressed, together with concern over Mrs Thatcher's personal association with the pro-Israeli lobby inside her own party. The one-sided statements made by Mrs Thatcher and by Chancellor Kohl of West Germany at Dublin are contrary to the European Community's Venice Declaration of 1980, which announced a much more balanced policy, including the security of all states in the Middle East and the involvement of the PLO as a party to negotiations. The British Foreign Secretary, Sir Geoffrey Howe, has said on a number of occasions that the Venice Declaration is the basis of British policy. So the Prime Minister, not for the first time, speaking impulsively and without due consideration for the effect of her words, contradicted the declared policy of the government she leads.

However, the position of a British Prime Minister in relation to the government and Parliament is more complicated than the positions of Arab leaders. In many Arab countries, the leader of the government exercises far stronger personal power than does the British Prime Minister. It is also usual in the Arab tradition to attach exceptional importance to the views and statements of individual leaders as being the views of governments, whereas in Europe and especially in Britain, there is a different approach. So, while Mrs Thatcher's statements are to be regretted, both because they are one-sided as well as because they are not entirely in line with the official policy of the British government of which she is the leader, they do not mean that Britain is not open to further influence.

For all its unfortunate subject matter, the British - West German accord at Dublin is of further interest. For all that there have been two terrible world wars with Britain and Germany as implacable enemies in each, there is an affinity between the two countries which goes back over many centuries and which is present today within the often uneasy relationships between the countries of the European Community. In an interview published recently in *Al Khaleej*, Mr David Steel MP, Leader of the British Liberal Party, expressed the view that Britain and West Germany should work together to influence the USA to take a less one-sided policy on the Middle East. That is a good proposition, although it may be aimed as much as anything at balancing out the rivalry in the Middle East between Britain and another powerful European partner, France. What is sad though is that at Dublin, Britain and Germany seemed more concerned to follow the American policy than to bring about the changes in it which are urgently required.

One of the features of the British system of government is that, for all the democratic system of the election of the government and the constant scrutiny of it by Parliament, a vast amount of government business is extremely secretive. Given that fact, there is reason to believe that the British government's policy in private is more positive than is indicated by its unfortunate public face. There is reason to believe that when Mrs Thatcher recently met President Reagan, after first meeting Mr Mikhail Gorbachev, one of the leading Ministers of the USSR, during his visit to Britain, (3) she did represent to the American President that he should adopt a more balanced policy towards the Middle East. Whether or not those representations will have any effect remains to be seen.

Whatever the secret talks, though, the British government's policy, like that of any government in any country, can only be judged by its public impact. Therefore, the clear task for Arab governments and the PLO is to express their concern strongly and forthrightly about the public direction of British policy. Having due regard to all the aspects of British policy as well as to the British system of government, that requires to be done both publicly and with private representations to British Ministers and to the Foreign Office. Britain has a long relationship with the Arab World and no small historical responsibility for the current situation. But Britain, like all Western Europe, has a major present-day interest in good relations with the Arab World. The British Empire has long passed into history and Britain's present-day economy is very weak and in need of friends wherever they can be found. Friendly relations with the Arab countries are more important than submission to the British section of the international Zionist lobby, with its sole aim of furthering the interests of the not particularly friendly Israeli state.

---

(3) Before he was appointed to the foremost position in March 1985.

# MOSSAD AND INTERNATIONAL CRIME

The Israeli intelligence service, Mossad, has a long history of being involved in international criminal activity. Some years ago, when educated and articulate PLO representatives were first starting to put the Palestinian case before the Western World, a number of them were murdered by Israeli agents. There have also been cases in Norway and in Germany, where Israeli agents have been shown to be engaged in murder against those on the Mossad list of persons to be assassinated. The European operations were at one time co-ordinated from Britain. London only ceased to be the European headquarters when, some years ago, the Israeli Embassy was warned that certain Mossad agents posing as diplomats would be expelled and their activities exposed publicly if they did not stop. A recent case at the Central Criminal Court in London has demonstrated that there is no sign that Mossad involvement in international activities of a criminal nature is diminishing.

Three Israelis, recruited through Mossad, were sentenced to long terms of imprisonment for kidnapping a Nigerian named Umaru Dikko and attempting to take him by force from Britain to Nigeria. Dikko, a Minister in the Nigerian government which was overthrown just over a year ago in a military coup, was badly wanted in Nigeria on charges alleging that he had enriched himself by corruption on a spectacular scale. But that did not in any way lessen the crime of his kidnapping, nor did it lessen the Israeli involvement.

On 5 July, he was kidnapped in London. He was drugged and an attempt was made to take him to Lagos in a crate on a Nigerian Airways cargo plane. The British police were alerted by his secretary, who witnessed the kidnapping, which took place as he was leaving his home. The police acted swiftly and the British Foreign Office, in what had to be top level decision, taken at very short notice, ordered the crate, which was labelled as diplomatic baggage, to be opened at the airport. Dikko was inside, bound and deeply drugged, accompanied by one of the Israelis. A second crate was also opened and it was found to contain the other two Israelis, who were also planning to go to Nigeria to hand their victim over to the government. The Israelis were Alexander Barak, the leader of the gang, who was sentenced to fourteen years in prison; Lev Arie

Shapiro and Felix Abitbol, who each received ten years imprisonment. The judge recommended that all three should be deported from Britain when they had served their sentences. They must, of course, have had one or more accomplices, to seal them into the crates, but the police did not succeed in bringing any such to justice.

Barak, the leader of the operation, was a wealthy businessman who had been involved in business deals with Nigeria. He held a Nigerian as well as an Israeli passport and also had a forged French passport. In 1982, the year of the horrendous invasion of Lebanon and of the Sabra and Chatilla massacres, he had been a Mossad agent in the occupied part of Lebanon. Abitbol was a business friend of Barak's. Shapiro was a Russian immigrant into Israel, a senior consultant anaesthetist and head of the intensive care unit of a leading hospital in Tel Aviv. He had been recruited for the kidnapping by Mossad and he it was who was found in the same crate at the airport as the victim. The evidence presented at the trial showed that Shapiro was in no doubt that the kidnapping was an official Mossad operation and that he took part believing that he was acting in the interests of the Zionist state. Both the Nigerian and Israeli governments denied being involved in the kidnapping but the evidence against both is strong and, as has been shown so many times over so many years, if the Israelis officially deny any particular course of action, it can usually be assumed that the truth is quite different from what they say.

In looking at the motives for the crime, there are a number of circumstances to be considered. For example, the Israelis could well have calculated that the return of Dikko to his own country at the hands of Mossad could have led to a resumption of diplomatic relations. There can be little doubt that, if the crime had succeeded, the worldwide Zionist propaganda machine would have hailed it as a triumph of bringing a criminal to justice. In its desperate search for oil, the Zionist state would especially value good relations with a major Black African, oil producing country like Nigeria. Israel also sees Nigeria as a valuable export market and Barak had entered into a number of deals for the export of Israeli manufactures to Nigeria.

At first, the gang planned to lure Dikko to Paris to take part in a television interview to be set up by Barak. They would then have kidnapped him in France. Also to be interviewed in the television programme was Nissim Gaon, an Israeli living in Geneva, who was owed a large sum of money by Dikko. Gaon may not have been fully aware of the plans to kidnap Dikko but that did not alter the fact that he was involved in Israeli politics at top level. He was the chief financier of the Israeli political party called Tami, which caused the 1984 election in Israel by withdrawing from the ruling Likud coalition government. Gaon's daughter was married to the son of the President of Israel and when Gaon was away from Geneva, the President's son managed his office for him.

When the judge passed sentence at the trial, he stated that he accepted that Barak thought that he was acting in the interests of his country. He was less charitable towards Abitbol but more so towards Shapiro. He spoke of Shapiro's "blind loyalty" to Israel and said that he had heard in the evidence that Shapiro was "honest, upright, dedicated to his patients and a true patriot." It was curious that the judge should go out of his way to speak in such a manner. For the facts were that Shapiro, by involving himself, apparently with pride, in an act of international conspiracy and crime by drugging and incapacitating the victim for the purposes of handing him over to a military dictatorship, had acted in betrayal of his oath as a doctor, which obliges doctors to act at all times for human wellbeing.

The trial followed shortly after another trial at which the same judge presided and in which his conduct of the trial aroused heavy criticism. That trial created a huge sensation and caused major embarrassment to the British government by showing them to have acted to mislead Parliament. That was the trial of a man called Clive Ponting, a senior civil servant accused of a breach of the law by revealing embarrassing, official government secrets to a Member of Parliament because he could not support what the government was doing. At that trial, the same judge had wanted to direct the jury to find Ponting guilty. Only intervention by the prosecution itself had persuaded him not to do so. Even so, he had summed up the case to the jury by advising heavily in favour of a verdict of guilty, which was what the government wanted. The jury responded with a unanimous verdict of not guilty.

# "THIS ACCURSED COUNTRY"

"What the writing on the wall says is that we must leave this accursed country quickly and without getting our hands even more dirty." Those were the recent words of a writer in the Hebrew language newspaper *Ha'aretz.* He likened the Israeli army to a furious, bleeding giant, committing what he called "a new series of mistakes" in Lebanon. He talked about progress from grand strategy to the responses of a wounded animal. By "grand strategy" he meant the war of aggression launched in 1982, of which the aim was to eliminate the PLO, turn Lebanon into a fragmented state under Israeli control and make it the probable launching place for the next war of aggression, against Syria. The so-called "new series of mistakes" were the daily atrocities being committed against the civilian population of southern Lebanon, under what the Israelis called the "iron fist" policy.

On the day when the article appeared in *Ha'aretz*, another Israeli paper *Ma'ariv,* described the reactions of Mr Uri Lubrani, the official who carried the sinister title of Co-ordinator of Israeli Activities in Lebanon. Mr Lubrani was described as being convinced that the Israeli army should behave even more harshly. Every day, the atrocities which he did not consider harsh enough continued, with murders, mass arrests, disappearances of citizens and the destruction of people's homes. To that could be added the systematic destruction of places of worship and the planting within them of delayed action bombs timed to explode when the buildings were filled with unsuspecting people at worship. That happened in the mosque at Maarakeh, near Tyre and, after the explosion, the Israelis broke into the largest hospital in Tyre and arrested a line of blood donors who were waiting to give their blood to save those who had been wounded.

The Director of the hospital was taken away and beaten senseless by Israeli soldiers, the third time, he said, that he had been treated in that way. Some of the blood donors and others who were arrested were detained overnight in appalling conditions and also beaten up. They were only released after being forced to pose "smiling" for Israeli propaganda photographs. This is mindful of the conduct of the Nazis in the countries they occupied in Europe during the second world war.

By a coincidence, my attention has been drawn recently to copies of some wartime documents from the German archives. These include reports sent back to Germany by the then German Ambassador in Turkey. The reports give an account of discussions held in 1940-41, when the Nazis were at the height of their power and the defeat of Britain seemed imminent. The documents show that at that time, in the Middle East, German officials were meeting officials of the Zionist terror group, the Irgun Zvai Leumi. The documents contain favourable comments on the philosophy of the Irgun Zvai Leumi as being compatible with the philosophy of the Nazis. That was before the Nazis had decided on their policy of genocide against the Jewish people and the papers describe proposals by the Irgun whereby the European Jews would all be sent to Palestine where, with German military backing, a Nazi-type Jewish state would be set up which would be Germany's ally against Britain. (4)

For the long term, the "grand strategy" at that time was to be that after the defeat of Britain, the Nazi-type Jewish state would control the Middle East on behalf of Nazi Germany, whose close and permanent ally it would be. The leader of the Irgun Zvai Leumi was Menachem Begin, who became the Prime Minister of Israel responsible for the invasion of Lebanon. With the defeat of the Nazis, the grand strategy of the early nineteen-forties was fortunately never realized, but the philosophy of the Irgun Zvai Leumi seems to have changed little and its influence in Israeli politics, through its successor political party, Likud, seems to have increased markedly.

Resistance to the Nazis grew throughout the years of the second world war in all the occupied countries of Europe. In Czechoslovakia, Hitler appointed a man called Heydrich as the "protector" and co-ordinator of German activities. Heydrich was assassinated and in revenge the Nazis totally destroyed the village of Lidice. In 1948, the Irgun Zvai Leumi, in co-operation with other terrorist groups, including the Stern Gang, of which Yitshak Shamir was a leader, perpetrated their own version of the atrocity against Lidice with the cold blooded murder of men, women and children of the village of Deir Yassin, as part of their campaign to terrorize the Palestinians out of their homeland. And in 1985, official terrorism against the people of southern Lebanon remains

---

(4) A translation of the key document is appended at the end of this chapter.

the policy as the defeated and retreating Israeli army seeks to extricate itself from "this accursed country." Brutal repression against people in their own homeland by occupying forces does only one thing. It stirs up ever greater anger and resistance and as all history shows, it unites the people and leads to the defeat of the oppressors. Europe in the second world war, Vietnam, Afghanistan and Lebanon all show that even the most sophisticated military forces cannot win in such circumstances.

When the Israelis first entered Lebanon, there was no shortage of people in that sadly divided country who were not averse to their presence. Among those were the large Shia population of the south but, from the start, the looting, pillaging and mass killing by the Israelis turned potential friends into implacable enemies. Now, the "iron fist" policy has created an entirely new dimension of hostility which poses long term factors of vital importance in the Arab-Zionist conflict, The so-called South Lebanese Army, under the nominal leadership of the Lebanese General Lahad, is disintegrating. Its purpose was to provide the Israelis with a Lebanese force under Israeli control, to subdue the population between the Israeli border and the Litani River and so create a buffer zone between the Zionist state and Lebanon - on Lebanese territory. That force originally recruited many Shia soldiers, but those soldiers, sickened by the Israeli atrocities against their own families, deserted in droves and many joined Amal, the militia of the Shia Lebanese community, in order to defend their own people. Shia leaders in Lebanon announced publicly that, not only would the resistance to the iron fist terrorism of the Israelis be stepped up but that, if and when the Israelis finally withdraw to their own border, then raids into Israeli territory would become a regular feature of Shia resistance.

So the government of Israel is now faced with an appalling dilemma of its own creation. It has alienated even the Phalange forces which connived openly in its invasion of Lebanon and who were its willing partners in the Sabra and Chatilla massacres. It has turned the Shia people of the south, who were prepared passively to accept the invasion, into enemies as implacable as the Palestinians. When the war was launched in 1982, it was cynically called "Operation Peace in Galilee." It was supposed to prevent rocket and guerilla attacks in the Galilee area although in fact no such attacks were taking place, the PLO having strictly adhered to the previously agreed casefire.

The war was the final, blatant and bloody breach of the ceasefire which the Israeli government had been looking to make over a year long period. All that the war has assured is that for the future there will be less "peace in Galilee" than there was before. It has also assured a greater awareness in the world community of the nature of the Israeli state and its "grand strategy" of constant expansion. All the atrocities which have been referred to in this article, and many more, have been prominently reported in the British and other western media - something which would not have happened only a few years earlier. In Israel itself, with growing economic crisis and growing concern over the conduct of the Israeli force in Lebanon, it is not only Lebanon but Israel itself, for more and more of its own citizens which is becoming what one of its own writers in Ha'aretz called "this accursed country."

# DAYS AND EVENTS TO REMEMBER

There are certain days when events combine by coincidence to mark the day as one to be remembered because of the way in which its events mark important trends. Such a day occurred for me on Sunday, 14 April, when I was in Saudi Arabia as a member of a CAABU delegation. Three particular items from that day remain especially in my memory. First, it was the day when the British Prime Minister, Mrs Thatcher, also visited Riyadh. Second, it was the day when the Saudi *Arab News* English language newspaper carried a report of an article in an American magazine written by the Secretary of State, Mr George Shultz, telling the world how grateful it should be for the Reaganite version of how the world ought to be run. Third, *Arab News* carried a letter from a reader right alongside the Shultz report, deploring what the reader termed "the onslaught" in the Middle East of that western culture which Reagan and Shultz think is so good. There was a fourth item on that same day, but I will come to that later.

Our CAABU delegation was not connected with Mrs Thatcher's visit. Like her, we had been invited by the Saudi government but it was coincidental that we were there at the same time. Mrs Thatcher stopped in Riyadh for only three hours on her way home from a tour of South East Asian countries which was criticized in Britain because of certain of her remarks in those countries. By contrast, she made no public remarks at all in Saudi Arabia and it is clear that in the meeting she had with King Fahd and the Saudi government, nothing was exchanged except pleasantries which, desirable as they may be, do little to help resolve the dangerous situation in the Middle East. The talks were described as "frank and successful." For those who understand the coded statements of diplomacy, that almost certainly means that there were differing viewpoints on what should be done about the Middle East situation, that little common ground was found on what to do next and that the talks probably ended exactly where they started.

What is likely to have happened is that the Saudi authorities pressed for a strong British and Western European stand to back up the Arab initiative, which had included King Fahd's visit to President Reagan, to seek a less one sided American policy and to try to create American moves to bring the Israeli state to the negotiating table. It is likely that Mrs Thatcher responded less positively than the Arab World would have wished because of the continuing official European deference to the USA. Mrs Thatcher is said, probably correctly, to have urged President Reagan in private to change his Middle East policy along the lines desired by the Arab countries and which are self-evidently necessary for the settlement of conflict. There is, though, little indication that the Reagan administration attaches any urgent priority to securing justice in the Middle East by exerting the pressure which it alone can exert on the Israelis. Without a change in the Israeli policy, there can of course never be justice in the Middle East and so long as there remains the deliberate denial of justice, there will not be peace.

To move to the second of the coincidental events of that fourteenth day of April, it falls strange upon many ears in the Middle East to hear of Mr George Shultz's eulogy of Reaganite policies. "America" Mr Shultz had written in his American magazine article "must not abandon those seeking democracy." That must seem strange indeed in every place where the Palestinian struggle for democracy is supported. For it is the USA's support for the Israeli denial of democracy to the people of Palestine and the Israelis' ever-increasing turning of the West Bank and the Gaza Strip into South African, apartheid-type bantustans which enables the denial of democracy to be sustained. Mr Shultz had also written that, as a result of American policy, Europe was evolving into a strong position in world affairs. Yet the reality is that throughout Europe, there is apprehension over American policy while, in America, little notice is taken of that apprehension. It is especially notable that Europe seems to have so little impact on the American policy in the Middle East which it knows to be so disastrous.

How much better it would have been if Mrs Thatcher could have used her visit to Riyadh to announce that she, together with President Mitterand of France, Chancellor Kohl of West Germany and other heads of governments in the European Community were going, publicly and in unison, to represent to President Reagan how urgent it is for him to change his Middle East policy. Had she been able to do something like that, it would indeed have demonstrated that there was a foundation for Mr Shultz's claim that Europe was evolving into a stronger position in world affairs.

Right alongside the report in Arab News of Mr Shultz's article was a letter from a reader which made the third of the interesting and related coincidences of that day. The reader was complaining about what he felt to be the over westernization of the English language channel of Saudi television. He wrote that many Muslim expatriates who had gone to Saudi Arabia to escape "the onslaught" of western culture in Europe and America and to find a safe haven in which to bring up their children, were finding it hard to do so. That was because of the way the television, as he put it "digs through the western trash baskets" to provide, among other undesirable features, "the monotony of western crime or cowboy serials."

During my visit to Saudi Arabia, I was not able to spend sufficient time watching television to be able to form any judgement of my own about the programmes, but I have a good deal of sympathy for the general point the writer of the letter was making. In the West also, among discerning television viewers as well as among discerning newspaper readers, similar complaints are frequently made about the trashiness of most of the western media. These complaints are not only about the so called "entertainment" provided but also about the often quite distorted view the media present both of the western world and of the world outside the west. The trashiness is, sadly, only another manifestation of the society for which Mr Shultz told us we should all be so grateful and which seems so incapable, among other things, of advancing the cause of peace and justice in the Middle East.

As I have already said, there was a fourth item on that day, to which I would come at the end of this article. That item, ominously, was that 14 April 1985 was the seventy-third anniversary of the day in 1912 when the Titanic struck an iceberg. The Titanic, in her day the greatest ship ever built and claimed to be unsinkable, struck an iceberg on her maiden voyage from Britain to the USA and sank with the loss of more than fifteen hundred lives. From the perspective of history, the sinking of the Titanic is sometimes looked upon as an omen of the terrible first world war to which mighty Europe was then drifting.

Many of those who were drowned were poor British and Irish emigrants on their way to a new life in the USA. Britain at that time was a rigidly class divided society as, indeed, it still is, and the emigrants, travelling in the cheapest accommodation in the lower decks, were actually locked below so that the first-class passengers could get to the lifeboats first. To bring together all the coincidental items of a single day referred to in this article, a western policy which gives increasing cause for concern and which connives at the deliberate locking down and suppression of a dynamic people in Palestine, must be challenged both in the West and in the East for, otherwise, it could prove to be an omen of even greater conflict to come.

# PROPHECY AND POLITICS

At one of the recent regular meetings of CAABU, the speaker was The Very Reverend Victor de Waal, Dean of Canterbury. Dr de Waal, a senior clergyman of the Church of England and a distinguished Christian theologian who has served the Church in the Middle East, spoke on "Palestine and Israel: the Reality of Myths." With Palestine a holy land for Judaism, Christianity and Islam, there is an inescapable religious dimension in its turbulent politics. In recent years, in all three of the great monotheistic religions which were first revealed in the Middle East, the growth of a new and simplistic fundamentalism has added new and dangerous aspects to conflict in the region and it was against that background that CAABU invited its distinguished speaker.

The greatest stronghold of the new fundamentalism in Christianity is the USA, but the fundamentalists there are trying to export their views throughout Christendom. They contend that the Israeli state is the expression of God's purpose as foretold in ancient biblical prophecy and must therefore be upheld in everything it does. But they go further than that, for they also contend that humankind is moving rapidly to Armageddon, the ancient biblical prophecy of the ultimate and final battle between good and evil. The place where the battle was prophesied to take place is southern Lebanon, but the fundamentalists claim that something is now approaching which is far more apocalyptic even than the terrible killings which have already taken place in Lebanon. Their version of Armageddon is that Israel and the USA are the forces of good and that they are ranged against the forces of evil which are represented by the Soviet Union and Arabia. Therefore the final battle will be nuclear warfare between the superpowers and when it takes place, which they say it inevitably will, Christians alone will be saved from destruction.

Such evil nonsense is wholly contrary to Christian teaching, for Christ taught that you should do to others as you would have them do to you [5] . It has also been the universally accepted doctrine of Christianity for centuries that the life of Christ was itself the fulfilment of God's purposes according to ancient prophecy. Zionist

---

(5) Matthew 7, 12 (from the Sermon on the Mount).

politicians have accepted the new fundamentalism in America with enthusiasm as a means to their end of securing an endless supply of armaments for Israel. They seem to be as unmoved by the prospect that they could trigger off a nuclear war as they are by the final point of the fundamentalist theory that, when the nuclear Armageddon takes place, all Jews will convert to Christianity or, if they do not, then like the "godless" Russians and all others, they too will be destroyed.

Contrary to the fundamentalist view, Zionism is wholly a political movement and not in any way religious. Its founder, Theodor Herzl, was not a religious man and in his theory he was seeking a political solution to European persecution of Jews, not any fulfilment of ancient religious belief. Many of the founders of the state of Israel were atheists. The Prime Minister Mrs Golda Meir once told the Israeli Parliament that the majority of Zionists accepted that their identity (as a nation) depended on a religion in which they did not believe. Herzl's theories were rejected by religious Jews and it was only later that a false religious dimension was added, for the double purpose of gaining support among religious Jews and for deceiving Christians in the Western World into supporting Zionism. It is now, in the nineteen-eighties, that the falsehood is working out in the crazy views of the fundamentalists.

In the United States, those views are pumped out every week on commercially sponsored television programmes to millions of people and President Reagan himself appears to be one of those who accept them. In October 1983, he said to Thomas Dine, the Executive Director of the American-Israel Public Affairs Committee, the most powerful and influential organ of the Israeli lobby:

> You know, I turn back to your ancient prophets in the Old Testament and the signs foretelling Armageddon. I find myself wondering if we are the generation that is going to see that come about.

The extent to which a nuclear war might be brought about by Reagan's own policies, of which Israeli expansion is a part, is itself a matter for serious debate, but the very fact that the President of the United States subscribes to such views is a measure of the power of the fundamentalists, as well as a matter for serious and urgent alarm.

All this is the frightening reality of the myths which Dr Victor de Waal made the theme of his address to the CAABU meeting in London, He made a telling comparison between the mentalities of the Americans who settled in western states of the USA, the Afrikaaners who settled in South Africa and the Zionists who settled in Palestine. When the western states of the USA were settled in the second half of the nineteenth century, many of those who went there were refugees from persecution and exploitation in Europe and they were mostly religious people. They believed that they were settling in a God given country and that, in taking it away from the "heathen" Indians whose country it had been for centuries, they were fully justified in responding to Indian resistance by massacring the resisters and driving such as survived into small and controlled reservations.

The Afrikaaners who went from Holland to South Africa had a similar outlook and from their outlook has grown the racist system of apartheid, whereby the majority, black population are herded into bantustans, abominably treated and exploited for the benefit of the white settlers. The perpetrators of this system subscribe to a fundamentalist version of Christianity in which they actually claim that apartheid is an expression of the Will of God, even though, in fact, it is in contradiction of everything that Christ taught. And of course exactly the same attitude prevailed among the Zionists who settled in Palestine, who sought and continue to seek to treat the Palestinians as the Americans treated the Indians and as the Afrikaaners treat the Africans. It is not surprising that there is a fellow feeling among the American settlers, the Afrikaaners and the Zionists and that America and South Africa are Israel's closest allies. In his address, Dr de Waal commented acidly and accurately that Israel needs enemies in order to overcome its internal doubts and that it is good at making new enemies.

As telling a point as any he made was that the Jewish contribution to world civilization has been noticeably diminished by the establishment of the Jewish state and by its history since its establishment. How sadly true that is. When one looks for instance at the outstanding Jewish scientists, doctors, musicians, political thinkers and others of the nineteenth century, one has to ask "Where are their equivalents in the second half of the twentieth century?" What a tragedy that the huge contribution of such talented people should have been so sadly dissipated into the endless and ever more dangerous conflict created by the establishment of Israel.

Among responsible Christians, as well as among responsible Jews and Muslims, there are those who see the dangers of the new fundamentalists and who are working to counteract them. The British Council of Churches, the British section of a worldwide movement which seeks to bring together the various branches of Christianity, sent a special delegation to the Middle East in 1981 and has since unanimously approved a statement on the region which is vastly different in tone and content from the ravings of the fundamentalists. In that statement, the Council examines the complex politics and conflicts of the region. It states that the tragedy of the situation must deeply trouble all people of conscience and it emphasizes that "There are great dangers in giving support to a particular party or policy in the Middle East solely on the basis of biblical prophecy."

One of the most effective passages of the statement is that :

> Fellow Christians in the area are not to be thought of as outposts of European Christianity in a foreign land. The great majority belong to indigenous Christian communities going back to the very beginnings of Christianity. Their grasp of the issues is immediate and direct. Members of their congregations have suffered and continue to suffer in the conflict; and they have opportunities to promote reconciliation. We have an urgent responsibility to learn from their traditions and their experience, to support them with our prayers and practical aid, and to make clear our sense of solidarity in their witness for peace and justice.

That seems infinitely more sensible than the ravings of the new fundamentalists and infinitely more in accord with the universal nature of all the great religions.

# *APPENDIX*

This is the translation of a memorandum (reference E234155-8) which was enclosed with a letter dated 11 January 1941 which the German Naval Attache in Turkey, Admiral von der Marvitz, wrote to the Ambassador, Franz von Papen. The Admiral's letter (ref, E234152) and the memo are lodged in the archives of the German Federal Republic. I am grateful to CAABU member Mr Brian Pearce, who obtained copies of these documents.

Principal features of the proposition of the National Military Organization (Irgun Zvai Leumi) regarding the solution of the Jewish Question in Europe - and the active participation of the NMO in the war on the side of Germany.

It has on numerous occasions been prominently expressed in speeches by leading statesmen of National Socialist Germany, that a new order in Europe would assume a radical solution of the Jewish Question through evacuation. (A Europe cleansed of Jews). The evacuation of the Jewish masses from Europe is a prerequisite to the solution of the Jewish Question, which can only be finally and completely attained by emigration of these masses into the Home of the Jewish people - to Palestine - and through the establishment of the Jewish state in its historic boundaries. To solve the Jewish problem in this manner, to free the Jewish people permanently and finally is the goal of the political activity and the fight of many years of the Israeli Freedom Movement, and National Military Organization in Palestine (Irgun Zvai Leumi).

The NMO, who are aware of the sympathy of the German Reichs-Government and of its departmental authorities towards the Zionist activities within Germany and towards the Zionist plans for emigration, is well known and is of the opinion that:

1. There could exist a common interest between the affairs of a new order in Europe on German ideas and the true national aspirations of the Jewish people who are represented by the NMO.

2. Co-operation between a new Germany and a renewed, national Hebraec people would be possible.

3. The establishment of a historic Jewish state, based on a totalitarian, national basis, which would stand in contractual

relationship with the German Reich, would strengthen and continue the future interests of German power in the near East.

Resulting from the above considerations, the NMO in Palestine, under the conditions of the acceptance of the above mentioned national aspirations of the Israeli Freedom Movement by the German Reichs-Government, will offer them active participation in the war on Germany's side.

This offer on the part of the NMO, whose activities in the military, political and information areas could be extended in and with particular organizational preparation also outside Palestine, would be bound to the military training and organization of the Jewish manpower of Europe under the leadership and control of the NMO into military units whose participation would be sought in campaigns to conquer Palestine, should such a front be formed.

The indirect participation of the Israeli Freedom Movement in the New Order in Europe, already in its preparatory stage, in conjunction with the positive radical solution of the European Jewish problem in the sense of the above mentioned natural aspirations of the Jewish people, would in the eyes of mankind incomparably enhance the moral basis of the New Order. The co-operation of the Israeli Freedom Movement was also to be found in references in one of the last speeches of the German Reichskanzler, in which Herr Hitler stressed that he would use every combination and coalition to isolate and defeat England. (6)

Short summery of the origin, the character and the activity of the NMO in Palestine

The NMO was formed in part out of the need for Jewish self defence in Palestine and the Revisionist Movement (New Zionist Organization) with which the NMO was loosely linked through the person of Mr V Jabotinsky until his death. The pro-English stance of the Revisionist Organization made a renewal of the personal link impossible and led, in the autumn of that year, to the complete break between themselves and the NMO, and to the ensuing split in the Revisionist Movement. The goal of the NMO is the establishment of the Jewish state in its historic boundaries.

(6) In the German style, the documents refer throughout to the United Kingdom as "England."

Contrary to the prevalent direction of ideas of the Zionists, the NMO leans towards a colonialist infiltration as the only means to the opening up and eventual possession of the fatherland and raises to its eventual attainment the fight and the sacrifice as the only true means for the conquest and liberation of Palestine.

Through its militant character and its anti-English attitude, the NMO is forced, under constant persecution from the English administration, to conduct its political activities and military training in Palestine in secret. The NMO, whose terrorist activities began in the autumn of 1936, intensified these activities in the summer of 1939 after the publication of the White Paper,(7) particularly its campaign and sabotage against British property. These activities, together with the daily secret radio transmissions, were registered and discussed by most of the world press.

Until the outbreak of war, the NMO kept independent political offices in Warsaw, Paris, London, Geneva and New York. The office in Warsaw was concerned in particular with military training and the organizing of the national Zionist youth and was in close contact with the Jewish masses who - particularly in Poland - followed with enthusiasm the fight of the NMO in Palestine and supported it in every way. Two newspapers belonging to the NMO appeared in Warsaw (*The Deed* and *Jerozalima Wseljona*). The office in Warsaw supported a close relationship with the former Polish government and the military circles, who showed great sympathy and understanding of the aspirations of the NMO. Consequently, groups and members of the NMO from Palestine were sent to Poland where they completed their military training at local barracks under Polish officers. The negotiations which took place between the Polish government in Warsaw and the NMO with regard to activating their help to greater results, reference to which is easily found in the archives of the previous Polish government, were brought to an abrupt end by the outbreak of war.

The NMO is closely related in its philosophy and structure to the totalitarian movements of Europe. The ability of the NMO to wage war could not be suppressed by either the harsh disciplinary measures of the English authorities, by the Arabs, nor by the Jewish Socialists.

---

(7) Cmnd. 5479, 1939. The Report of the Peel Commission, the first proposal for the partition of Palestine.

# 8

# THE RAMBO PERIOD

## THE REALITY BEHIND THE RHETORIC

The more President Reagan fulminated over the hijacking of the TWA aircraft which was held at Beirut, the more he exposed his helplessness in the international trap of his own making in which he was caught through nobody's fault except his own. There could only be international condemnation for the taking of the plane by an international act of piracy, for the sadistic murder of one young American passenger and the holding as hostages of the other passengers and crew. But there was equal cause for censure of the Reagan administration's part in creating the situation which was the cause of the hijack. As the London published magazine *Middle East International* pointed out, the Americans had only to ask themselves one question, "Would the TWA aircraft have been hijacked if Israel - with American connivance - had not invaded Lebanon in 1982 and remained in occupation of the largely Shi'ite south of the country for the next three years?"

That appalling invasion, with its attack on the civilian population, using American supplied weapons of exceptional horror, coupled with the terrorist methods of the Israeli army, which got ever worse as the defeated and disillusioned army retreated, turned the Shia people of Lebanon into the most implacable and most effective yet of Israel's self-created enemies. Yet the hijackers limited themselves to just one relatively modest demand. All they demanded was the release of some seven hundred Lebanese civilians who had been taken from their homes by force, carried illegally into Israel and held as hostages - an act of hijacking every bit as illegal as the seizure of the American aircraft and carried out with greater brutality and far greater loss of life.

Ronald Reagan defeated Jimmy Carter for the Presidency of the United States in 1980 by exploiting Carter's helplessness when American hostages were held in Tehran under the Khomeini regime. Reagan assured the American voters that such things would not happen again if they made him President. The facts are, first, that his policy of world domination by American military and economic intimidation, which was supposed to prevent such happenings, has served only to increase their likelihood and, second, that it was the Israeli dimension in his global policy which provided the main reason for that particular hijack. The reality behind his rhetoric is that he is as helpless to stop such incidents as was Carter.

Meanwhile, the absurd attempt to enforce an international ban on Beirut airport and on the Lebanese national airline, Middle East Airlines, turned into a self-inflicted humiliation. The only support came predictably, from the British Prime Minister, Margaret Thatcher, Reagan's sole admirer among European heads of government. Asked in the House of Commons (2 July 1985) by the Member of Parliament who was the Chairman of the Conservative Friends of Israel, if she would join with President Reagan in banning Middle East Airlines, she said that such action would "certainly" be supported by the British government and she hoped that it would have "the widest international backing." The following day, when the US Vice-President George Bush arrived in London, seeking international backing for the ban, he duly received it from Mrs Thatcher. Everywhere else in the world, there was scepticism or hostility. The airlines of the Eastern European countries, sensing the obvious embarrassment in the West, rushed in gleefully to provide new services to Beirut.

However, even in Britain, there were serious reservations and almost before the words were out of Mrs Thatcher's mouth, some furious back pedalling started so as to leave as many opportunities as possible for Britain to extricate itself from the Prime Minister's embarrassing undertaking. One embarrassment was that Middle East Airlines operated important joint services with British Airways which would be seriously affected by any banning of MEA. Furthermore, due to the situation in Lebanon, a great deal of MEA's maintenance and repair work was done in other countries, with Britain taking a major share. The loss of the work carried out in Britain would mean a large loss of revenue for BA and that alone would be detrimental to one of the most central of the Conservative government's policies, the sale of national assets to speculative capitalists. There had already been a number of embarrassing financial scandals arising from that policy and the government simply could not risk another self inflicted wound by jeopardizing BA's profitability in the eyes of potential purchasers. The projected sale of the British national airline had already been long delayed through a legal action in America arising from the spectacular collapse in 1982 of Laker Airways, itself formerly a speculatively owned British airline.

One irony in the American ban on MEA operations to the United States was that the only service affected was that between Beirut, London and New York. Inaugurated in happier times, mainly as a prestige service, it had long been running only half full or less. So Reagan provided a good opportunity for the withdrawal of the service without embarrassment to the airline. But the practical impossibility of any European part of the proposed ban went wider than that, with France, Greece and Switzerland announcing their opposition without even waiting for a visit from Mr Bush. It was inconceivable that the French government would be prepared to ban the Paris-Beirut service for, quite apart from considerations of French foreign policy, both global and in relation to Lebanon, with which France had close and historic ties, the French national airline, Air France, owned twenty-eight and a half per cent of MEA.

MEA had played a major part in building up and running other importance Arab airlines and that also contributed heavily to making it an indispensable part of the world air network. It was hardly surprising when the announcement of the proposed ban brought immediate and well deserved Arab warnings of retaliation against American air services. The more the proposed ban was examined, the sillier and more impractical it was seen to be. The political implications were even wider.

Within days of Mrs Thatcher's statements in London, the Arab

Ambassadors, like their colleagues in Washington, were calling in person on Ministers of the government to register the official and unanimous opposition of their own governments. In a special statement, the Lebanese Ambassador, General Ahmed Al Hajj, pointed out that the people of Lebanon had for so long been affected by the consequences of international terrorism that they were exceptionally qualified to evaluate the American proposal. And the perceptive evaluation he gave was that the proposal would be wholly counter productive. It would strengthen the tide of extremism, create a widespread reaction which could well threaten the interests of any governments involved in the ban and would certainly not stop any further hijackings.

As for the Reagan allegation that the hijacked aircraft was allowed to land at Beirut because the airport was a centre for terrorism, the Ambassador stingingly pointed out that when the plane was allowed in, permission to land was granted absolutely on humanitarian grounds and that the airport authorities could not possibly have acted callously and indifferently with human life at stake in the way it was at that crucial point. For good measure, he added that it would be more useful for the international community to undertake a concerted effort in helping Lebanon to restore its sovereignty and stability by assisting the legitimate government to impose its authority on all the unruly elements in the country.

The latter point went to the very heart of another reality behind the Reagan rhetoric. For one thing which emerged from the whole episode more clearly even than before was that stability could not be restored in Lebanon, any more than the hijacking itself could be resolved, without the involvement of Syria. That reality did not by any means please all "the unruly elements" in Lebanon itself, but it was bitter anathema to the Reagan administration, because Syria had been on their priority list of countries to be hated ever since the breakdown of the unworkable, so-called withdrawal agreement into which Lebanon was manoeuvred by America on 17 May 1983. The agreement was designed solely for the advantage of Israel, the aggressor, and Syria was not even consulted. The administration's hatred against Syria rose even higher after December 1983, when the US tried unsuccessfully to bomb Syrian forces in Lebanon into acquiescence, provoking uproar among America's European allies and leading to the collapse of the entire American policy in the Middle East.

What the administration had to come to terms with, following the hijacking, but what it found very difficult to swallow, was that if it had not been for the help of President Hafez Al Assad, there was every probability that the hostages held in the aircraft would not have been released. And that was forcing the administration to another reality it could not stomach - that sooner or later, its policy of trying to freeze Syria out of negotiations on wider issues would have to be changed. The experienced diplomats in the US Embassies in Beirut and Damascus had been transmitting that message back to Washington for years but, so great was the power of the Israeli lobby that the administration refused to accept the message or, for that matter, to accept any advice from any of its own experienced diplomats in any Arab country unless the advice was acceptable to and approved by the Israelis. It must have been galling for Reagan that, throughout the hijacking, he received absolutely no help from his "ally" Israel, whereas he did receive help from Syria, without which he could not possible have got out of the dilemma created by his own policies.

# CONFERENCE IN GENEVA

When the Second United Nations International Meeting of Non-Governmental Organizations on the Question of Palestine took place in Geneva from 9 to 12 September 1985, one hundred NGO's participated, with seventeen others represented by observers. A number of the NGO's, such as the Parliamentary Association for Euro-Arab Co-operation and some of the religious organizations were, themselves, international in character; so the spread of representation was even wider and more international than the figures suggest. With the meeting taking place in Switzerland, it was not surprising that Switzerland. with nineteen NGO's present, was the country with the largest number. Next in order of numbers was the USA with sixteen and there were nine from Israel.

It was especially important that countries like the USA and Israel, whose governments were hostile to the whole idea of the conference, should be so well represented. Two years earlier, when an inaugural meeting of governments and NGO's was held, on a resolution of the General Assembly of the United Nations, the United States and Israeli governments did their utmost to prevent it from taking place and ever since they had worked to prevent further meetings. The presence in Geneva of distinguished delegations from NGO's in both countries in such strength was an indication that, when government spokespersons of those countries speak and act against the cause of justice for the people of Palestine, they do not by any means represent the views of all the citizens of their respective countries.

On the day the conference started, the Israeli Knesset voted for a new law to sentence any Israeli citizen who met with any member of the PLO to three years in prison. It was on the initiative of Israelis at the conference that a telegram of protest was sent to the Israeli government to express unanimous objection to such repressive legislation. Geneva was formerly the headquarters of the League of Nations, the forerunner of the United Nations Organization. At a meeting of the League in the nineteen-thirties, held in the Palais des Nations where the NGO's met, a representative of the then Nazi government of Germany showed his government's contempt for the League by thumbing his nose to the meeting. Successive governments of Israel have shown their contempt for the United Nations ever since the creation of Israel in 1948. By passing their repressive law on the opening day of the Geneva conference, it was almost as if they were repeating the physical gesture of contempt for the international community of that nineteen-thirties Nazi.

The conference met against a gloomy background. In mid August, Mr Richard Murphy, the Assistant Secretary of State in the USA, visited Amman and it had been widely expected that he would at least informally meet a Jordanian-Palestinian delegation as a first move in the painfully constructed Hussein-Arafat initiative for peace talks. It was not expected that such a meeting would indicate any commitment by Mr Murphy on behalf of his government but that at least it would give him something to report back for further action, In the event, he had no such meeting and so the initiative was set back seriously. The gloom was added to by the advance made in Israel's unfair trading advantages with the European Community. When the first NGO meeting was held a year earlier, the European section had been much concerned at the developments then taking place. Since then, all tariffs on Israeli exports to the European Community had been removed although Israel was still retaining tariffs on products imported from the Community. So there was the absurd situation that Israel had unrestricted access to the huge European market while Europe had to pay tariffs to export to the relatively tiny Israeli market.

In a brilliant paper presented to the conference, Dr Mohammed Shadid of An Najah University, Nablus, showed how the occupation of Gaza and the West Bank had transformed Israel into an imperial economy, with all development projects in the occupied areas subject to military approval and with official theft of the wealth of the territories taking place on a massive scale. The USA had inaugurated a programme of so-called "aid" through private voluntary organizations, supposedly "to improve the quality of life" in the occupied territories. What the programme really demonstrated was that the American government had accepted permanent occupation and Dr Shadid showed how Israeli pressure turned even projects which were supported by such aid, supposedly to benefit the Palestinians, into aid for Israel. On top of which every dollar in that programme was matched by $476 of direct aid to Israel. All that was accompanied by a sharp and growing increase of Israeli terrorism against the people of the occupied territories.

The conference was much occupied with ways and means to implement General Assembly Resolution 38/58C, calling for an International Peace Conference, and there was an outstanding speech on that subject by Dr Matti Peled. Dr Peled, who retired from the Israeli army after the 1967 war, with the rank of general, was the first to expose the myth that it was a defensive war and to show that it was in reality a war of open aggression. He went on to become a major member of the peace movement in Israel and a Member of the Knesset. In his speech to the conference in Geneva he strongly affirmed that an international conference held out the most practical prospects for peace, as compared with any attempted unilateral approaches. Camp David, he pointed out, had led to the Israeli bombing of the nuclear power station at Tarmuz in Iraq and to the 1978 and 1982 invasions of Lebanon. The USA had tried to use the peace process to further its own interests at the expense of the USSR and Israel had used it to further its interests at the expense of the Palestinians.

Dr Peled saw many Jewish people, inside and outside Israel, adopting a Nazi ideology of racism. He described that as the terrible and ironic revenge of Adolf Hitler against the Jewish people. He revealed that Israel then already had fifteen to twenty nuclear warheads which it could deliver by aircraft. Not surprisingly, Arab countries were starting their own nuclear weapons research and so the nuclear arms race had spread to the Middle East, to the danger of the entire world. There were crazy elements in Israel who might come to power and who would not hesitate to start a nuclear war. It was a matter of the utmost urgency to stop the flood of insanity which was rising within Israel.

The conference met at the height of the mid nineteen-eighties cold war and the sombre nature of the problems it considered was added to by the divisions among those present over the structure and composition of the co-ordinating mechanism which it was proposed to establish. Those divisions reflected not only the tensions between the eastern and western power blocs but also those between the developed and the developing countries. In addressing the conference myself, I pointed out that everyone there was united in a belief in justice for the Palestinians and that, while there were differences in approach which all had to respect, what was most important was to emphasize what united rather than what divided the conference. The new International Co-ordinating Committee (the ICCP) would obviously have to pay attention to the differences which arose from genuine and unsurprising differences of approach in the varied cultures and experiences of the differing regions of this world in which, if we did not all live together in peace, we should all die together in war. That was rather coolly received at first but the theme was taken up by others and proved in the end to be the basis for a consensus in the election of the ICCP. (1)

Outside the conference, on the second day [10 September 1985], I heard two separate English language radio broadcasts which strongly demonstrated the differences in presentation and approach to international problems. They were reports by the Voice of America and by the BBC World Service on the decision of European countries to impose sanctions against apartheid South Africa. The voice of America gave it as the number one item in the news, stating that nine of the ten European Community countries, plus Spain and Portugal [that was prior to their entry into the EC] had agreed to impose sanctions. Britain, the report added, had declined to do so. Only a few minutes later, the BBC World Service made it item number six in the news and put it in the form that the Foreign Ministers of the EC countries "had failed to agree" on sanctions. It was necessary to listen very carefully to the BBC version to realize that it was the shameful decision of the British government, alone, which was the cause of the so-called "disagreement."

Yet, if the conference met against such a sombre background and demonstrated that there were so many difficulties, the essential striving of humankind towards peace and justice still shone through the gloom. One of the most inspiring speeches was the keynote address delivered by Dr Bruno Kreisky, the former Chancellor of Austria and senior statesman of world renown. He pointed out that, in his own country, democracy had disappeared due to Austrian fascists, first under the influence of Mussolini and then of Hitler. In 1939, the outbreak of the second world war was the result of incompetence in the governments of Western European democracies and, in 1940-42, the future of democracy had seemed hopeless, but it had revived. Dr Kreisky told the conference that after the second world war, the then American Secretary of State, John Foster Dulles, had opposed the neutrality of Austria, wanting instead to incorporate the country into the western bloc but, on more rational consideration, Dulles had accepted Austrian neutrality.

---

(1) See also Chapter 6 .

It can now be seen how crucial and far reaching that decision was. In later years and especially under the leadership of Dr Kreisky during his years as Chancellor, Austria, as a neutral country, played a crucial role in world affairs and nowhere more so than in the Middle East. From his triumphs in office to his noble endeavours after office, Dr Kreisky clearly showed how the world community could reconcile its differences and disagreements.

## RAMBO POLITICS

"Rambo" is the title of an American film which is an improbable story of an ex-soldier who returns to Vietnam and, in a single handed orgy of killing and destruction, compensates - at least among simple minds - for America's humiliation in the Vietnamese war. It is not a very good film and it has been severely criticized by every reputable film critic. However, President Reagan, the former Hollywood actor, has expressed admiration for it. As a president, Ronald Reagan is no Abraham Lincoln, as an actor, he is no Laurence Olivier, and a combination of those shortcomings seems to have persuaded him to introduce a new form of foreign policy which is being widely described as Rambo politics.

This new approach seems to have been triggered off in the momentous events of the first fourteen days of October, which started on the first day of the month with the Israeli air attack on the PLO offices in Tunis. Events then proceeded from the piracy of the Italian ship Achille Lauro to the piracy of the Egyptian aircraft which was carrying the perpetrators to Tunis for trial, and culminated with the collapse of the British initiated talks in London on the fourteenth day of the month. All those events were inter-related and the first was especially related to the last. From the very start of the Hussein-Arafat peace initiative, the Israelis sought to destroy it. When the American diplomat Richard Murphy failed to talk with any Palestinians during his visit to Amman in August, when the object was to explore the putting together of a joint Jordanian-Palestinian team for peace negotiations with Israel, as was envisaged in the initiative, the Israelis must have thought that they had succeeded in their objective of destroying the whole project.

However, then came Mrs Thatcher's proposal for talks in London, to which the Israeli government reacted with hysterical fury. It stretches credulity too far to accept that the attack on Tunis, one of the objects of which was to kill Arafat and to do so at the exact time when Hussein was talking with the American government in Washington, was not carefully timed to ensure the final destruction of the Hussein-Arafat initiative. Nor could the attack have been carried out without American knowledge and complicity for, from the moment they left the ground, the attacking aircraft, as well as their refuelling planes, would be monitored automatically on the radar screens of the American controlled NATO alliance.

The question has not been answered as to why no counter action was initiated, why for example no warnings were issued and NATO aircraft were not put into the air to intercept the aggressive expedition against Tunisia, a country friendly to the NATO alliance. For nearly thirty years, President Habib Bourguiba of Tunisia had been one of America's closest allies in the Arab World yet, when it came to that attack on his country, Ronald Reagan's reaction was one of public approval. Rambo politics, perpetrated in the first place by the Israelis with White House approval, meant that the supposed closeness of Tunisia to the USA counted for nothing when set against American support for Israeli aggression.

What never seems to get through to perpetrators of violence, whether they are individuals, small groups, larger organizations or governments, is that violence not only achieves nothing except death and destruction, but that it causes inevitable counter violence and still more death and destruction. The general failure to realize that in the closing decades of a century which has seen more violence than any other in history, and in which mankind has armed itself with weapons of destruction which can destroy the world, is as incomprehensible to thinking people as it is potentially disastrous for all of us,

As in the case of Tunisia, two friendly countries, Egypt and Italy, were treated with open contempt in a flagrant breach of international law. The fact that Italy is one of the countries of the NATO alliance, even a base for American nuclear missiles, made the conduct of the Reagan administration all the more deplorable. The four accused murderers from the Achille Lauro who were en route from Cairo to Tunis ought perhaps to have been sent by Egypt to Italy to face trial, rather than to Tunisia. The crime had been committed on an Italian ship so, arguably, it was to Italy that they should have been sent for justice.

However, the American pirating and forcing down of the Egyptian plane at the Italian NATO base at Sigonella in Sicily was itself a gross violation of international law, which did not even have any saving grace in that it had any pretensions to bring criminals to justice in the appropriate country. The purpose was to kidnap the accused persons and also Mohammed Abbas of the PLO Executive

Committee, who had acted to bring about their surrender, and the objective was to take them all away to the United States, which had no internationally recognized jurisdiction over them at all. There was a parallel with the recent case in Britain, which I wrote about in an earlier article, in which three Israeli Mossad agents were brought to trial for kidnapping a Nigerian (2) citizen and attempting to take him illegally to Nigeria. Can it be seriously suggested that those agents should have been sent to Nigeria for trial instead of being tried in Britain? Both in principle and in practice, the American action in the Mediterranean resembled the Israeli action in London.

In Italy though, not only did the American planes invade Italian air space and land at Sigonella without permission. They took with them two additional plane loads of commando troops who were only prevented from storming the Egyptian aeroplane after it had landed because the Italians surrounded it with defending soldiers. It was only last minute orders from the highest level which stopped the American commanding officer from opening fire on the soldiers of a country allied to his own. Nor did Rambo politics end there, for they then continued with the organized destablilization of the Italian government because it had refused to act as an American satellite. All in all, against Egypt and in Italy, there was the application of the sort of military force and political destabilization which had been seen already in Latin America, the Caribbean and Lebanon.

It was against that background that the Thatcher move to try to revive the Hussein-Arafat initiative moved to its sorry conclusion in London. While there was not the open, physical application of Rambo politics in that instance, there could not really be any doubt, for all the dutiful denials of the British government, about American pressure behind the scenes. With the hysterical Israeli opposition to the proposed talks and Israel's control over United States policy, it was clearly necessary to look beyond the face value of the denials.

The tragic farce in London was compounded by unforgivable mix-ups both there and in Amman. On Thursday, 10 October, four days before the meeting, a document was drawn up in Amman between the Jordanian government and the British government. There was no proper consultation with the PLO. One of the two distinguished Palestinians who were to go to London, Mayor

---

(2) See above pp 114 - 117 .

Mohammed Milhem, was in the USA at the time. The other one, Bishop Elia Khoury, was in Amman and he was informed of the document. But a crucial factor was that the consultations were verbal and the two men did not see the actual document until they arrived in London on Sunday, 13 October, in readiness for the meeting the next day. While the Bishop felt that he could still accept the draft with which they were presented, the Mayor felt unable to do so. So they both very properly declined to accept it without modification.

It was an especially sad thing that the required modifications were relatively minor matters of wording. The two distinguished Palestinians had arrived under the impression that the draft was for a communique to be issued after the meeting and that it was open to amendment. What they found however was that, far from being a draft for a final communique, it had to be accepted in advance as their ticket of admission to the meeting. The draft had been drawn up to meet the requirements of the American government rather than the requirements of negotiations for peace and the entire procedure was an extraordinary breach of normal diplomatic practice.

The haste with which the British Foreign Secretary, Sir Geoffrey Howe, rushed to announce the cancellation of the meeting could not be attributed to any cause other than a desire to meet American requirements. How much more sensible it would have been to hold the meeting and announce frankly that there had been certain matters of disagreement. But the need to appease the American administration was seen as paramount and so the first fortnight of Rambo politics reduced British standing to a new low in the Arab World. None of that was likely to do anything at all for the cause of justice for the Palestinian people. Until the time comes when that cause is made political reality, there can and will be no peace. The inauguration of the era of Rambo politics seemed likely to usher in a new period of tension and violence.

# A NEW PHASE

It is now clear that the Middle East, is moving into a new phase. Major changes are taking place in relations among Arab countries and, with the introduction of Rambo politics, almost all the Arab World is reviewing its relations with the USA and much of it is reviewing relations with the USSR. It remains to be seen what will be the outcome of all this, just as it remains to be seen what will be the outcome of the Reagan-Gorbachev summit meeting (3). So far as the Middle East is concerned, the summit needs to be seen in its perspective as just one among a number of current events likely to shape the future and not as something likely immediately to change the course of history on its own, disappointing though that may be to the sense of self importance of either or both the superpowers. What is already clear though is that the long period in which the USA sought to be the arbiter of the Middle East, trying to impose its own pattern on events there, is coming to its end.

Ever since the 1973 war, America has sought to determine the pattern of events, but its policy has been to advance what it has seen as American interests rather than to establish a peace acceptable to the countries in the region. That policy was skillfully exploited by the Israeli lobby in Washington to further what successive Israeli governments saw as Israeli interests. With the election of the Reagan administration in 1980, with its policy of worldwide confrontation with the Soviet Union, the result was to turn the Middle East into the most dangerous area of superpower confrontation in the world.

That apart however, there is a growing realization, even in the White House, although not in every part of the administration and certainly not in the United States Congress, of what has been obvious everywhere else for a long time, that the United States' Middle East policy has lost it virtually every friend it formerly had in the region. The culmination in Rambo politics, with secret connivance in and open approval for the Israeli attack against Tunis, then the hijacking by the American air force of the Egyptian aircraft bound for Tunis and the near shooting match between American and Italian forces at the NATO base in Italy where the plane was

---

(3) The first meeting, held at Geneva, November 1985.

forced down, brought a dramatic crumbling of increasingly precarious friendships.

Far from achieving its essential objective of freezing the Soviet Union out of the Middle East, the American policy finished up by substantially accelerating the growth of Soviet influence. It is of particular note that it is the conservative Arab states who are taking the lead in reviewing their position and establishing more friendly relations with the USSR. Among the six conservative countries which constitute the Gulf Co-operation Council, Kuwait was long alone in having diplomatic relations with Moscow. In a move which took some by surprise, Oman, one of the countries most closely associated with the West, established relations in September and, shortly afterwards, the United Arab Emirates did likewise.

Meanwhile, it was confirmed that the exploratory talks between Saudi Arabia and the Soviet Union, about which there had been rumours for months, were indeed under way, although they seemed to be moving slowly because of divided opinions in the kingdom. Not surprisingly, there are those in Saudi Arabia who have their doubts about establishing relations with the USSR. According to the influential London weekly *Mideast Markets*, they include the Defence Minister, Prince Sultan bin Abdul Aziz. The Saudi Ambassador to the United States is Prince Sultan's son, Prince Bandar, and it is fair speculation that what is happening is that the American government, aware of its crumbling stature in the Gulf, is exerting all possible pressure through the Washington Embassy to prevent the talks from progressing.

But no pressure can overcome the fact that Washington's open-ended support for Israel has brought growing disillusion in Saudi Arabia and almost everywhere else, and it certainly cannot overcome the fact that disillusion was increased by the dramatic events in the Mediterranean in October. All of which prompted the conservative Arab states more fully to recognize the need for Soviet involvement as a precondition for progress towards a settlement of the Palestine question. For all of them, that question is of basic importance, they rightly recognize it as the most fundamental of all the questions in the region, without the settlement of which there can be little hope of stability anywhere.

However, it is not only in Arab relations with the superpowers that the Middle East is moving into a new phase. Inter-Arab relations are also changing dramatically. The resumption of diplomatic relations between Jordan and Syria, after a break of four years and accomplished under the patient mediation of Saudi Arabia, is of obvious importance for the Palestine question and the stability of the region. There were those in Israel and the USA who. given the hostility of Syria towards Yasser Arafat and the uneasy relations between him and the Jordanian government, saw the resumption of relations between the two countries as a hoped for blow to the PLO and as an opportunity to try to damage the Jordanian-PLO relationship. Their wishful thinking, following the grave damage done to the Hussein-Arafat initiative by the fiasco in London, was that Jordan could be persuaded to abandon the PLO and to negotiate separately with Israel. Another part of the same wishful thinking was that Egypt could also be persuaded to abandon the PLO and join in such negotiations.

That was fallacy-based wishful thinking of a high order. The idea that Jordan would contemplate such a course of action after such an important move towards resolving differences with Syria, was ridiculous. Equally ridiculous was the idea that Egypt, immediately after the bombing of Tunis by the Israelis and the treatment it suffered at the hands of the Americans over the Achille Lauro affair, could be persuaded to throw away all the progress it had made over several years in its relations with the rest of the Arab World. The Israeli-American wishful thinking was soon blown sky high by firm statements from President Mubarak, King Hussein and Chairman Arafat.

In the changing pattern of Arab relationships, there was another development, in the resumption in early November of friendly relations between Syria and Sudan, which had been broken off during the Numeiry regime. No less important than the establishment of relations between the two was the potential in their agreement for the development of better relations between Syria and Sudan's neighbour Egypt. Nor could the importance be overlooked in terms of Arab relations with Black Africa, not least because Sudan, with the legacy of frontiers drawn in the earlier age of British imperialism, is the huge country where Arab Africa meets Black Africa under one government. (4)

---

(4) In late 1985, when the above was written, the overthrow of the Numeiry dictatorship and the event of a democractic government under Prime Minister Sadiq Al Mahdi, gave hopes of moves to solve Sudan's many, huge problems. Unfortunately, Al Mahdi failed to solve anything, not least the long-running civil war in the Black south, and he went down in the military coup in mid - 1989.

Meanwhile, there is even talk of another attempt to restore relations between Syria and Iraq. That may well prove to be wishful thinking on the Arab side,[5] but for all the formidable difficulties, such a restoration would be one of the most important developments of all if it could be brought about. It is an exceptional tragedy that two powerful countries, each of which has applied, with some success in the face of enormous difficulties, a conscious philosophy of trying to deploy national resources for public benefit, should be so tragically locked in a hard line, modern version of the ancient rivalry between Baghdad and Damascus, which is not only detrimental to each but also to the unity and progress of the whole Arab World.

Some years ago, there was in the United States a broadcast programme which featured a game of questions, in which people competed for a prize which started at one thousand dollars and doubled at successive stages and with increasingly difficult questions to a maximum of sixty-four thousand dollars. It gave rise to a phrase still current - "The sixty-four thousand dollar question." Now, the sixty-four thousand dollar question may be said to be "What will be the outcome of the new phase in the Middle East?"

The answer is very difficult. Inter-Arab relations are notoriously volatile and it could all too easily go horribly wrong again. But if it goes right, then the serious and damaging difficulties of recent years could be resolved, even if only in part, and that would enable what has been for too long a divided and quarrelsome Arabia to produce a more united and more effective approach to the rest of the world. In spite of everything, both superpowers are changing their attitudes towards each other and that, in conjunction with a more united Arab approach, could lead more favourably towards the vital issue of a full international peace conference on the Middle East under United Nations auspices. Approaching events will determine whether the scenario of the new phase is pessimistic or optimistic,

---

(5) It did !

# DIVISION IN THE ZIONIST STATE

Although the last article, about changing relationships among countries in the Middle East and changing attitudes towards the superpowers, did not deal with changes in Israel, the fact is that there are major developments and disagreements in that country which are also an important part of the developing new phase in the region and which mark important pointers to the future. There are changes in the economy and in the political situation, while there are growing revelations of failure in the attempted colonization of the territories occupied outside the 1967 borders; all of which is causing deep internal divisions in an already divided country.

In any country, the condition of the economy is arguably the most fundamental consideration of all because it affects everything else. The state of the Israeli economy can be judged from a recent front-page headline in the London *Jewish Chronicle,* "Israeli Economy is Facing Collapse." The Israeli economy is an entirely artificial one, only kept going by huge American subsidies and, even in the United States, so acquiescent to the demands of the Israeli lobby, voices are starting to be raised to question those ever increasing subsidies. Consequently, the government in Washington has started to ask for Israeli measures to control the huge rate of inflation as a condition for further help. It is the first time that any effective questioning voices ever have been raised in the USA on the subject of the unending subsidies and that has set alarm bells ringing both in Israel and within its lobby in America.

One result has been an attempt in the last five months to try to control the enormous rate of inflation. The attempt has partly succeeded in that it has brought down the rate from sixty-five per cent a month to five per cent a month. By any standard that is still a huge figure but, even so, the government measures have produced all the classic problems of deflation, with bankrupt businesses, inadequate wages and growing unemployment. The main enterprises have run up a combined deficit of well over $3 billion and the Histadrut, the so-called "trade union" movement (which is in reality not trade unionist at all but a huge concern which employs one quarter of all the workforce) is calling for government subsidies to cover the deficit. If the government should change policy and provide such subsidies, it would have to do so without American underwriting and so could only do it by printing worthless money and returning to hyper inflation. It is little wonder that the London *Jewish Chronicle* should be talking about the collapsing state of the economy.

Sitting on this economic volcano in a divided country, the so-called "government of national unity" begins to look increasingly like a government of national disunity. In October next [1986], the Prime Minister and Labour leader Shimon Peres is due to hand over to the Likud leader Yitshak Shamir. Mr Peres wants very much to be able to call an election before then, to try to secure a majority to enable the Labour Party and its allies to form their own government. To achieve that objective, he has first to create a climate sufficiently favourable to the Labour Party, which is why he is engaged in a complicated political exercise which falls broadly into three parts.

First, he seeks to keep inflation under control to ensure American support but without losing support at home from the working people who are the basis of the Labour vote but who are increasingly hostile to the fall in their living standards brought about by the efforts to control inflation, Mr Peres knows only too well that it was disillusion with the earlier years of Labour government among the lower paid Israelis who ought to form the Labour Party's natural voters, which put the Likud government into power under Menachem Begin in 1977. He knows too that sympathy is still strong among them for extreme rightwing and racist policies. That leads to the second part of his political exercise, which is to try to disembarrass himself of the Likud half of his divided and unworkable coalition and discredit the Likud and its allies in the eyes of the electorate at the same time.

A classic demonstration of the disunity of the government was when one of its Likud Ministers, Ariel Sharon, made an open attack on the Prime Minister, who responded by attempting to dismiss Sharon. That very nearly brought down the government but compromise was reached when both sides realized that neither could win an election, and so the government continued on its uncertain way. Meanwhile, Sharon also remains engaged in a bitter battle within his own party, to remove Shamir from the leadership and take it for himself. He sees himself as a future Prime Minister whose policy would be to annex the occupied territories, drive out the Palestinians and subdue the Arab World with a renewed policy of aggressive military expansion. He seems to have learned nothing from the disastrous war in Lebanon of which he was the main architect. Neither, it seems, has anything been learned by the section of the Israeli population for which he is a hero and which he hopes would provide the votes to put him into power.

All of which leads to the third part of Prime Minister Peres' complicated manoeuvrings. Peres realises the crazy reality of Sharon's plans and that they would be likely finally to test American support beyond breaking point and so endanger the very existence of the Zionist state. Peres would like to be elected as Prime Minister of a Labour-led government with a policy of negotiating for peace but, like most Israeli leaders, he lives in a fantasy world which precludes him from recognizing the importance and the representative nature of the PLO and the absolute necessity to involve it in negotiations.

Following the fiasco in London when the British Foreign Secretary, Sir Geoffrey Howe, refused to meet Bishop Elia Khoury and Mayor Mohammed Milhem, a situation for which the Israeli government and its international agents had worked very hard, Mr Peres really seemed to think that the PLO could be discounted and that Jordan would be prepared unilaterally to enter into Camp David type negotiations. The timing of his co-called "peace" initiative based on that premise and his slap-down of Sharon were designed to precipitate an election which he hoped he could win with a "peace" appeal to the Israeli electorate. In the event, he realized the depressing fact that the proportion of the electorate which supported peace was not big enough to guarantee him a victory. So the internal manoeuvres of both sides of the disunited "government of national unity" continue, with the date of the handover of the premiership to Yitshak Shamir getting steadily closer without any sign of any shift away from a state of national deadlock.

Meanwhile, in the occupied territories, the colonization programme is not going according to plan. About a year ago, the respected Israeli scholar and geographer Elisha Efrat completed a study which showed that the target of getting four hundred thousand settlers into the West Bank by the year 2000 was so far behind schedule that, to quote his own words "The chances of succeeding now look so dim as to raise doubts about the whole enterprise." Now, another respected scholar, Professor Arnon Sofer, Head of the Jewish-Arab Centre at Haifa University, has stated bluntly, in another survey of the settlements, that "there are no settlers for them" and that in spite of the most strenuous efforts at colonization, some people are now actually leaving the settlements and moving back behind the 1967 borders.

The colonization drive has included grandiose building schemes and the extension of control to something like fifty-two per cent of the land in the West Bank. Yet Professor Sofer found that many of the settlements were occupied by only a few families who, he said "Will pack up and leave at a hint of favourable compensation." Despite all the efforts to colonize the territories ever since 1967 and in spite of campaigns by the fanatical Gush Emunim settlers' group, the total number of settlers to date is only about fifty thousand, compared with the three quarters of a million Palestinians of the West Bank and the half million of the Gaza Strip, whose numbers, with a high birth rate, are increasing all the time. A recent, much publicized rally to attract new colonists to the Eli settlement in the West Bank was attended by thousands of people and that was projected as showing how eager people were to settle there. Professor Sofer showed that the reality behind the propaganda was very different, for of the thousands at the rally, only forty-six families were actually prepared to sign an undertaking to settle there.

So, for all its military might and American backing, the Zionist state faces economic and political problems of its own making, all of which weaken it and all of which are significant for its relations with other countries and likely to affect the course of events in the Middle East as a whole. Not least significant is that, for all the repression in the occupied territories, the initiative there, no less than the moral right, is really with the Palestinians. What a well-deserved irony it would be if those carefully constructed settlements were to prove in the end to provide homes for the Palestinian citizens of an independent state in the West Bank and Gaza Strip.

# 9

# DEADLOCK

## AN AWKWARD IMMIGRANT

The saturation coverage in the western media for the arrival of Anatoly Shcharansky in Israel after his release from imprisonment in the Soviet Union died into sudden silence within a few days. The silence was an eloquent testimony to growing realization that, unless the independent, libertarian-minded Shcharansky undergoes a remarkable personality change, he will no more fit into the bigotry of the Zionist ruling class than he fitted into the prejudices of the former Soviet rulers who imprisoned him. His release, together with that of a number of persons convicted of spying for the USA in the USSR, and in exchange for a number of persons convicted for spying for the USSR in the USA, was one of the results of the Reagan-Gorbachev meeting in Geneva in November 1985.

Middle East issues as a whole were studiously avoided by the two superpower leaders - a matter for special regret now that such flickering hopes for peace as did arise during 1985 seem to have been extinguished. Had Reagan and Gorbachev been prepared to face up to the real issues in the region and to make joint efforts in the cause of peace there, we would not have the current dreary situation of seemingly immovable deadlock. As things stand, the release of Anatoly Shcharansky and his arrival in Israel is seemingly the only positive outcome of the summit. Yet his arrival in Israel could prove to have different consequences from those expected and he could prove to be an awkward immigrant.

According to Zionist propaganda, he had been imprisoned because he was a campaigner for the release of the allegedly persecuted Jewish citizens of the Soviet Union. How this alleged persecution on racist grounds squares with the known facts is something of a mystery. In the first place, there is the very matter of emigration. Given the restrictive parameters of Soviet society, Jews seem to be a privileged rather than a persecuted minority for, of the many minorities in that vast country, they are the only one to have been given rights of emigration on a substantial scale. Then again, the many thousands who have emigrated over the years have not exactly been poor, deprived and underprivileged. On the contrary, they have been well-off, highly-educated scientists, administrators and professional people in general.

There has been another widespread common factor among them in that the overwhelming majority have demonstrated very clearly that, while their choice was to leave the USSR, it was certainly not to settle in Israel. The majority preferred to settle in western countries, especially in the USA. Even among those who went to Israel, many left subsequently. Of the total who left their own country, only a derisory fifteen per cent, less than one in seven, made permanent homes in the Zionist state. Some of the explanation for that was to be seen in the very nature of the welcome extended to Shcharansky on his arrival. His wife, who had lived there for some years, greeted him with a public announcement that it was a day to give thanks to God and to pray for the land of Israel to be filled with immigrants, never to be divided and never to be given up by those immigrants.

Mrs Shcharansky was a member of one of the extreme right-wing political groups, central to whose philosophy is an egocentric, fundamentalist version of the Judaic religion. For that group, the million and a half Palestinians living in the West Bank and Gaza, whose families have lived there for centuries, should be driven from their homeland in the same way that another million and a half already had been driven out, to be replaced by foreign immigrants. Now, while it is only the right-wing politicians who publicly express such sentiments, the same sentiments also have a strong place within the Israeli Labour Party. The only basic difference is that the Labour Prime Minister of the coalition government, Shimon Peres, and other Labour politicians are more skillful in gaining acceptance for such policies in the Western World.

Anatoly Shcharansky suffered years of imprisonment, not in support of Zionist imperialism, but in support of basic human rights. That he could settle into a society where the ruling circles are so contemptuous of Palestinian rights seems doubtful. Many of the liberal-minded Russian Jews like him who went to Israel have already left in disgust. At least one, Edward Kuznetzov, who arrived after five years imprisonment, divorced his wife soon afterwards because she too held similar views to those of Mrs Shcharansky. The whole purpose of the campaign about the alleged persecution of Russian Jews was, of course, to try to sustain the Israeli state by the immigration of colonists. Western Jews notoriously refused to go there in any numbers and the campaign to persuade Soviet Jews to go there has been aimed, above all, to provide colonists for the West Bank and Gaza in the absence of colonists from the West.

However, on top of the refusal of both western and eastern Jews to go there, the colonization programme has gone wrong in other important aspects, as Meron Benvenisti, the former Deputy Mayor of Jerusalem, now the respected Director of the West Bank Data Base, has revealed in a recent press conference. Benvenisti revealed that among the more than one hundred settlements (all of which are of course illegal in international law), only about fifteen are viable, all of them in a small area clustered around Jerusalem or near the border close to Tel Aviv, and the only reason for the comparative success of those is that they provide dormitory suburbs for people working in the big cities.

Meanwhile, the Palestinian population is increasing rapidly. Benvenisti showed that at the end of 1984, it stood at 787,000 , an increase of no less than one third of what it was at the time of the occupation of 1967. Apart from anything else, that meant that the population growth had already gone far towards replacing those who were driven out in the 1967 war. It meant too that there was overwhelmingly a young population. The rate of increase during 1984 was one of the highest ever, at thirty-one per thousand people. The increased number of Palestinians was not confined to the West Bank. Within the 1967 borders, inside the Israeli state, the

Palestinians were also increasing rapidly as a percentage of the total population, of which they already [1986] number a rising eighteen per cent.

Meron Benvenisti showed that in the total area of Israel and the occupied territories, the Jewish majority was falling steadily, from sixty-five per cent in 1969 to sixty-three per cent in 1984. He predicted that the figure would be down to fifty-eight per cent by the year 2000. Predictions of that sort are always problematical but there are other factors in that, with the continuing emigration of Jews out of Israel, which has had a net and rising emigration rate for some years; with the refusal of foreign Jews to go there and with the rapidly increasing Palestinian population; Jews could become a minority in the "Greater Israel" which it is every Israeli government's policy to establish. There lies the reason for the desperate attempt to attract immigrants. That was why the government led by Shimon Peres was seriously suggesting that future immigrants from the USSR should be compulsorily flown direct from the Soviet Union to Israel, instead of being staged via Vienna, from where the large majority opted out of Zionist plans and went somewhere else.

In 1862, the statesman Otto von Bismarck, who was then already engaged in the policy which was to lead to the uniting of a number of small countries under Prussian leadership to create Germany, said that the policy could not succeed through talking, having shooting matches and singing songs, but by iron and blood. A quarter of a century later, in 1886, when the then united Germany was becoming a great world power, he said the same thing, except that he reversed the key words, so that it became a policy of "blood and iron." He has been depicted ever since as an advocate of the bloodshed and armaments of war. To an extent he was, but his original reference to iron was to the iron machinery of industry and the increased output it could produce to enrich humankind, while his reference to blood was not to bloodshed but to the growth of population.

Ever since its creation in 1948 by bloodshed in Palestine accompanied by deceitful propaganda throughout the world, the state of Israel has followed the military side of Bismarck's famous double-edged statement by a policy of blood and iron against the Arabs and, from his original, it has even derived its own phrase "the iron fist." It has attempted to solve the population side of the equation through the massive immigration of colonists, but that policy has become a growing and demonstrable failure. Not the least of the reasons for the failure is the distaste of growing numbers of Jewish people, both outside and inside the country, for the iron-fisted, apartheid nightmare which is the reality of the Zionist dream. And that is unlikely to be lost on fighters for human rights like Anatoly Shcharansky. There are time bombs ticking away for the Zionist state, not only in population trends and in the brave resistance of the Palestinian people to the iron fist, but also in distaste among its own more libertarian-minded people for what it has become.

## CAN EUROPE WAKE UP?

Does the apparently sleeping giant of Western Europe intend to awake from the uneasy but deliberate slumber into which is seems to have fallen over the Middle East? Does it mean to try to do anything effective to get the search for peace out of the dangerous swamp within which it is now stuck? There is an urgency and a tragedy about the current situation and the tragedy is made worse by Europe's continuing failure to use its considerable potential to show some independence of the United States and to advance the cause of peace. It is now nearly six years since the member countries of the European Community issued the famous Venice Declaration, in which they declared that they were obliged by traditional ties and common interests with the Middle East to work towards peace. It is nearly six years minus a few weeks since they backed away from that obligation under Israeli and American pressure.

In the Venice Declaration, they said that the necessary guarantees should be provided through the United Nations for the security and peaceful existence of all states in the region within recognized borders, and that the EC countries would participate in maintaining the guarantees. They called for Israeli withdrawal from the occupied territories and referred to the colonizing settlements as illegal in international law and as constituting a serious obstacle to peace. They attached special importance to Jerusalem and stated that no unilateral change in the status of the city was acceptable - an outright condemnation of the Israeli annexation and despoliation of East Jerusalem.

The EC countries called for a just solution for the Palestinians, fully involving their right to self-determination, as an essential requirement for peace. The achievement of peace, they declared, required the support and the involvement of all parties, including the PLO, who must be a party to negotiations. Finally, against the background of those ringing declarations, they announced that they intended to make contact with all parties to the conflict, with a view to determining what form an EC peace initiative could take. It is interesting to take the salient points of the Venice Declaration and to compare them with the actual situation six years later.

Guarantees for the security and peaceful existence within recognized borders for all states in the region?

Lebanon has been invaded and destroyed as a viable, governable country. Israeli occupation continues in the south with regular incursions further north to perpetrate atrocities against the civilian population. Tunis has been bombed. Israeli militarists are discussing when would be the best time to launch a new war against Syria. Israeli politicians are talking about driving the Palestinians into Jordan.

United nations guarantees with European Community participation?

In Lebanon, the UNIFIL force is too weak to do anything and is itself subject to constant Israeli harassment. The only EC participation was that by Britain, France and Italy in Beirut in 1983-84 in the so-called international peace keeping force which was destroyed by American policy.

Israeli withdrawal from the occupied territories (which was first called for as long ago as 1967 in Security Council Resolution 242)?

The only withdrawal has been from the largely desert Sinai, under the terms of the Camp David arrangements which, by neutralizing Egypt, prepared the way for the invasion of Lebanon. At least fifty-two per cent of the land in the West Bank is now Israeli controlled, Jerusalem is ringed with fortress like buildings and more than one hundred colonizing settlements are in existence. Arbitrary arrest, detention, torture and illegal deportation under a brutal apartheid system is accelerating. The Golan Heights have been annexed.

Palestinian involvement and self-determination with the PLO as a party to negotiations?

With American backing, the Israelis are refusing absolutely to recognize the principle of self-determination. To avoid it, they propose at best the appointment of their own nominees as Palestinian mayors, with minimal responsibilities for running local services which are deliberately starved of funds although Palestinians are forced to pay heavy taxes. At worst, they propose to crush Palestinian aspirations to self-determination by brute force.

From the very day when the Hussein-Arafat working arrangements were finalized, to try to find a way through the Israeli and American barricades to PLO involvement in negotiations, the Israelis set out to ensure that no such way would be found. Whenever any barricade looked like being removed, they put up several new ones. Whenever there seemed even the remotest possibility that the team which wanted peace might score a goal, they moved the goalposts.

So, nearly six years after the Venice Declaration, not one of its points has been achieved and they look further away from realization than when they were put forward. With the Hussein-Arafat initiative run into the sand and with a worldwide campaign to discredit the PLO, it is worth looking at what is happening to the Palestinians who are under Israeli apartheid.

According to one reliable Israeli commentator, Meron Benvenisti, the Director of the West Bank Data Base, the occupation regime under the coalition government led by Shimon Peres is even more brutal than it was under the earlier Likud government headed by Yitshak Shamir. There is a large increase in detention without trial, sealing of houses, demolition of houses and deportation. Under international law, deportation is wholly illegal. Article 49 of the Fourth Geneva Convention, which deals with the situation under occupation of "protected" - that is civilian - persons, sets out the position with unmistakable clarity, It states:

> Individual or mass forcible transfers. as well as deportations of protected persons from occupied territory to the territory of the occupying power or to that of any other country, occupied or not, are prohibited, regardless of their motive.

Yet such deportations are a regular and increasing method of repression. A favourite method is to take deportees to a lonely desert area south of the Dead Sea and abandon them. Their only hope of survival is to be picked up by a Jordanian patrol.

The so-called "trials" which sentence victims to this treatment are also in breach of every recognized or recognizable principle of justice. The prosecutors use so-called "secret proofs" against the victims which are not communicated to the defence. Not only are defending lawyers not allowed to see such so-called "evidence" but they actually have to leave the court when it is presented and they cannot in any way challenge it. Re-arrests for deportation have been made among prisoners released within the terms of the agreement made last May [1985] in Geneva under the auspices of the International Committee of the Red Cross and guaranteed by the Red Cross and the Swiss government. The, in some cases instant, re-arrest and illegal deportation of persons released under a guaranteed agreement of amnesty is yet another breach of international law as well as of every conceivable principle of justice.

With all that proceeding apace under his direction, Prime Minister Peres, during his visit to Europe in January, made a speech at the Royal Institute of International Affairs in London under the title "Peace: the Next Step Forward." His speech contained such gems as that the only way to resolve the Palestinian problem was through diplomatic means and that he had learned from Britain how to apply the wisdom of compromise and how to preserve what is precious to humanity as a whole! Hardly surprisingly, a speech of such hyprocrisy made little impact and when Peres went on to Bonn, he received a well-deserved rebuke from the West German Chancellor, Helmut Kohl, for his denial of the centrally important issue of self-determination. It was a pity that he was not similarly and publicly rebuked by the British government.

At least, however, some stirrings seem to have started among the EC governments in the aftermath of Peres' visit. Every six months, the Presidency of the Council of Ministers and with it the Presidency of the Council of Foreign Ministers of the member countries rotates. The current President of the Foreign Ministers is Hans van den Broek, the Foreign Minister of The Netherlands, another country in which Peres made his speech. Shortly after Mr van den Broek was appointed, he met a delegation of European members of the Parliamentary Association for Euro-Arab Co-operation, who were agreeably surprised to be told by him that he definitely did not advocate a European attitude of hiding behind the USA in the Arab-Israeli conflict. That was exactly what the Association and a great many other groups in Europe had long been pressing for. The Minister went on to tell the delegation that he would prefer to try to bring all the parties concerned closer to each other and that he thought that Europe could actively contribute to narrow the gap between the call for an international peace conference and the USA-Israeli demand merely to negotiate within an "international context."

Shortly after that meeting, the EC Foreign Ministers met in Brussels and agreed that the Dutch Foreign Minister, on behalf of the EC, should set about meeting the various parties to the conflict. That is no more than a belated and hesitant step towards implementing one small part of the Venice Declaration and whether or not it will achieve anything positive, and whether or not Western Europe will jump back into line when the USA cracks the whip remains to be seen. The European Community still insists that the Venice Declaration is its policy and if it adheres to that, the PLO will have to be included in the meetings upon which the Dutch Foreign Minister is to embark on behalf of his colleagues. With the sixth anniversary of the Venice Declaration very close, why not invite the Chairman of the PLO and colleagues from the Executive Committee to meet members of the EC Council of Ministers in Venice on the anniversary?

## MRS THATCHER'S GRAVE MISTAKE

The British government's support for the United States air raids against Libya during the night of 14-15 April, through allowing the use of British bases, aroused a storm of protest in Britain such as had not been seen for many years. Not for a long time had people taken to the streets in such numbers to demonstrate their disapproval. Every public opinion poll in the country showed that around seventy per cent of the British people disapproved of the use of the British bases, while the massive vote against the government in the municipal elections and in the two parliamentary by-elections held on 8 May also owed much to public anger over the bombing.

It has to be said that the government was already unpopular before the bombing, as had been demonstrated in a parliamentary by-election in the Fulham constituency, when the government was defeated in a previously Conservative held seat. Parliamentary by-elections and municipal elections are almost always contested on issues of home politics and seldom on issues related to foreign policy so, with the government already in low standing, it was to be expected that the elections on 8 May would go against them. However, candidates and canvassers in every party were forced to recognize that Mrs Thatcher's subservience to Ronald Reagan's demand for the use of British bases was a factor which was important in the elections and which increased the swing against the Conservative Party. Mrs Thatcher's support for the bombing of Libya was a grave mistake and the great majority of the British people, including supporters of the Conservative Party, sickened by the pictures on their television screens of dead and wounded children and other civilians, felt deeply shocked and angry over the conduct of their government.

Among my duties as Director of CAABU, an all-party organization, is to represent the views of CAABU to the government, irrespective of which party is forming the government and, on behalf of CAABU, I conducted a correspondence with the government which expressed a fair sample of the widely held objections to the government's conduct. My first letter was to Sir Geoffrey Howe, the Secretary of State for Foreign Affairs. The letter arose from a meeting of the Executive Committee of CAABU on 27 March, shortly after hostilities had been exchanged when American warships had crossed the line in the Gulf of Sirte which the Libyan government had unilaterally declared to be the limit of its territorial waters. On the unanimous decision of the CAABU Executive Committee, I wrote to express "the strongest disapproval of the United States action against Libya in the Gulf of Sirte and, also to express grave concern at the official British support."

The American claim to have embarked on the adventure in order to uphold rights of navigation in international waters did not bear examination. It was not in dispute that Libyan claims over the waters in the Gulf of Sirte were untenable in international law but, for the United States to despatch a large naval force towards Libya was an obvious act of provocation, designed to create hostilities. For that matter, official American sources made it clear that the real objective was nothing to do with freedom of navigation but was to weaken the position of Colonel Qadhafi. In practice, it had the opposite effect and the evidence was that Qadhafi's position was strengthened rather than weakened.

By its one-sided approach to the issue of the Arab-Israeli conflict and its brushing aside of Arab interests, the United States government had already gravely damaged prospects for peace. With the Gulf of Sirte affair, it appeared, in the words of Cyril Townsend, Conservative Member of Parliament and Joint Chairman of CAABU, to have replaced what the Americans themselves had once called "the peace process" by a war process.

In the CAABU letter to Sir Geoffrey Howe, I pointed out that the American action would increase the probability of retaliatory acts of terrorism around the world. That proved only too sadly true and it was in retaliation for such acts - the killing of an American soldier in a discotheque in West Berlin and the shootings of innocent people at Rome and Vienna airports - that the USA launched its air raids against Tripoli and Benghazi. Sir Geoffrey did not reply to the CAABU letter until after the raids had taken place. His reply did not attempt to answer the arguments, simply stating that the British government supported the American so-called naval exercise and stating that Libya had attacked US forces and that the US response in "self defence" had the support of the British government.

By then, I had written directly to the Prime Minister "to condemn the attack on Libya by the United States as an outrage against international law" and also to "express strong condemnation of the official British support and the use of British bases to launch the attack." That letter proved to be one among thousands sent to Mrs Thatcher by outraged British citizens. Even though some wrote in to support her, she was forced to admit in reply to questions in Parliament that the letters of criticism outnumbered the letters of support by three to one.

So great was the volume of protest that Mrs Thatcher's office had to produce a standard letter of reply. The letter did not attempt to answer the criticisms but simply reiterated the statements she had made in Parliament to try to justify the American attack and her support for it. The main claim was that the USA was under attack through a concerted Libyan terrorist campaign, was defending itself and was fully justified in international law, under Article 51 of the Charter of the United Nations.

Such arguments simply did not stand up to examination. In the first place, no proof of any such concerted Libyan campaign was ever produced. Mr Reagan and Mrs Thatcher seemed to think that "proof" was provided simply because they kept on repeating the allegation. They were on equally untenable ground in claiming an act of self defence in accordance with international law. Article 51 of the UN Charter refers to "the inherent right of individual or collective self defence if an armed attack occurs against a member of the United nations." That clearly refers to an armed attack against the territory of a member country. Any county so attacked can then very clearly and properly defend itself and is required also to report its defensive action to the Security Council. In actual fact, Libya had a much stronger case to report the USA to the Security Council and, being unable to defend itself against the superpower, to ask for international defensive action on its own behalf.

Article 51 was, of course, drafted long before what came to be termed "international terrorism" had become such a major and tragic issue, but that did not in any way alter the argument, for the Article could not be used to justify retaliatory actions against individual acts of terrorism, however abhorrent. Neither the killing of the American soldier in Berlin nor the outrages at Rome and Vienna airports, which were given as justification for the attack on Libya, could possibly be correctly regarded as an armed attack against the USA.

Nor did the USA report its supposedly "defensive" action to the Security Council, a breach of international law made all the more distasteful when it is recalled that the USA is a permanent and indeed a founder member of the Security Council. What happened was that Article 51 was taken out of the context of the Charter and out of the context of international law as it had developed since the Charter was drawn up, and was then misinterpreted to try to justify an internationally illegal action.

What was no less extraordinary than the specious arguments put forward to try to justify the attack and official British support for it, was Mrs Thatcher's personal conduct, for she seemed to have acted entirely on her own to do President Reagan's bidding, without properly consulting even her most senior colleagues in the Cabinet.

On Monday afternoon, 14 April, only hours before the attack and days after Reagan had indicated his intentions to the British, Sir Geoffrey Howe was at a meeting of the Foreign Ministers of the countries of the European Community, where he added his support to the EC ministerial appeal for "caution and restraint" in relation to Libya. At first glance, it seemed inconceivable that he could have been ignorant of what was planned and so he would appear to have been guilty of flagrant deception and untruthfulness. Yet the evidence which came out afterwards seemed to indicate that he really did not know the full situation because Mrs Thatcher had not told him what she was authorizing, even though he was one of the most senior Cabinet Ministers and, as Foreign Secretary, one of the most directly involved. The Prime Minister only informed the British Cabinet of what was happening at a meeting called two hours after the American aircraft had taken off from the British bases.

The Labour Party's principal foreign affairs spokesman and Shadow Foreign Secretary, Denis Healey, acidly expressed what most British people felt. He said that when President Reagan cracked the whip, Mrs Thatcher's response was to ask "how high do you want me to jump?" It was clear that Mrs Thatcher had gravely damaged her own and the Conservative Party's standing. What was more serious was that she had undone many years of work in improving Arab-British relations and had set them back to something like they were in the aftermath of the disastrous Suez affair - another grave miscalculation by another Conservative Prime Minister, almost exactly thirty years earlier.

## RACISM AND THE AUSTRIAN PRESIDENCY

A wave of anti-Arab racism is being organized in the Western World. There is also the campaign to depict Kurt Waldheim, the newly-elected President of Austria, as a Nazi war criminal. At first sight, the two may not appear to be related, but a closer examination reveals interesting links.

The campaign of racism is especially strong in the United States of America, where citizens of Arab descent and first generation Arab immigrants, who number something between two and a half and three million, and who have only in the last two or three years even started to refer to themselves as "Arab Americans", are increasingly victims of abuse and physical assault. The law enforcement authorities have moved to try to protect victims of such assaults, but they have to try to do so in an official climate which is not helpful. In both Houses of Congress, the votes against President Reagan's request to sell a very modest package of arms, worth $354m, to Saudi Arabia - modest indeed in comparison with the billions going to Israel - provide their own evidence of how anti-Arab the Congress has become. The vote against was 72 to 22 in the Senate and 356 to 62 in the House of Representatives. It was the first time in the entire history of the USA that both Houses of Congress had voted down a presidential request to sell arms. President Reagan and Secretary of State Shultz made efforts to reverse the rebuff but their efforts were based in their own damaged egos and not in any friendship for the Arab World.

The wave of anti-Arab racism is by no means confined to the USA. The *Sun* newspaper of London recently published a report about the return to his home in Britain of a Libyan who had earlier been deported, under the front-page headline in large letters "Arab pig sneaks back in." When a complaint was made to the Press Council about the racist nature of the headline, the Council made the strange ruling that the headline was not racist because of the paper's claim that the phrase "Arab pig" referred to only one individual and not to all Arabs. The paper responded by immediately publishing a cartoon depicting a group of pigs objecting to being called Arabs. (2)

---

(2) See above, page 78 .

Although the campaign by the worldwide Zionist agencies against Kurt Waldheim, the former Secretary-General of the United Nations Organization and now President of Austria, might not at first sight appear to be a part of the wave of anti-Arab racism, it is, as always, very advisable to look below the surface of whatever campaigns the Zionist machine organizes.

Their campaign against Waldheim suddenly emerged during the Austrian election. He was accused of having been a war criminal, involved directly in the Nazi genocide against the Jews when he was serving as a junior officer in the German army in the second world war (when Austria was incorporated into Germany and all Austrian men of military age were obliged to serve in the German army). No convincing evidence was produced and, the alleged incidents having occurred more than forty years earlier, it seemed strange, to say the least, that he could have served as Secretary-General of the United Nations without the matter ever having been raised before. He denied the charges and treated them with a probably well-deserved contempt. However, in the eyes of the world outside Austria, he did not appear to handle the matter well and with the worldwide Zionist propaganda machine in top gear, he appeared less than convincing, with the result that the allegations against him increased by the day.

In looking below the surface of this campaign, there are two special features to be taken into account. The first is that, from the start, Waldheim was the favourite to win the election and become President. The second was the special role which Austria had built up in Middle Eastern affairs and also as a neutral bridge between the eastern and western power blocs. Under the inspired and inspiring leadership of the former Chancellor, Bruno Kriesky, himself Jewish, Austria, although a small country, had come to play a major role in drawing to wider European and world attention the appalling suffering inflicted upon the Palestinian people by Zionism.

Kriesky had also, to the fury of the Zionist state and its foreign agencies, met Yasser Arafat, introduced him to other leading European statesmen and strongly advocated the necessity to include the PLO in negotiations for a peaceful settlement. In addition, Austria had come to play a special role in the campaign to encourage Jews to leave the Soviet Union and go to Israel, and Vienna was the staging post where they first stopped on their journey. But what infuriated the Zionists was that the majority of the emigrants, on arrival in the Austrian capital, refused to go on to Tel Aviv and went instead to other countries, most preferring the United States.

For the past thirty years, Austria had been a major east-west meeting place. It was in Vienna that Kennedy met Kruschev in one of the earliest summit meetings and where there had been a long series of meetings between the US and USSR foreign ministers. The 1985 first meeting between Reagan and Gorbachev might very well have taken place in Vienna in preference to Geneva. One of the major Israeli policy aims is to prevent any agreement between the superpowers, because if the USA and the USSR were to come to an agreement and give their joint attention to peace instead of confrontation in the Middle East, the Zionist state's era of expansion would be ended and a just order of society and of international relations could then be established. So, with Kurt Waldheim likely to be elected as President, there was seen to be a strong opportunity, which was seized upon eagerly, to damage Austria's vital role, both in the Middle East and in East-West relations.

Within Austria, there was widespread and understandable resentment at the Zionist interference in the election and more people voted for Waldheim than would have done so if the campaign against him had not been waged. The Austrian voters made it plain that they were not taking orders from the Israeli state as to whom they should vote for to be President of Austria. Consequently, Waldheim's standing was increased and he won the election with a bigger majority than expected. Naturally, that led to the usual Zionist branding of the Austrian people as "anti-Semitic." But that again is an essential part of Zionism, the very foundation of which is a false theory that all non-Jews are automatically hostile to Jews and, therefore, all Jews must leave the country of their birth and go to live in a Jewish state. So, where anti-Jewish feelings do not exist, it is an essential part of Zionism to create them.

The undoubted anger among the Austrian people at the Israelis' determined attempt to dictate who should or should not be their president could prove to have wide implications. Not least in the United States where, after years of subservience, there is starting to be resistance to the all-powerful Israeli lobby. So far it is small but it is growing and it is starting to be recognized that the lobby lacks credibility in that it exists solely to sustain the interests of a foreign power, at high financial and political cost to the citizens of the United States.

As the present wave of anti-Arab racism shows, there is a very long way to go before the challenge really becomes effective to the lobby's stranglehold on North America and to its power in Western Europe, while the lobby will fight with every weapon and every dirty trick in its formidable armoury to maintain its power. Sooner or later, though, the dangerous excesses of the Israeli state and the coercion exercised by its worldwide agencies will come to be recognized and contained. With international law and justice and world peace itself in the balance, it requires to be sooner rather than later.

# 10

# DECADE'S END: SO MUCH HAPPENING

From the day it started on 9 December 1987, the Palestinian Intifada created a sea change. The sight, on television screens worldwide, of young Palestinians defying the Israeli war machine with only stones and personal courage, brought a wave of support such as had never been known before. CAABU was inundated with messages and calls for supportive action. On Thursday afternoon, 17 December, we decided to hold a public meeting, very conscious that with the imminence of Christmas. it had to be held quickly. The following Monday, 21 December, was the only possible day; the intervening, pre-Christmas weekend would make organization difficult. Fortunately, a room was available at Friends' Meeting House, Euston Road; Faisal Aouidha, the PLO Representative in London, was available to speak. Every available stop was pulled out to publicize the event.

A few hours before the meeting, a fault developed in the lighting in the room we had reserved and we had to use another room which was more than twice as big. It was a good thing that fault occurred. People came in hundreds and we had difficulty getting them all even into the bigger room. By a happy coincidence, a senior PLO spokesman, Khaled Al Hassan, Chairman of the Political (Foreign

Affairs) Committee of the Palestine National Council, was in London on the day and Faisal Aouidha was pleased to give way to him as speaker. I chaired the meeting, Khaled and I had shared platforms and I had chaired meetings for him on numerous occasions. He had worked long and hard to make a reality of the Hussein-Arafat initiative, only to see it brought to nothing by Israeli obstruction, and for many months, he had been worried and depressed by the seeming hopelessness of the situation. That evening, he was inspired and he received a tremendous ovation.

His performance, its reception and the attendance at the meeting were symptomatic of the effect of the Intifada, not only in Palestine, but among Palestinians and sympathizers throughout the world. Within weeks, the brave people of the Intifada came to do more to focus attention on the injustices suffered by the Palestinians than the entire world community had done in forty years. Suddenly, the stultifying deadlock was over, everything seemed possible and it soon became clear that this was much more than resistance to military occupation. It was the struggle of a proud people for self-determination and independence. It was also the struggle of a generous people, who were prepared to be astonishingly forgiving towards the oppressors whose aim was to usurp the whole of their homeland, for they were prepared to be independent in only a small portion of their own land and to live in peace with the Israelis in a two-state solution of the two peoples' common problem,

Another point which the Palestinians made clear was that they were no more prepared to live under any form of suzerainty by the King of Jordan than under Israeli occupation, King Hussein himself was finally forced to recognize that and to renounce all claims to sovereignty over the West Bank, an action which led directly to the Palestinian Declaration of Independence on 15 November 1988 and to the subsequent conferring of the title of President on Yasser Arafat. The turgid wording of the Declaration of Independence may not have measured up to the standards of the American "We hold these truths to be self-evident,..." but it encapsulated the same ideals and was of comparable significance,

In the dying days of the Reagan administration, the final and arguably most stupid act of the Secretary of State George Shultz was to deny Arafat a visa to enter the United States in order to address the United Nations. That led to the UN's special session in Geneva and Arafat's speech there on 13 December which led, after a night of mediation by Sweden, to the American decision to open talks with the PLO at ambassadorial level.

When the talks actually commenced in Tunis,. the American Embassy did not know where to start and had to consult the British Embassy, who produced the PLO representatives with whom the talks opened. One might be forgiven for asking where, on that night of mediation in Geneva, was Britain with its "special relationship" with the USA and all the British experience and historical responsibility in the Middle East. As it was, the Americans briefed the British government on their change of policy, mediated by Sweden, a day or so later. It was an indication of how marginalized Britain had become.

Not one of those historic events would have happened without the courage and endurance of the people of the Intifada. On the first anniversary of the uprising, 9 December 1988, the United Nations Relief and Works Agency (UNRWA) calculated that the Israeli Defence Force had already killed 313 people and wounded an estimated 20,000. Throughout 1989, the methods of repression became more harsh as the Israelis turned the Intifada into a long war of attrition. The Palestinians showed no sign of weakening but by mid 1989, it was becoming clear that the US-PLO talks were getting nowhere and that Israeli obstruction and their power over American policy was succeeding in its objective of creating yet another situation of deadlock and delay. I will return to that but first, a debating speech at Cambridge on the day after the Declaration of Independence and an analytical examination of the situation given at Oxford a little over two months later.

## SPEECH AT THE CAMBRIDGE UNIVERSITY UNION DEBATE

***Presiding, Piers Pressdee, St. John's College, President of the Union***

In winding up in support of the motion that "This House believes that the first condition for peace in the Middle East must be an independent Palestinian State" I wish, first, to support the Hon. Member who so ably moved the motion [Simon Bourne, Sidney Sussex College], especially in his comments on the fortuitous timing of this debate. He wondered, referring to the Palestinian Declaration of Independence which was made only yesterday in Algiers, if the sponsors of the motion had a direct line to Mr Yasser Arafat. For my part, recalling that the motion was formulated and the date of the debate decided months ago, I find myself wondering if those who formulated the motion and decided the date possess powers of prognostication which are denied to the rest of us, for the terms of the motion and the timing mean that, outside the Palestine National Council - the Palestinian Parliament - this House is probably the first assembly in the world to debate and to have the opportunity to endorse the historic Declaration of Independence made little more than thirty-six hours ago, in the early hours of yesterday morning.

The basic nature of the problem of the Palestinians is a long standing problem of human rights - the problem of a people dispossessed of their land, their dignity and their identity. When the state of Israel was established by force of arms on the soil of Palestine in 1948, one million Palestinians were forcibly dispossessed. They were dispossessed of the homes they lived in, of the land upon which they depended for their living and which they had cultivated successfully for generations, and they were dispossessed of the very country which they loved - and love - so dearly.

There is a long standing, carefully created and carefully cultivated myth that they left voluntarily or that they were ordered to leave by Arab governments. That piece of mythology has long since been destroyed - except in the minds of those with a vested interest in perpetuating it. Very recently, it has been destroyed by the distinguished Israeli historian and journalist Dr Benny Morris.

When my colleague, Mr Cyril Townsend (MP, Bexleyheath, Conservative) referred in his speech, supporting the motion, to the distinguished Jewish writer, I. F. Stone, certain opponents of the motion purported not to know who I. F. Stone was. I trust that even their lack of knowledge of distinguished Jewish writers does not also extend to Dr Benny Morris who, in his recent book *The Birth of the Palestinian Refugee Problem, 1947-49*, has provided a devastating and superbly documented account of how the Palestinians were, in fact, terrorized by Zionist forces into leaving their homeland. That the book is published by the Cambridge University Press - even if at an exorbitant price - adds even more to its credibility.

I want to quote something else from Dr Morris. He very recently served three weeks in prison, on grounds of conscience, for refusing military service in the occupied territories. In his statement to the court which sentenced him, he said:

> What we are doing in the occupied territories is a crime. I refuse to take part in it. We must get out of the territories.

That statement is in line with the thinking of other enlightened Israelis and it clearly predicates Palestinian independence. It is also entirely in line with the worldwide consensus which has been developing over a number of years, a consensus for Palestinian self-determination and independence in the West Bank and the Gaza Strip, in accordance with the right to self-determination and independence which is one of the most basic rights of all peoples.

I want now to turn to the Palestinians themselves. The great uprising in the occupied territories is much more than a protest against years of brutal occupation, of brutal repression and of the organized theft, not only of their personal property but of the natural resources of their country. Even if the uprising was on those grounds alone, it would be entirely justified, but it is much more than that. It is, as the people of the occupied territories have made clear over and over again, a clear call for self-determination and independence. And it demonstrates several things.

In the first place, it demonstrates that the Palestinians have completed the process of nation building and are now ready to have their own nation state. Then, again, it demonstrates also that the very large majority reject rule from Jordan by King Hussein and demand their own chosen leadership. And they have made very plain that their chosen leadership is that of the Palestine Liberation Organization. That was the background against which, on 31 July [1988] King Hussein withdrew all claims to sovereignty over the West Bank. That means that there is now no legal sovereignty over the West Bank except that of the Palestinian inhabitants. In the Gaza Strip, the legal niceties are different but the principle is exactly the same. So the case for independence is also made in terms of international law.

What is most remarkable is the generosity of the Palestinian people. For all their loss of human rights at the hands of the Israeli state; for all they have suffered; they are still prepared to live alongside Israel. That message, too, is coming loud and clear, both from the occupied territories and from the Palestine National Council, meeting in Algiers. It is profoundly to be regretted that the response of Mr Yitshak Shamir and his fellow rejectionists has been, as usual, totally negative. The reality, which he and his like are incapable of seeing, is that it is in Israel's own vital interest to have a free and independent Palestinian state in the West Bank and Gaza.

At this point, I want to refer to the speech made earlier in this debate by the Hon. Member of Parliament who opposed the motion [Ivan Lawrence QC, MP, Burton Upon Trent, Conservative]. During the debate, his speech has been heavily attacked. I have no wish to twist the knives that have been pushed in. I enjoyed his speech, especially that lesser part of it in which he actually addressed himself to the motion. In that part, he told us that an independent state in the West Bank is in no way practical. "It is too small, it has no resources and it is not viable" he told us. Yet he also told us that an independent Palestinian state would be a threat to Israel's security. Now, the state of Israel surrounds the West Bank on three sides. The state of Israel also boasts constantly that it is the fourth, or at the very least, the fifth greatest military power in the world. Yet we are asked to believe that this "too small", "resourceless" and "unviable" state constitutes a threat to Israel. What a ludicrous argument that is!

What are the alternatives to a free and independent Palestinian state alongside Israel? If Israel continues the occupation, there will be endless conflict and ever worse crimes by the occupiers. There will also be growing demoralization and conflict inside Israel -

something which is already being manifested there on an increasing scale. There are powerful calls there to annex the occupied territories and incorporate them into a greater Israel. If that were done, it would create serious demographic problems. By the twenty-first century - and in historical terms, that is not very far off - it would create an Israel with more Palestinians than Jews. There would then be just two alternatives; apartheid like that in Israel's close ally South Africa; or the expulsion of the Palestinians.

There are, of course, growing calls in Israel to annex the territories and expel the Palestinians. That is a suggestion as wicked as it is impractical. It would certainly lead to war in the Middle East which would be more destructive than any yet seen even in that war torn region of the world. So the reality is that it is as much in Israel's interest as it is in the Palestinians' interest to have an independent Palestinian state. And it is certainly in the interest of the peace, justice and stability of the whole Middle East, which means the peace and stability of the whole world. So, to sum up and conclude; on grounds of justice and of peace, in the cause of ending the longest running conflict of the twentieth century, there is an unanswerable case for an independent Palestinian state as a first and basic condition for peace in the Middle East. I commend the motion for the support of the House.

## THE MIDDLE EAST:
## A TIME FOR EVERYTHING

***Address to Oxford University Strategic Studies Group, 24 January 1989*** (1)

What may seem to be the slightly cryptic title I have selected for this address is taken. as is easily recognized, from those stirring, poetic words of the first verse of Chapter 3 of *The Book of Eccliastes* in The Old Testament: "There is a time for everything, and a season for every activity under heaven." To explain the theme of this address more fully, I quote additionally the second and eighth verses:

> A time to be born and a time to die,
> A time to plant and a time to uproot.
>
> A time to love and a time to hate,
> A time for war and a time for peace.

Those brilliant words could hardly be more applicable to the current situation in the Middle East. They were referred to last week in the House of Commons by William Waldegrave, the Minister of State at the Foreign and Commonwealth Office. To avoid any suspicions of plagiarism on my part, let me make clear that I had selected the title of this address long before that as, Mr President, my letter to you of 23 November last will verify. It is notable that William Waldegrave quoted the words when reporting on his recent meeting with Yasser Arafat. There was as near to a unanimity of view on the value of the meeting as Parliament ever gets to and it is further to be noted that the Minister was replying to a private notice question from the Shadow Foreign Secretary, Gerald Kaufman,(2) who had also met Mr Arafat a few days befor Mr Waldegrave.

The words are so applicable because a whole series of dramatic events in 1988 - which is continuing - has changed not only patterns of events but also perceptions of events which had previously endured for forty years, and those events have produced a situation with a huge potential for life and death, for war and peace. I am always wary of making over-dramatic statements - although not

(1) Repeated, in substance, one week later at Durham University, meeting organized by Durham CAABU Branch.
(2) House of Commons, 17 January 1989.

quite so much so as Sir Geoffrey Howe (3) - but current events have brought the Middle East to a point where there are crucial choices to be made and where, whatever choices are made, the consequences are unpredictable. But the situation is also that. if the world should choose to remain as if standing indecisively at a cross roads and uncertain of what to do or which direction to take, then the consequences are still unpredictable. So, indeed, this is a time for everything.

Of course, I am referring especially to the Middle East in terms of the Arab-Israeli conflict although that is, sadly, far from being the only dispute in that conflict ridden region of the world. There is the situation in the Gulf where, although the long and bloody war between Iran and Iraq has ended, there is at best only an uneasy truce, with long and difficult negotiations to be undertaken and major internal conflicts in both countries. Then there are great stresses and conflicts, both between and within many countries in the region. One must never over simplify but a cautious analogy might be made with medieval Europe, emerging from dark ages into the Rennaissance and the Reformation, with all the huge conflicts which then resulted from new ideas and new perceptions of humanity. The Middle East, too, is emerging from something resembling its own dark age of colonialism and its own form of feudalism. However, because events now move so much faster, where Europe had several centuries to evolve, the Middle East has only decades in which to come to terms with late twentieth century technology and the great flood of invention and discovery which marks our own times. Returning to the context of the Arab-Israeli conflict, I want first to consider some of the dramatic developments of 1988 and their portents for the future, before going on to wider international aspects, especially the involvement and the policies of the two superpowers, upon whom greatly depends the ultimate outcome.

Nineteen eighty-eight has been notable above all for the sustained Palestinian uprising or "Intifada" - which continues as strongly as ever. Most of the other events connected with the Arab-Israeli conflict have flowed from that and would not have happened if there had not been the Intifada. For example, the Intifada was directly responsible for bringing a much greater United

---

(3) The then Secretary of State for Foreign and Commonwealth Affairs, noted for his unexciting style.

States involvement. In the first half of the year, Mr George Shultz, the Secretary of State until only a few days ago (I have to confess that I find myself with an already developing and embarrassing tendency to think of him as "the late" George Shultz), made no less than four visits to the Middle East which would certainly not have taken place had it not been for the Intifada. Yet, in all four visits, he met no representative Palestinians. His not meeting with representative Palestinians was a classic demonstration of the perceptions of what Professor Kenneth Galbraith dubbed thirty years ago as "the conventional wisdom," which might now be more appropriately referred to as "the established prejudices." In this case, these refer to the perceived idea that you could solve the Palestinian problem, which is the core and crux of the whole conflict, without direct reference to the Palestinians themselves, or to their chosen representative body. And one thing the Palestinians have made absolutely clear through the Intifada is that their chosen body is the PLO. Finally, in the closing weeks of 1988, the USA had to recognize that it must talk with the PLO. Western Europe is now also actively doing so. This coming weekend, Yasser Arafat is to be received in Madrid, to meet the Foreign Ministers of Spain, France and Greece. And they are not just meeting the Chairman of the PLO in their own right, but as the designated representatives of the Foreign Ministers of all the twelve countries of the European Community.

Another development of fundamental importance is that the Palestinians have made very clear that they no more wish to be ruled by King Hussein of Jordan than by the Israelis. On 31 July 1988, King Hussein finally recognized that he did not have the confidence of the Palestinians and he withdrew all claims to sovereignty over the West Bank. That was a change of policy as dramatic as any and it had early and far-reaching consequences. It led directly to, although it was not the cause of, the Palestinian Declaration of Independence on 15 November by the Palestine National Council, which is in effect the "Palestinian Parliament in Exile." The Declaration of Independence did not evolve from the Jordanian withdrawal. It is the other way round. The Declaration of Independence was being talked about months before King Hussein's announcement.

Since the Declaration of Independence is an important matter of debate, we should look at its implications in international legality and I would refer you to the cogently argued essay on that subject by Professor Robert Charvin, Professor of Law at the University of Nice, which has just been published [4]. The Israelis have always claimed that the West Bank and the Gaza Strip were never sovereign territories, on the grounds that they were occupied territories before the Israeli occupation of 1967. Their argument is that the West Bank was territory occupied by Jordan and that the Gaza Strip was territory occupied by Egypt. Among other contentions, they argue that therefore the Geneva Conventions on the treatment of the inhabitants of militarily occupied territory do not apply. That has always seemed to me to be a tortuous exercise in semantics and one that certainly does not excuse the Israeli conduct in those territories, which has been in the most blatant disregard of the Geneva Conventions, both long before and since the Intifada. King Hussein's withdrawal of claims of sovereignty left the West Bank without any internationally recognized legal sovereignty. So the legal sovereignty, in accordance with the fundamental principle of the self-determination of peoples, which is embodied in the Charter of the United Nations, became invested in the indigenous inhabitants, The situation in the Gaza Strip differs only in minor matters of international legality and is self-evidently identical in principle. Now, since the indigenous inhabitants, the Palestinians, have made absolutely clear that they accept only the PLO as their representative organization, the Declaration has unanswerable claims to legality and it is not surprising that over sixty countries have already recognized it. [5]

Near the end of 1988, in the remarkable sequence of events in that year, came Yasser Arafat's speech to the General Assembly of the United Nations in Geneva, which was followed almost immediately by the United States decision to reverse its longstanding policy and to talk with the PLO, after a night of mediation by Swedish diplomats. Where, one wonders, was the British "special relationship" with the USA at that crucial point? All these, then, have been some of the major, dramatic developments in this "time for everything." in the Middle East.

This has been a time which has brought Israel, more than any other country, to a cross roads and to a growing sense of bewilderment as to where to go next. Israel now has a large section

---

(4) Robert Charvin, *The "Intifada": from Palestinian People's Self-Assertion to Statehood,* published in Palestine and Law, International Association of Democratic Lawyers, Brussels, 1988.

(5) As at 24 January 1989. The number was then increasing almost daily.

of its armed forces tied down in the occupied territories, where the brutal nature of the attempted suppression of the Palestinians is having deep and demoralizing effects throughout the country, as well as causing worldwide revulsion. The 1988 election revealed a deeply divided country - divided by whether to rule by brute force or to come to terms with Palestinian aspirations. Many weeks of political manoeuvring after the election finally produced a government which is refusing to talk with the PLO and which is refusing to recognize any Palestinian right to self-determination and independence and which is, itself, deeply divided. Only within the last few days, there has been an extraordinary symptom of the divisions in the government. Under the terms of the agreement which finally produced the Likud-Labour coalition, it was agreed that eight new settlements should be established in the occupied territories. The Labour Party was opposed to any new settlements. The Likud Party wanted many more. The eight were an uneasy compromise reached to allow a government to be formed. Shimon Peres, Leader of the Labour Party and Minister of Finance, is refusing the money to fund these settlements. Consequently, the Prime Minister, Yitshak Shamir, is asking those ministries which have Likud ministers to find the money from within their budgets, which have already been allocated. That open conflict between the Prime Minister and the Minister of Finance must surely demonstrate one of the most extraordinary internal situations within any government anywhere.

Israel is facing unenviable options of its own making. It can continue the occupation, in which case there will be ever more conflict, deeper divisions within Israel and deeper alienation from the rest of the world. It can annex the territories, and there is no shortage of voices in the country calling for that, in which case, by the end of the century, which is close in historical terms, it will be a country with as many Palestinians as Jews. It will then either cease to be a Jewish state, which was the whole reason for its establishment, or it will become a full apartheid state, trying to hold down the Palestinians in the same way that South Africa is trying to hold down the black people. It can, of course, attempt to expel the Palestinians, and there is no shortage of voices on the extreme right calling for expulsion. If such a course of action were to be embarked upon, it would create conflict on a scale never before seen even in this war-torn region of the world and with incalculable consequences for the very existence of Israel. Alternatively, Israel can come to terms with the reality of its situation. For many, even among those who advocate that very policy, it will be no less difficult. It means recognizing that Israel's very future depends on an accommodation with the Palestinians. It means negotiating - properly and on equal terms - with the PLO in an international peace conference.

The Israeli government now remains the only government opposed on principle to an international conference. Even members of the government like Shimon Peres, who supports some sort of conference, only supports one at which no real negotiations could take place and he refuses any role for the PLO. Israel apart, there is now universal support for the idea of an international conference. But there are very different ideas about what form it should take. It is only likely to take place, leave alone to succeed in producing results, if the two superpowers reach agreement about its priority, about what form it should take and about what should be its terms of reference. One idea currently being canvassed at diplomatic level is that it should be convened by the five permanent members of the Security Council. That is an idea which has been around for quite a while. An additional suggestion is that it should be under joint USA-USSR chairmanship. That idea has been around for even longer, since it first arose from the famous Security Council Resolution 338, about which we so constantly hear so much without reference to its actual content.

Over the years, the Middle East has become a major area of superpower rivalry and manoeuvring. Eight years ago in the United States, the Reagan administration was elected on a policy of worldwide challenge to the Soviet Union and it came to regard the Middle East as a vital sector for confrontation. It was in that context that on 29 September 1983, the USA concluded an agreement with Israel which gave unprecedented support for Israel, even in the long and close association between the two countries. That agreement remains very relevant in the current situation and its terms need therefore to be recalled.

There was to be, and there is, joint military planning and joint naval manoeuvres in the Mediterranean, with intelligence sharing and US military stockpiling in Israel. American military aid was to be no longer in repayable loans but in outright grants. Currently, and now for some years, those grants are at a rate of about $3.5 billion a year. There was also instituted a free trade agreement which exempts all Israeli exports to the USA from all US tariffs. In

1983, the Israeli Lavi fighter-bomber aircraft was in an advanced planning stage and ready to go into production. It was to be heavily subsidized by the United States. That provision of the agreement was eventually discontinued because of heavy lobbying in Washington by the American aircraft industry, which objected strongly to US subsidization of an aircraft which would be in competition in the world markets with the products of America's own aircraft industry. The aircraft had to be cancelled. Consequently, there are currently highly secret negotiations going on between Israel and South Africa to see if the Lavi, or an equivalent can be jointly produced in that country. All the terms of that far reaching Israeli-American agreement arose largely because, following the fall of the Shah and the advent of the Khomeini regime in Iran, Israel was seen by the United States as a main base for enforcing its policy and exerting control over the Middle East.

Resolution 338, which followed the 1973 war, set up what came to be called the "Geneva Conference" which was to be under joint United States-Soviet chairmanship, with the object of bringing together all parties to the conflict, including the Palestinians. The Geneva Conference broke down very quickly because the Israelis refused to negotiate with any Palestinians - not with the PLO but with any Palestinians. It was to no small extent out of Egyptian and American frustration over the failure of the Geneva Conference that the Camp David Conference was born,

However, the USSR regarded Camp David and the Egypt-Israel Treaty which came from it in 1979 as a breach of the joint approach of Resolution 338 and as a policy to increase American power and influence at the expense of the Soviet Union. As worsening relations became the cold war of the mid nineteen-eighties, the Soviet government sought to maintain influence in the region through knife-edge diplomacy with Iran and Iraq throughout the war between the two, which enabled it to retain more or less reasonable relations with both countries. It also set out on a policy of steadily extending diplomatic relations with the Gulf Arab countries. It had longstanding diplomatic relations with Kuwait and established them with Oman and the United Arab Emirates in 1985, and with Qatar in 1988. For years, it has engaged with Saudi Arabia in a kind of "will they - won't they" dialogue on diplomatic relations, which continues.

If the events of the 1980's demonstrate anything at all, they demonstrate very strongly the potential danger of the Middle East as a flashpoint for worldwide conflagration; and they demonstrate the absolute need for superpower confrontation in the region to be replaced by co-operation, not only for the avoidance of superpower conflict but as a vital requirement in settling the regional conflict. Fortunately, at this time when everything seems to be happening, the measure of detente in the global context also gives encouraging signs of greater co-operation over the Middle East. Both superpowers now accept the need for at least some sort of international conference under United Nations auspices. The USA is talking with the PLO and although these are very early days to make a judgement, there are some signs that the Bush administration could have a more concessionary policy than its predecessor on Palestinian rights and on the requirement to involve the PLO in a peace conference. The USSR has long recognized the PLO and it has used its relationship to exert pressure on the PLO to modify its policy to make it more acceptable to the United States.

Unfortunately, Israel, under Shamir's premiership, remains obdurate in rejecting Palestinian rights. Early in the New Year, for example, Sir Geoffrey Howe, during his tour of the Gulf countries, made a very reasonable call for an Israeli response to the PLO's changes in policy announced by Yasser Arafat in his Geneva speech, only to have his call instantly rejected. Then Yitshak Shamir's furious response to William Waldegrave's meeting with Arafat was an instant statement that, not just Britain, but Europe "has no role in the peace process." That is a pretty astonishing statement by any standards, given Europe's geographical proximity to the region; to say nothing of its centuries-old cultural relationship and its huge political, strategic and commercial interests in the Middle East.

This address has been based in two main themes - the remarkable series of continuing events and the involvement of the two superpowers as well as the evolving nature of their policies, and it has also explored several sub-themes related to both main themes. The series of events in 1988 has created a completely new situation with wide possibilities. Above all, there has been the sustained Intifada from which all the rest has flowed - King Hussein's withdrawal from claims of sovereignty over the West Bank; the Palestinian Declaration of Independence; the USA talking with the PLO; and increased co-operation between the USA and the USSR. The result of all that is that the world may now be on course, even if only at the start of the course, for an international peace conference. When such a conference takes place and whether it produces anything is likely to depend on the willingness of the United States and the Soviet Union to make it happen.

A great deal depends on whether Israel can be reassured that its interests will be enhanced by participating. On the other hand, Israel cannot be allowed indefinitely to obstruct a conference, nor to refuse to recognize the grave injustice it has inflicted on the Palestinians, nor to refuse to come to terms with the PLO. The PLO has greatly modified its position. The leadership has gone to the limit of what its constituency will take - and that constituency makes with Israel the equally important one of the two most crucial constituencies involved. It cannot be expected that the PLO can go on making all the concessions and never getting anything in return, or to go on finding that the goalposts have been moved every time it concedes anything while, at the same time, its people continue to endure brutal repression and persecution which is not only internationaly illegal but a matter of moral concern to the entire world community.

In this address, I have not attempted to come up with glib solutions. There are none, and we are deceiving ourselves if we think there are. But we are at a point where profound changes are taking place, both in events and in long entrenched perceptions of events. The course of events in the foreseeable future depends on how this new situation is handled and it is a situation which is not capable of resolution without global involvement. What is certain is that it can only be resolved when right is done to all parties to the conflict and is seen to be done by those parties, themselves.

# 11

# QUESTIONS FOR THE NINETIES

## 1. The Iron Fist

"We are at a point where profound changes are taking place, both in events and in perceptions of events." I have to admit that when I said that in concluding the foregoing address in January 1989, I had little idea of just how prescient it really was. By December of the same year, the cold war was over. Half a dozen long established dictatorships in Eastern and Central Europe had been ended in a breathtaking series of revolutions. Almost everywhere, there was a new perception of the world and hope that the nineteen-nineties could hold out a prospect of worldwide change for the better, such as had not been seen before in the entire twentieth century.

However, at least one place where that did not apply was the Middle East. There, the hopes for progress were actually less than they had seemed a year earlier. The euphoria of 1988 had disappeared and the Intifada was turning into a long, hard war of attrition in which the oppression of the Palestinians was more brutal than it had ever been. Even in South Africa, things were changing, but the historic release from prison of Nelson Mandela on 11 February 1990 evoked not the slightest response from Israel, South Africa's closest ally and fellow apartheid state. It could be argued that Mandela's release, after twenty-seven years in prison and at the age of seventy-one, was a move calculated to preserve white domination rather than to abolish it and it might well have been a tactic in procrastination learned during the close relationship between the two governments. Even so, it was a major move. Far from making any comparable gesture of conciliation to open the new decade, the hardline ruling circles in Israel moved in the directly opposite direction and intensified their efforts to oppress the Palestinians and ultimately to drive them out completely.

By the second anniversary of the Intifada, 9 December 1989, well over 750 Palestinians had been killed by the occupation forces and their agents (border guards, police, prison guards and interrogators using torture, as well as settlers and collaborators using Israeli-issued weapons). Included in the total killed were nearly 200 children aged sixteen and less, 135 of them killed by gunfire, and there were nearly 80 women and girls, 34 of them also killed by gunfire. It was not possible to make an exact count of the injured because a high percentage were treated anonymously in homes and emergency places to avoid the regular practice of the Israeli army of invading hospitals and dragging patients from their beds and even from operating tables for interrogation. 45,000 people were treated in hospital but it was reliably estimated that there were at least 80,000 seriously injured.

During the two years, more than 1,200 Palestinian homes were demolished or sealed up to prevent their use. Since the householders were not permitted to rebuild, they were forced to camp out in the open as best they could, including, in a society of young marriages and a high birthrate, many children. Among pregnant women, there were hundreds of miscarriages induced by toxic gas, used not only in the streets but also inside buildings, including homes and hospitals. Prolonged curfews were regularly imposed and while farmers were thus prevented from harvesting their crops, the army and armed gangs of settlers regularly destroyed whole fields of crops and whole fruit orchards. Huge areas of seedlings and plants were uprooted, burned or destroyed by chemicals. More than 77,000 mature olive trees, vital to the economy and representing years of careful cultivation, were uprooted.[1]

---

(1) Statistics of deaths, injuries and destruction taken from the December 1989 Report of the Database Project on Palestinian Human Rights, Jerusalem and from figures supplied by Al-Haq (Law in the Service of Man), an affiliate of the International Commission of Jurists.

Another method of oppression was the imposition of punitive taxes, which were wholly illegal in international law, The town of Beit Sahur, near Bethlehem in the West Bank, a place of twelve thousand, mainly Christian inhabitants built on the site where traditionally the birth of Christ was announced to shepherds watching their flocks, became especially famous for its resistance to those taxes. In May 1988, the townspeople began refusing to pay. The army of occupation then imposed a series of lengthy curfews and instituted a heavy military presence. The citizens responded with a sit-down strike in the streets, which resulted in further curfews, beatings and mass arrests. In the summer of 1989, the Israelis began systematically to raid homes, shops and the small factories of the town; frequently, in typical police-state fashion, in the middle of the night, beating up the people, taking hostages and confiscating possessions, often to a value much in excess of the amounts supposedly owed in taxes. There was also a great deal of individual looting by Israeli troops.

To try to prevent public knowledge of what was happening, Beit Sahur was surrounded and subjected to a siege which went on for six weeks, during which no-one was allowed into the town and all food, medical and other supplies were also excluded in an attempt to starve the people into submission. Eventually, on 5 November 1989, with the lifting of the siege, a many hundreds strong assembly of sympathetic Israelis and people from western countries managed to reach the town, marched through it en masse and held a Judaic-Christian-Muslim ecumenical prayer service. A message of support was read out from former President Jimmy Carter of the USA (2). In the face of such a demonstration of international protest, even the Israeli army did not dare to interfere but the demonstration did not prevent the continuation of the savage oppression throughout the occupied territories.

In the last days and hours of 1989, when the people of Romania were celebrating the overthrow of the Ceausescu dictatorship, while the German people were celebrating the end of dictatorship in East Germany and the end of the Berlin wall, and people everywhere were hoping for a new decade of peaceful progress, Israeli forces broke up an international, non-violent demonstration in support of peace and goodwill which took place in Jerusalem.

The idea of the demonstration, an outstanding example of

---

(2) *News Report*, Middle East Council of Churches, October-November 1989.

international NGO co-operation, originated at the European Nuclear Disarmament Convention held in Spain in July 1989. It was called "1990, Time for Peace" and the preparatory committee, which was based in Rome, announced it as an initiative for "a decade of peace for all peoples at a time when the road of disarmament has been undertaken but when many conflicts are still tragically unsolved." Based in "support for the Palestinian people struggling for their rights and for the forces of peace and realism in Israel" it was based on the principles of "negotiations for peace and respect for human and civil rights, two states and two peoples." The 1989 European and International NGO meetings on the Question of Palestine, held in Vienna, endorsed the initiative and a great deal of preparatory work was done in Europe, America and the Middle East. In Israel, the arrangements were co-ordinated by Peace Now in co-operation with other Israeli peace and conciliation organizations. The principle features were to be a women's peace march from West to East Jerusalem on Friday, 29 December and the formation of a chain of people linking arms the following day round the walls of the old city of Jerusalem, a distance of four kilometres.

Five thousand women, predominantly Israelis, participated in the march and they were harassed throughout by security forces. Among participants who were beaten up was an Italian Member of the European Parliament, Dacia Valent. A number of Palestinian bystanders, although taking no part, were beaten up and arrested. Major Derek Cooper of CAABU, whose wife Pamela was in the march, repeatedly remonstrated with security forces and on asking why they did not arrest him, was told "Because you are not an Arab."

On Saturday, 30 December, twenty-two thousand people gathered to link arms round old Jerusalem. One witness, Ian Black, Jerusalem correspondent of *The Guardian* newspaper, described them as:-

> ... linking hands happily ... Coloured balloons, T-shirts and sprigs of olive branches mingled in a golden bright winter's afternoon, a colourful, almost carnival scene where Hebrew, Arabic and a dozen other languages babbled a message of peace for 1990 ... monks and nuns, Jews and Muslims, old and young, chanting, singing and united in a rare moment of hope.(3)

---

(3) *The Guardian*, London and Manchester, 1 January 1990.

There had been ominous signs though. Peace Now's application to hold the demonstration had been granted only grudgingly. Jean-Marie Lambert, Executive Director of the office in Geneva of the International Co-ordinating Committee on Palestine, and Mikko Lohikoski of Helsinki, Chairman of the European Co-ordinating Committee of NGO's on the Question of Palestine and a driving force behind the initiative, were both turned back at Tel Aviv airport and denied access to Israel. A Soviet delegation were denied visas.

As the final links were formed in the chain at Herod's gate, the demonstrators were attacked with gunfire, water cannon and toxic gas. Police and border guards, the latter particularly noted for their brutality, lashed out indiscriminately with heavy batons. At least seventy people were injured. Among those attacked were representatives of the media seeking to record the event. Seventy-eight people were arrested. Scores of road blocks were set up and thousands of Palestinians from outside Jerusalem were prevented from attending (4).

Throughout 1989, to parallel the physical suppression of dissent in Israel and Palestine, there was also an Israeli political offensive to delay progress towards negotiations, aimed principally at the USA, where Ronald Reagan had been succeeded by George Bush and where the Israeli lobby remained more powerful than in any other country. Thoroughly alarmed by the US-PLO talks, even at the low level in Tunis, the Israeli government produced its spurious plan for elections to appoint Israeli approved Palestinians to talk about the future of the occupied territories. It was basic to the plan that there would be no question of self-determination and that the purpose of any talks would simply be to ensure the subjugation of the territories under permanent Israeli occupation. The plan was designed to exclude the PLO, to destroy the US-PLO talks and to lead to the sort of stalemate which had served the Israeli establishment so well in the past.

President Mubarak of Egypt put forward "ten points" to try to resolve the deadlock. That came to nothing and then came the "five points" of the American Secretary of State, James Baker. The

---

(4) Eyewitness accounts given to the author, including the estimated 22,000 demonstrators, usually reported as 30,000 in the international media. Also reported by Daoud Kattab, Jerusalem correspondent of *Middle East International,* London, No. 366, 5 January 1990.

Baker points amounted to little more than an endorsement of the Israeli "election" proposal and a by-passing of the PLO. So the nineteen-eighties, which had at one stage seemed to hold out hope for progress, ended in deadlock and continuing bloodshed. By then, the Palestinian Declaration of Independence had been recognized by more than one hundred countries, the Palestinian people, who were continuing to suffer so much, remained undefeated and as united and determined as ever but, not surprisingly, they were increasingly demanding to know why it was that while they were sacrificing so much, the rest of the world seemed immobilized and uncaring.

Israel was deeply divided, with an important minority very conscious of the immoral path upon which the country was set. But they were a minority and survey after survey indicated that the majority, especially among the younger generation, held racist, anti-Arab views and favoured the expulsion of the Palestinians by force. That was, in fact, the ultimate although hidden objective of the government, as the Deputy Foreign Minister, Benjamin Netanyahu, revealed when he said, in reference to the massacre of Chinese students who had campaigned for democracy in Tiananmen Square, Beijing, in the summer of 1989 :-

> Israel should have exploited the repression of the demonstrations in China, when world attention was focused on that country, to carry out mass expulsions among the Arabs of the territories. Regrettably, there was no support for this policy, which I put forward then and still recommend. (5)

The ultimate objective was blatantly confirmed by the Prime Minister, Yitshak Shamir, in a speech to Likud Party members in Tel Aviv on 14 January 1990, on the subject of the immigration of Jews from the Soviet Union. He announced that for the next five to seven years, they would be entering at a rate of 100,000 to 120,000 a year. It would be imperative therefore, he said, to retain the West Bank and the Gaza Strip to house all those people. Israel, he said, was required to be big and, within five years, the country would be bigger and stronger and changed demographically beyond recognition.

What he was announcing was no more than the latest

(5) Reported, *Hotam*, Israel, 24 November 1989. English translation *Israeli Mirror* No. 793, 30 November 1989.

development in a long standing plan. Not least among Israel's problems, right from its establishment, had been the massive refusal of Jews from the West to settle there. So a campaign of hate had been organized against the USSR, based in the alleged persecution of its Jewish community and calling for "the release of Soviet Jewry." But, when Jews had started leaving the USSR in substantial numbers in the late nineteen-seventies and through the eighties, the very large majority, eighty-five per cent or more, had not settled in Israel. They were, on the whole, educated, highly-skilled professional people more concerned to find a rewarding outlet for self-fulfilment in a freer society than to settle in the Zionist state and they simply refused to go there. The migrants' route was via Vienna and, once arrived in that city, the large majority opted not to go to Israel. Their choice of destination was overwhelmingly the USA.

In 1989, the Bush administration surrendered to prolonged and persistent Israeli pressure and restricted their entry severely. Hence Shamir's claim that hundreds of thousands would be forced into immigration into Israel. As the American restrictions started to bite at the turn of the year, there was a dramatic increase although it did not measure up to Shamir's claims. During 1989, 13,000 out of 71,000 who left the Soviet Union entered Israel (of whom about 2,000 subsequently re-emigrated); in December, the monthly average of entrants quadrupled and a further 4,000 arrived in January 1990. The Jewish Agency estimated that 50,000 were to be expected in each of the first two years of the new decade (6). That was a far cry from Shamir's forecast but even so it indicated a very significant change, especially since the placing of those people in the illegal settlements in the occupied territories was set in hand immediately.

There was another aspect to the whole undertaking. Shimon Peres, in his days as Prime Minister, had proposed that Soviet Jews should be transferred compulsorily in non-stop flights from the Soviet Union to Tel Aviv, so that they would be deprived of the choice offered by the staging post in Vienna. In February 1990, James Baker, during consultations in Moscow and on the instructions of the President, formally requested the Soviet government to institute an "air bridge" of direct flights to Israel, a request which the Soviet authorities emphatically rejected, pointing

(6) *Middle East International,* London, No. 368, 2 February 1990, article by Haim Baram.

out that emigrants from the USSR were free to go where they wished. That the President and the Secretary of State could be so used as mouthpieces of the Israeli lobby was a striking demonstration of the power of the lobby in the United States. It was also a commentary on how the world was changing, when the President and the Secretary of State from "the land of the free" could propose compulsory transfer to the government of what Ronald Reagan had called "the evil empire."

What remained was that there was serious cause for concern over the huge planned increase in immigration, for it was a plan for the calculated wrecking of any hopes of justice for the Palestinians, upon which ultimately rested all hopes for peace. Shamir's speech could have been a last ditch stand by an aging and beleaguered Prime Minister for the Greater Israel of his life's dreams but whether that was so or not, it indicated a massive new problem for the nineteen-nineties.

Yet another cause for concern lay in the likely impact inside Israel. The arrival of such large numbers of mainly unwilling immigrants would put a severe strain both on the divided society and on the shaky economy. The chairman of the Immigration and Absorption Committee of the Knesset, Michael Kleiner, admitted that there would be huge difficulties. He estimated that the cost of absorbing just 300,000 would amount to one third of the Israeli budget, which would mean severe and unpopular cuts in living standards while, if Israel failed to provide housing and funding for their settlement, it would drive the immigrants to leave and lead ultimately "to the destruction of Israel." Immediate demands were placed on world Jewry to finance the immigration, including £20m. on the British Jewish community and $420m. on the American - a singular irony given the American role in creating the situation which was supposed to be so good for Israel.

What Kleiner said he feared most of all was that the defence budget would have to be cut to pay immigration costs, which would mean cutting the defence budget of "the state whose survival depends on military force." (7) Like Natanyahu's reference to the massacre of Chinese students, it was a frank and ominous admission of the real policy of the Zionist state. From every aspect, the new development was an ominous pointer for the new decade.

---

(7) Reported, *Palestine*, PLO Information Bulletin, Vol. 14 No. 101, 16 February 1990.

So, although the nineteen-nineties opened with turbulent changes and growing hopes in many places, they opened with deadlock and foreboding in the Middle East. As so often in the past, official Israeli policy was successfully blocking all international moves which might implement the world consensus for Palestinian self-determination and independence. Much of the world outside the Middle East, upon which so much depended and which had been so stirred by the bravery of the Palestinians, seemed, superficially at least, to have lost interest and to be more concerned with developments in Europe.

By any standards, what was happening in Europe was of the most profound importance. But what was happening in the Middle East was no less important for, there too, there was a great surge to replace dictatorship with democracy. Just like those in Europe who were struggling against tyrannies established in their countries forty years earlier. The Palestinian people were struggling against a tyranny originally established in their land at about the same time. In Europe, only in Romania did a long standing dictatorship try to put down the people's rising with comparable methods but, whereas the dictatorship there had already been defeated, that in Palestine had not.

## 2. The New Europe

During the cold war, the Middle East was an arena for superpower confrontation, with the Reagan administration seeing it as a vital region for "the containment of Communism." Well before that, successive administrations had seen the Shah of Iran as the principal policeman of American interests in the region. With the replacement of the Shah by the virulently anti-American Khomeini regime, Washington saw Israel as replacing Iran in the role of American policeman. That suited Israel very well and successive Israeli governments, backed up by their immensely powerful lobby in the US, had exploited the situation, not only to obtain huge American military and financial support, but virtually to control American policy for the furtherance of their own expansionist plans.

It has been an essential part of American strategy to keep the Soviet Union out of the Middle East and excluded, like the PLO, from negotiations on the Palestine issue. With Israel seen as a vital "strategic asset" the US opposed criticism of Israel in the United

Nations and vetoed every move in the Security Council to pressure Israel to negotiate, and that continued to be American policy even as the cold war was thawing out, notwithstanding that in that period, the Soviet Union had exerted heavy influence on the PLO to modify its policy to make it more acceptable to the United States. But, as the PLO found, whatever concessions it made, the rules were promptly changed to make the concessions unacceptable.

By 1990, even the United States was becoming impatient with Israeli intransigence. On 16 January, Senator Robert Dole, the influential Republican leader in the Senate and one time aspirant for the Presidency, opened a new approach when he suggested in an article in the *New York Times* that there should be a five per cent cut in American aid to the most favoured recipients and that the money should be used instead to help the newly emerging democracies in Central and Eastern Europe. By far and away the most favoured recipient of American aid was Israel. Senator Dole went further, referring, indirectly but unmistakably, to the Israel lobby as a pressure group which had turned the aid given to Israel virtually into an entitlement. It was the first time in many years that a senior political figure had dared openly to challenge the lobby. The challenge was quickly supported in a White House statement with a clear implication that American aid could be cut if Israel continued to obstruct efforts for peace.

The implication was only related to the Israeli refusal to participate in the American-Egyptian-Israeli talks proposed in the "five points" put forward by James Baker, who might well have been the real initiator of the Dole letter. The Baker talks were little more than a signpost to a blind alley, irrelevant to the basic requirement for Palestinian self-determination and the involvement of the PLO, but the significance was that the huge American support, without which Israel could not survive, could be reconsidered and used to pressure Israel if it continued refusing to respond to American attempts at mediation. Another indication that thinking in powerful circles was moving that way came just a few weeks later in a pointed statement to the *Wall Street Journal* on 8 February by Senator Robert Bird, Chairman of the Senate Appropriations Committee, who said "Some countries, certainly the largest of our historic aid recipients, can probably take cuts substantially larger than five per cent. Somewhere between ten and twenty per cent would be more realistic."

With the end of the cold war, not only were American priorities changing but Israel's claim to be an American asset in the Middle East was losing credibility. Without the massive injection of American aid, the Israeli economy would collapse. So it was in the power of the United States to bring Israel to the negotiating table. Talking had never worked as a method of persuasion and the question for the nineteen-nineties was whether the will would develop in Washington to use the sanctions which were well within its power to bring peace to the Middle East.

No less crucial was whether real co-operation could develop with the Soviet Union for the settlement of the Palestine question. It was in the vital interests of both powers to have a peaceful Middle East and Palestine was the key whose turning could open the way for progress towards settling all the other conflicts and problems of the region, thereby releasing a huge potential to benefit the whole globe. The Middle East, having been an area for confrontation between the superpowers, was now an area crying out for their co-operation.

But the nineteen-nineties opened with the Soviet Union deeply pre-occupied with other problems. Its economy was in a parlous condition and for all the political reforms instituted by Mikhail Gorbachev, there were serious shortages of basic necessities among an increasingly impatient population. The Baltic republics were demanding greater freedom from Moscow and even secession from the Union. The overthrow of the Romanian dictatorship had brought demands for the secession of Moldavia and its re-union with Romania. There was serious trouble in Armenia and in other, predominantly Muslim, southern republics. If there were questions for the USA for the new decade, there were profound questions for the USSR and, together, those questions seriously hampered prospects for co-operation between the two countries to resolve the situation in the Middle East.

There were those for whom the ending of the cold war was not welcome. The economy of much of the western capitalist world was geared to a military-industrial complex for which a cold war of some sort was a necessity. Cold warmongers, with all their basic assumptions under challenge, were neither capable of understanding the significance of what was happening nor of accepting it. One camp among them gloated at the Soviet difficulties and took a line that "the wounded bear in the death throes of the Communist empire" could provide a continuing and arguably even greater threat to the "democratic West." Another camp was busily creating a new international ogre in the shape of "the hordes of Islam" who were supposedly massing to overwhelm "Western Christendom." For that camp, this was to be the new threat in the nineteen-nineties against which a new cold war would be maintained thereby preserving the military-industrial complex and conceivably even giving it room for expansion, by uniting an ailing and frightened Russia with the West because the Soviet Union had its own problems related to its large Muslim population. Both scenarios boded ill for any possibility of settlement in the Middle East. The second scenario was even more ominous than the first for it envisaged the Middle East becoming more, not less, a region for confrontation.

In Europe, by the advent of the nineteen-nineties, the centuries old civilization which had come close to self-destruction in the first half of the century, was vigorously re-establishing itself. Visionaries were already referring to earlier decades as the period of "the European civil war," The European Community was moving to full economic union and becoming a de facto Confederate States of Europe. The overthrow of the dictatorships in Central and Eastern Europe, the end of the artificial, cold war division of the continent, East and West Germany moving towards re-unification, all this was paving the way towards the re-establishment of Europe as the centre of gravity of global politics. Immense problems remained and new ones were being created, not least in the re-unification of Germany and the attitude of the right-wing West German Chancellor Kohl that re-unification meant a West German capitalist takeover rather than a merger on a basis of an equal coming together of the divided German peoples. However, feelings which were widespread were summed up by George Schopflin, who wrote of 1989:-

> It was the year when Europe grew up and shook off the legacy of the Great European Civil War of 1914-45 and began to redefine itself in its own terms and against the now declining superpowers which had exercised tutelage over it for so long[8].

To what extent could this new, invigorated Europe redefine itself for an active role to bring peace in the Middle East?

---

(8) Article in *International Affairs*, Royal Institute of International Affairs, London, Vol. 66, No. 1 January 1990.

A decade earlier, the Council of Ministers, the policy making body of the EC, had made an attempt to do so in the Venice Declaration, but that attempt had come to nothing. It had been declared at Venice that the Community countries were obliged by traditional ties and common interests with the Middle East to work towards peace and that they intended to make contact with all parties to the conflict with a view to formulating an EC peace initiative. The Venice Declaration had called for Israeli withdrawal from the occupied territories and had described the colonizing settlements as illegal in international law and a serious obstacle to peace. The Declaration had called for justice and self-determination for the Palestinians and for the PLO to be a party to negotiations.

Within days. the Israelis had launched an international campaign to destroy the Venice Declaration. Through their embassies and their lobbies, it was attacked and undermined in the individual EC countries and also in the USA, with the assertion that it was an impediment to the Camp David "peace process" which had been initiated under President Carter in 1978. Under American pressure, the European countries fell obediently into line and within months the Israeli government was announcing that the Declaration was dead. But the humiliating collapse of American policy which came after the Israeli invasion of Lebanon showed that it was Camp David, not Venice, that was dead and in March 1984, the Foreign Ministers of the EC countries issued a strong, updated reaffirmation of the Declaration. However, for the rest of the decade, such initiatives as they attempted amounted to little more than ineffective attempts to persuade the USA to take a less one-sided approach.

By the turn of the decade, though, the newly-invigorated Community was taking a stronger and increasingly independent line, not only reiterating constantly that the principles of the Venice Declaration remained the basis of its policy, but adding to those principles. In a declaration issued in Madrid in June 1989, the Council of Ministers not only called for recognition of the right to self-determination of the Palestinian people "with all that this implies" but they also called for an international peace conference under United Nations auspices in which the PLO should participate. They also stipulated that any elections in the occupied territories would have to be set in the context of a process towards a comprehensive, just and lasting settlement, would have to take place under adequate guarantees of freedom and must also include the Palestinians, whom Shamir proposed to exclude, of the (illegally annexed) territory of East Jerusalem. The European Parliament, too, was becoming highly critical of Israeli conduct, and the breaking up of the peace demonstration in Jerusalem, in which Members of the Parliament had participated, with one of them being beaten up by the Israeli security forces, had turned spoken criticism into practical action.

The powers of the Parliament were limited. The policy making Council of Ministers were responsible to their respective national parliaments. There was a continuing argument over what powers the European Parliament should have, the various national parliaments, the British in particular, being wary of the extent to which the powers of the European Parliament might supersede their own. This somewhat begged the question of control over the Commission, the powerful executive body which controlled the vast bureaucracy and which was not elected, its members being appointed by the governments of the member countries, but over which the Members of the elected European Parliament felt that they should exercise greater control. However, one field in which the Parliament did exercise ultimate authority was the budget which, prepared by the Commission, was subject to parliamentary approval. The Parliament now moved to use its authority over budgetary allocations.

On 18 January 1990, they adopted a wide-ranging resolution which noted that the Palestinian people were looking to the international community and in particular the European Community, to play a more active role in the search for peace in the Middle East. Only a month earlier (14 December) the Parliament had strongly condemned the closure of the schools and universities in the occupied territories which had been enforced since the start of the Intifada. Now, they called on the Commission to freeze immediately the budget allocation for scientific co-operation with Israel. In response, the Commission announced the indefinite suspension of co-operation on high technology research (worth about £7m. annually), they cancelled an official visit to Israel by Abel Matutes, the Commissioner responsible for Mediterranean Affairs and postponed consultations designed to prepare Israeli exporters for the single European market of 1992. Meanwhile, the Community's contribution to UNRWA was increased and direct aid to the occupied territories was doubled.

In their resolution, the Parliament had also called on the

Commission to examine "closely" and to report on whether treaties between the EC and Israel were being observed, in particular with reference to products from the occupied territories. That, too, went to the heart of another aspect of community policy over which the Parliament exercised real power.

Israel enjoyed a highly privileged trading relationship with the Community, to which it sent thirty per cent of its exports and took fifty per cent of its imports. Its exports were exempted from community tariffs, although it imposed its own tariffs on imports from Europe. In 1988, the European Parliament had exercised its power to hold up the renewal of trade protocols which authorised this privileged relationship, until the Israelis agreed to allow access on equal terms for Palestinian produce from the occupied territories. Faced with the prospect of damaging sanctions, the Israeli government, after furious resistance, was forced to agree, but it then proceeded to do everything in its power to obstruct the exports, including destruction at source of Palestinian agriculture by burning and chemicals. It was a blatant example of how Israel was not observing its treaties with the European Community.

So the Community entered the new decade with all three of its governing institutions - the policy making Council of Ministers, the executive Commission and the elected Parliament - increasingly critical towards Israeli conduct and taking practical measures to curb it. Growing in power and in confidence, the Community was in a strong position to influence events. With the limitations on American capacity for action caused by the strength of the Israeli lobby and the limitations on the Soviet capacity caused by their internal economic and political situation, it was the European Community which was most strongly placed to take practical action in the cause of peace and justice. It was in the Community's power to make clear to the Israeli government that it was not prepared to tolerate Israel's brutal repression of the Palestinians, refusal to come to the negotiating table and contemptuous flouting of treaty obligations, and that Israel could not expect to maintain its highly privileged trading status with the Community if it persisted in such courses. What remained to be seen was the extent to which the Community would be prepared to exert its growing economic and political power to implement its declared intention to work towards peace in the Middle East.

What is required most fundamentally for peace is justice for the

Palestinians which does no injustice to the Israelis. It could be attained through a two-state solution. That is to say through an independent Palestinian state comprised of the West Bank and the Gaza Strip, with communication between the two via Israel and with the integrity of Palestine and Israel internationally guaranteed through the United Nations. Jerusalem is the natural capital for both countries and locating both capitals there would be an important factor to achieve full co-operation between the two. Such a settlement could lead ultimately to a Middle East Economic Community which, apart from its huge value to the region and the world, would guarantee Israel's acceptance by its neighbours.

Moves to attain such a peaceful settlement could only be brought about through negotiations between the PLO and Israel on equal terms and under international auspices. As the twentieth century moved into its final decade, there was a world consensus for both the solution and the means to achieve it, but although enlightened people in Israel were part of that consensus, the Israeli government remained resolutely outside it. Israeli citizens who met PLO representatives to talk about peace were put in prison and there was little sign, unless there should be changes as dramatic as those in Europe, that any government was likely to be formed which would be prepared for realistic negotiations.

Both main parties, Labour as well as Likud, refused to recognize that the PLO was accepted by the Palestinian people as their representative body and in effect as their government - as would manifestly be confirmed in any free and properly conducted elections in the occupied territories. The conflict could clearly not be settled by negotiations while the government of the one party to the conflict refused absolutely to negotiate with the government of the other party or to recognize its people's right even to live in, leave alone govern their own homeland.

With the official Israeli side so opposed to negotiations and with powerful voices in the country calling for the annexation of the occupied territories with the displacement of the inhabitants and their replacement by immigrants, it was clear that international intervention was essential for a settlement which would be just to both sides and prevent further and wider conflict. Both the United States and the European Community had the means to exert strong economic pressure for peace. The latter was the more advanced in inclination to use its economic power and in its perception of the nature of the conflict. With Europe no longer divided by the cold war, the centre of gravity of global politics was moving towards that invigorated and swiftly changing continent. What remained to be seen at the opening of the nineteen-nineties was if either Europe or America, and preferably both, had the political will to exert their economic power for peace in the Middle East.

# EPILOGUE

## VARIATIONS

### 1. Theme and Thoughts Arising

Not least among the products of the Palestinian struggle has been a growth of artistic creativity. It is an aspect of the struggle which is as important and interesting as the politics. It has led to art with a powerful social and political message and the growth is accelerating. I have long believed that artists who claim to be socially and politically uninvolved are the poorer for it and that there is a corollary in that to be in politics without some interest in the arts is also to be the poorer. Hence the bringing together of art and politics in this epilogue, through using an interest in listening to music which I mentioned in the prologue (P 9), as a theme for a set of variations. Certainly, these will move beyond the issue of Palestine but philosophically they will not be irrelevant to it.

My interest in the Middle East became active with the 1967 war when, as a recently elected Member of Parliament, I was shocked by the conduct of the Zionist lobby towards any MP who dared to question Israeli conduct. To become actively interested was to become involved inextricably but not to be consumed to the exclusion of all else, and in the same period, my interest in music which, like my interest in the Middle East, was previously rather peripheral, also broadened and deepened.

When I took over the directorship of CAABU in September 1983, awareness of the growth in Palestinian culture was already developing and CAABU was heavily involved in preparations for a Palestinian cultural festival. This was to be held in London and to last a week as part of the celebration of the United Nations International Day of Solidarity with the Palestinian People, which is observed annually on 29 November, the anniversary of the 1947 Partition Resolution. The idea for the festival had originated among Palestinians working and studying in Britain and CAABU had agreed to their request for help with the administration.

Organizing the festival proved to be a nightmare. Most of those who had thought up the idea had little capacity for advance preparation and they were riven with dissension into the bargain. Then there were people in Arab countries who accepted invitations to participate but who applied to British consulates for visas only a day or two before their scheduled departure and so could not obtain visas in time and thought that they then only had to telephone CAABU to get strings pulled so that they could get visas. Others did not reply to invitations but arrived nevertheless. Others who had not been invited arrived and expected to be accommodated in expensive hotels at someone else's expense.

Yet the festival was an astonishing success. Audiences attended the events in surprising numbers. On Tuesday, 29 November itself, in the middle of the festival, there were a thousand people at what was the high spot. Faisal Aouidha and I made brief speeches. I spoke on the way in which every great revolution had been accompanied by a wave of artistic creativity. Afterwards, a German lady who had made a point of travelling to London for the festival made a point of telling me how especially thrilled she was because I referred to the way Beethoven was inspired by the French Revolution!

The new growth of Palestinian creativity has been most notable in writing and painting. The trend in music has been mainly in song, although to my knowledge there is at least one interesting exploration of the European orchestral tradition in the work of the composer Youssef Khasho, who was born in Jerusalem in 1927. I was once given a set of records, two in number, of his fourth and fifth symphonies, performed respectively by the Rome Theatre Orchestra and the Naples Symphony Orchestra, both conducted by the composer. The two works are linked under the title *The Great Arab Revolution.* They may not provide strikingly innovative music to European ears, while the anonymous programme notes are over-eulogistic of the Jordanian Hashemite dynasty, but the music is very melodic and deeply reflective not only of the Palestinian struggle but also of the pan-Arab struggle against successive Ottoman, European and Zionist colonialism.

Every great, convulsive struggle for social justice has inspired its own surge of creativity. How much poorer the world would be without the huge inspiration derived by Milton from the English Civil War and Commonwealth, or that derived by Beethoven from the ideals of the French Revolution, or by Shostakovich from the ideals of the Russian Revolution. Like those and many others, well-known and lesser-known, the Palestinian writers, painters and musicians in the late twentieth century have an inescapable sense of involvement in the great events of their time and, not surprisingly, above all in the aspirations of their own people.

For that matter, no-one can opt out of the great issues of his or her times or out of the politics of those issues, creative artists less so than most. Richard Strauss despised politics and politicians. However, he had a lifelong and very legitimate concern to improve the status of musicians and, when the Nazis made him President of their Reich Music Chamber in 1933 because they wanted to exploit his great international reputation for their own purposes, he naively supposed from his apolitical stance that he could use the position to help fellow artists. Two years later he resigned, his resignation pre-empting his dismissal, because he was by then under Gestapo surveillance for his unswerving support for his librettist and friend Stefan Zweig. To the last days of the Nazi regime, he worked, at no small risk, to protect Jewish friends and his Jewish daughter-in-law, but his naive association with the Nazis in their early days in power did lasting damage to his reputation. It is an object lesson to demonstrate that there is no such thing as not being in politics, We are all in politics, whether we acknowledge it or not, because the decisions taken by politicians self-evidently affect the daily lives of each and every one of us.

Long before the Nazi era, Strauss when a young man played an important part in making known the music of Elgar, and there is a recording of one of Elgar's masterpieces *Serenade for Strings,* which dates from those early days and which for me has special associations. It is a recording in which Yehudi Menuhin conducts the English Chamber Orchestra (1). I have never met Sir Yehudi Menuhin but (at the risk of sounding like a bad parody of the satirical song about Lloyd George) I knew his father.

One of the most memorable days of my life, in September 1969, was spent with his father, Moshe, at his home in Los Gatos,

---

(1) Arabesque Z6563. issued 1986 (compact disc).

California. Moshe Menuhin was one of the greatest of all Jewish campaigners against Zionist excesses. Another is Dr Israel Shahak, a survivor of the Belsen death camp and long time President of the Israeli League for Civil and Human Rights. I have had the privilege of meeting both these great men, both assuredly cast in the mould of the prophets of old. When I visited Moshe Menuhin, he gave me a copy of his pamphlet *Quo Vadis Zionist Israel?* which was a "postscript" added after the 1967 war to his monumental book *The Decadence of Judaism in Our Time* (New York, 1965. Second impression, including postscript, Institute of Palestine Studies, Beirut, 1969). On the title page he wrote :

> To David Watkins, with hope that you will accomplish deeds of bravery in your struggle to bring justice to the innocent Arab victims of insane 'Jewish' nationalism. With all good wishes, Moshe Menuhin, Los Gatos, California, September 6 1969. The day we first met. I hope, not the last time.

Sadly, it did prove to be the last time, although we corresponded subsequently and he later sent me a copy of his book, which he inscribed :

> To David Watkins MP, in hopes that this book will strengthen your convictions about doing justice to the innocent victims of insane 'Jewish' nationalism!

When Yehudi Menuhin was only sixteen, he made the first ever recording of Elgar's violin concerto, with the composer conducting. The following year, he played it again in Paris, in a concert arranged by his father, at whose specific request Elgar again conducted. From my acquaintance with Moshe Menuhin, I feel a sort of link, however fanciful and distant, with Elgar himself. During his lifetime, Elgar suffered hostility and neglect from within a snobbish British musical establishment because of his humble origins in the rigid English class system. I shall come back to that later. Meanwhile, this seems an appropriate point to turn to Mahler - a contemporary of both Richard Strauss and Elgar in their younger days - another composer of gigantic talent who was also derided in his lifetime.

In the manner of a prominent parliamentarian who was once described to me by another as a teetotaller who had discovered the pleasures of alcohol late in life, I am a music listener who discovered the pleasures of Mahler late in life. I can however plead that latter-day addiction to Mahler is an international phenomenon. In his lifetime, he suffered ridicule and abuse. By the nineteen-eighties, practically every symphony orchestra in the world was playing and recording his works. Beethoven cast a long shadow all down the nineteenth century. Mahler has cast an even longer one all down the twentieth century.

A personal favourite among his works is his first symphony, which combines lyrical description of the beauty of nature with savage satire of the society which mankind has created in the midst of such beauty. Mahler wrote of the opening "Spring without end, the introduction depicts the awakening of nature in the early morning." The second movement gives a picture of people dancing and enjoying themselves in the country but Mahler's analysis is forcefully expressed when the dance rhythm goes on to become the steps of a funeral march. It is a grotesque funeral march, injecting deliberately vulgar Viennese dance music into a biting parody based in an old South German fairy tale, in which animals and birds dance with understandable joy as they follow the funeral procession of a huntsman. The last movement opens with a despairing outburst, expressing all the anguish of a deeply sensitive human being over the world around him. Then the movement gradually brings together all the conflicting elements and resolves the work in a stupendous expression of belief in a better existence. This remarkable symphony is among my favourites as much for its scathing expression of Mahler's view of society as for the outstanding brilliance of the music.

When Mahler conducted the first performance, in Budapest in 1889, it was greeted with jeering derision and the scene was set for the sort of reception his work was mostly to receive for the rest of his life. What upset the critics most of all was the scathing parody of the funeral march. The biting social comment may or may not have been fully understood at the time, making as it does a contrast between honest peasants and the effete aristocracy of the declining Hapsburg Empire. In that rigid, class-divided society, the middle-class critics were in a quandary. They were despised by the ruling aristocracy and they were frightened by the growing aspirations of the working class. On the credit side, one result was that they took refuge in the arts, where they were the supreme class, so that there was a remarkable flowering of creative genius in the last decades of imperial Vienna, not even surpassed in the freer society of Paris.

Critical inability to accept what appeared in his lifetime as difficult, radical music was by no means the only factor in the hostility towards Mahler. Another factor was the virulent anti-Jewish racism which was rampant in Imperial Austria-Hungary. His impressive and dignified personality, which to me seems to jump right out of photographs of him, and his huge achievements did not prevent his being referred to as "that dwarf Jew." It was the atmosphere which influenced Theodor Herzl, who was Mahler's contemporary in Vienna, to produce his pamphlet *Der Judenstadt* (*The Jewish State*) in which he set out the creed of Zionism, in 1896. The following year, Herzl founded and became the first President of the World Zionist Organization. It always seems to me to be instructive to compare those two remarkable contemporaries and their respective legacies.

Moshe Menuhin wrote of Herzl in The Decadence of Judaism in Our Time (p. 36) that :

> The disabilities, injustices and exploitations that the common masses of the Gentile world lived through and revolted against escaped him completely. He could not and would not see the evolution of history, the struggle for the emancipation of the entire world, the brotherhood of man that was evolving gradually and most painfully, but surely.

What a contrast there was between what that narrow, tunnel vision produced and what Mahler's vision produced. Herzl's reaction to anti-semitism was to set in motion what was to become one of the longest and most bitter disputes of the twentieth century. Mahler's vision encompassed all humanity and in his work he sought to express all human experience. His achievement was to create great music, essentially of the twentieth century but likely to live long beyond it.

During a musical package holiday in Austria in 1989, I saw, at the Bregenz Festival, a brilliant production of Saint-Saen's *Samson and Delilah* which was vividly remindful of the outcome of Herzl's theory. The tour company had provided programme notes within which it was stated:

> The action of the opera takes place in Gaza .... The Israelites are in despair because of their subjection to the Philistines, which involves forced labour. Samson gradually arouses them to defiance ...

What irony! - given the despair of the Palestinians, the contemporary "Philistines" in Gaza, descendants of those of biblical times, enduring the brutal subjection of the contemporary "Israelites" and finally aroused, after years of suffering, to defiance in the Intifada.

## 2. Andante - Accelerando

My interest in music started in schooldays, to reminiscences of which I turn for the continuation of these meditations.

When I was at school in the nineteen-thirties and forties in my native city of Bristol, the eleven-plus system of educational segregation was in full swing. At the age of eleven, you were subjected to an examination which was then known as "the scholarship." If you were lucky enough to be in the top ten per cent or so in this lottery, you qualified for a place in one of the Local Authority's "secondary schools" - which were subsequently renamed "grammar schools" in the post-war reconstruction. If you were luckier still and got into the top two per cent or so, you could even secure a place in a direct grant grammar school. The vast, ninety per cent or so majority, except for another small, select group within which I was lucky enough to find myself, were allocated to the Local Authority's "elementary schools" - which were subsequently renamed "secondary schools" and whose pupils finished their formal education at the age of fourteen.

The Eleven-plus system was an important pillar in sustaining the social order. At the pinnacle of the order were the ruling oligarchy who opted out of the state system completely by buying their children's education in the mis-named "public" schools. Grammar schools were run as inferior copies of the "public" schools; secondary schools were run as inferior copies of the grammar schools. Both grammar and secondary schools took a substantial proportion of children from fee-paying, middle-class families and eleven-plus segregation was an important piece of social engineering to separate potential working-class leaders from their fellows and make them safe for the retention of the established order.

My own educational speed was not among the sprinters. It was much more among the walkers, albeit at a faster rather than a slower walking pace and, when I took the eleven-plus in 1936, it was without expectation of any exceptional luck in the draw. The parents of the lucky ones were notified by post and the list of names, in order of achievement but with no details, was also published in local newspapers. Unsurprisingly, no notification came to my parents but, there, very close to the absolute top of the published list was my name, David John Watkins. I think the list must have been published during the short Whitsun holiday, because I recollect what seemed an interminable period before returning to school. I remained pretty unconvinced that it was me but the effect among parents, grandparents, uncles, aunts, cousins, neighbours and schoolmates was spectacular. All speculation centred around what school I might end up in. Then, as now, people were more concerned with where children were taught than with what they were taught.

When we duly returned to school, our class teacher asked who had heard their results. The sprinkling of lucky ones in the fifty-strong class proudly identified themselves. Everybody, including the teacher, looked at me and I clearly recall saying, very hesitantly, "My name was in the paper, Miss, but I haven't had any letter." Inquiries were telephoned to the Local Authority and it was the head himself who quietly took me aside and told me that it was not me but that I would be "offered a place in one of the central schools." In the years since, I have more than once wondered who my namesake was and what became of him.

Eleven-plus segregation took no account of late developers and it must have deprived the nation of a vast amount of talent. The principles upon which it was based still persist. Even in the apogee of educational reform in the mid-twentieth century, the drive was more to produce a bigger and better middle class than to create an educated democracy. The result is that in the late twentieth century, Britain is one of the worst educated and most socially backward countries in Western Europe. Even in the nineteen-thirties, there were some far-sighted educationists who saw the injustice and the folly of the system. One of the nationally outstanding among them, Robert St. John Reade, years later Alderman and Chairman of the Bristol Education Committee in days when I myself became a member of that body, became a good friend and someone among those who most influenced my thinking in formative years. By the nineteen-thirties, as a result of the efforts of people like him, "central schools" were well established in Bristol and elsewhere.

Their very existence was an early admission of the inadequacies of the falsely based selective system. They catered for a select group who missed out in the eleven-plus but who were thought to be "too good" for the elementary schools.

So I went to South Bristol Central School. The school was housed in slum premises which were so sub-standard that, finally, His Majesty's Inspectors ordered the Local Authority to move the school, lock, stock and barrel. It moved to premises in the centre of the city and, two years later, was moved to a third set of premises back in south Bristol. Both moves were within my four years at the school. In 1940, the year I left "South Central," Bristol's three central schools were abolished, being replaced with technical schools. In its short history, South Central produced two future Members of Parliament. The other one, older than me and now sadly and prematurely dead,. was a good friend and colleague, first on the Bristol City Council and subsequently in the House of Commons, Ted Bishop, later Lord Bishopston.

My form master in my first year at the South Central School was Mr A. E. Scillitoe, who was also the school's music master. He was a martinet, not much liked among the boys, but one thing he did was to arouse in me and in others a lifelong interest in music - even if, in my case, it has been a passive, listening interest rather than an active, participating one. He introduced us to Beethoven's fifth symphony and he taught us the concept of music as an international language - a concept soon made all the more vivid when that tremendous, hammering, "fate knocking at the door" rhythm of the fifth symphony, the morse code letter V (for victory) became a symbol and a rallying call for the resistance throughout Nazi-occupied Europe.

Every year, the school produced a Gilbert and Sullivan opera. As it was an all boys school, the youngest had to take the female parts and, in my first year, I was press-ganged into the chorus of "his sisters and his cousins and his aunts" in *HMS Pinafore.* It was the start of a lifelong devotion to Gilbert and Sullivan. More than twenty years later, I again met Mr Scillitoe who was then, if my memory serves me correctly, principal of a teacher training college in Bristol. I was a member of the Bristol Education Committee and prospective parliamentary candidate for the Bristol North West Constituency. The Gilbert and Sullivan copyright had not long expired and a post-copyright performance of one of the operas had just been given on television. We talked about it and I recall his remark that "South Central boys everywhere would have watched and said 'they did it very well.'" When the copyright expired, there had been an anguished outcry in some quarters, inspired at least in part by the D'Oyly Carte Opera Company, anxious about the loss of their monopoly. There were even calls for Parliament to extend the copyright. Fortunately, such calls were of no avail. Had they been, we could have been stuck for decades with productions frozen in the nineteenth century.

Parliament having no shortage of individuals "fond of uttering platitudes in stained-glass attitudes," Gilbert's wit and Sullivan's music are as applicable there as ever. Only once in my seventeen years membership did I take part in the pantomime of the procession from the Commons to the Lords to hear the speech from the throne, only once I watched the state opening from a seat in the Lords reserved for Members of the Commons, only once I walked in the procession to the Lords for prorogation. In each case the motivation was curiosity to see what it was like. My abiding impression is that these absurd processions would be enhanced if they were accompanied by suitable music and that nothing would be more appropriate than a selection from the brilliant, parliament-knocking *Iolanthe*. Turning to the more realistic side of parliamentary activity, in the division lobby during a late-night vote after a long day at the House, my mind would turn inevitably to Guiseppe's sparkling song from *The Gondoliers* :

> With a pleasure that's emphatic,
> We retire to our attic
> With the gratifying feeling that our duty has been done!

When I started at the South Bristol Central School in 1936, my parents had to contract with the Education Authority to keep me there until I reached the age of fifteen, which was one year later than the then minimum school leaving age. By the time I was fifteen, it was my parents' and my intention that I should stay an additional year in order to take the School Certificate Examination, the forerunner of the GCE and the later GCSE. Access to the "School Cert" was limited to the small minority who were able to remain at school to the age of sixteen. The central schools were not geared to provide for it but they had steadily developed facilities to enable those who wished and who were judged competent, usually not more than half a dozen in a class of forty, to stay an extra year to take the examination.

However, in 1940, the year I was fifteen, the central schools in Bristol were abolished and turned into technical schools. It was felt that these new schools would not be able to cope with aspiring school certificate candidates and a generous Local Authority decided that they were entirely in favour of transferring those who wished to continue their education to municipal secondary schools - provided their parents paid fees for the privilege. Fortunately, my father was able to pay and so I completed my full-time education as a fee-paying pupil at Merrywood Secondary School which, in the post-war reconstruction, became Merrywood Grammar School. I left in the summer of 1941 with what would be the equivalent in later years of six O levels.

Those were of course among the darkest days of the second world war. When I was in my final days at the South Central School, the British army had reeled back to Dunkirk and had been evacuated with the loss of all its equipment, the Battle of France had been lost and the Battle of Britain was beginning. When I started at Merrywood School, the Battle of Britain was at its height. Bristol, with its then great aircraft industry, docks and railway yards, was a prime target for the Luftwaffe and in my first weeks at the new school, we had regularly to take to the air raid shelters. Then, as the winter of 1940-41 approached, with the defeat of the German daylight air offensive, their night-time assault started.

The first night attack on Bristol was on Sunday, 24 November, just ten days after the great attack on Coventry. We lived on the southern edge of Bristol and when we emerged from cover at the end of that first raid, the entire skyline of the city seemed to be ablaze, an awesome, epic, Gotterdammerung scene. It was just the start to a long winter of aerial bombardment. During the longest nights of midwinter, there was one raid of twelve hours of sustained bombing. On the night of Good Friday 1941, there was a raid which hit the south side of the city with exceptional severity. One of my schoolmates at Merrywood and his family were all killed. At the height of the raid, an incendiary bomb hit the dividing wall between our terraced house and the one next door and fell blazing into the front garden. That was actually the second time that happened during that winter of air raids, a remarkable and for us fortunate coincidence. Had the bombs been a few inches either side and gone through the roof of either house, the house would have been gutted.

Britain was of course standing alone then against the might of a seemingly invincible Germany (and in Ankara, the Irgun Zvai Leumi were negotiating with the Nazis, see pages 162 & 173). "We can take it" announced Winston Churchill and every day the newspapers and radio were telling us how high our morale was. It was a myth. Morale was not high. The general feeling was of dispirited acceptance of a situation in which there was no choice except to endure. In later years, when the course of the war had turned, the feeling of the ordinary German people was the same. In 1940-41, we lived in daily expectation of invasion. Had it taken place, the country would have been occupied in weeks. The general feeling was a cynical one that the government and the royal family would decamp to Canada and the people would be left to face the occupation. In fairness though, had the invasion taken place, the war could not have been carried on otherwise.

By the time I left school in 1941, with the German attack on the Soviet Union, the air raids had abated but those were still among the darkest days of the war and remained so for a long time. One defeat succeeded another - Crete, the sinking of the "Prince of Wales" and the "Repulse", the fall of Singapore, the rout of the British army in North Africa. The defeat which remains in my memory as perhaps the most depressing and humiliating of all - just three days after the fall of Singapore - was when the German battlecruisers "Scharnhorst" and "Gneisenau", after being subjected to months of supposedly crippling British bombing at Brest, left harbour and sailed up the Channel, through the Strait of Dover and back to Germany, with Britain seemingly impotent to do anything to hinder them.

From those dark days, two voices remain in my memory as having played a special part in taking the national mood slowly from despair to a grim determination to win through, come what might. The first was the calm, gritty, Yorkshire voice of J. B. Priestley in his famous radio "postscripts." The second was the voice of Vera Lynn, who rose to a rare pinnacle with her wartime songs. Great hits like *Yours*, *When They Sound the Last All Clear*, *When the Lights Go On Again* and *We'll Meet Again* sustained a nation in dark days and gave an early vision of a brighter future. The words were often mawkish and the songs would qualify for what Noel Coward had in mind when he observed "Extraordinary how potent cheap music is," but there was no cheapness in the manner of their delivery or in their impact in the circumstances of the time. My favourite was and remains The White Cliffs of Dover, written by an American who never actually saw the white cliffs until 1989!

> There'll be blue birds over
> The white cliffs of Dove,
> Tomorrow, just you wait and see.
>
> I'll never forget the people I met,
> Braving those angry skies.
> I remember well as the shadows fell,
> The light of hope in their eyes.
> And though I'm far away,
> I still can hear them say
> 'Thumbs up!'
>
> For when the dawn comes up,
> There'll be blue birds over
> The white cliffs of Dover,
> Tomorrow, just you wait and see.
> There'll be love and laughter
> And peace ever after,
> Tomorrow, when the world is free.
>
> The shepherd will tend his sheep,
> The valley will bloom again.
> And Jimmy will go to sleep
> In his own little room again.
> There'll be blue birds over
> The white cliffs of Dover,
> Tomorrow, just you wait and see.
>
> There'll be blue birds over etc.

*The White Cliffs of Dover* is an unforgettable reminder of the mingled hopes, fears and aspirations of the war years and of the ultimate "tomorrow" which finally came. A.J.P.Taylor wrote :

> .....Future historians may see the war as a last struggle for the European balance of power or for the maintenance of Empire. This was not how it appeared to those who lived through it. The British people had set out to destroy Hitler and National Socialism -'Victory at all costs.' They succeeded. No English

> soldier who rode with the tanks into liberated Belgium or saw the German murder camps at Dachau or Buchenwald could doubt that the war had been a noble crusade. (2)

To that I would add the words of Wordsworth, who drew the same inspiration from the French Revolution as his contemporary, Beethoven.

> Bliss was it in that dawn to be alive,
> But to be young was very heaven!

But the song also serves as a reminder of how the price of liberty is eternal vigilance, because all that great national vision of the nineteen-forties had degenerated by the nineteen-eighties into the squalor of Thatcherism.

### 3. Affettuoso

Where there are pieces of music like *The White Cliffs of Dover* which especially evoke personal memories of stirring times as well as providing thoughts for the present and the future, there are other pieces which recall certain places and thoughts associated with those places, and I turn now to two such pieces, both by outstanding British composers.

Not until the twentieth century have any native-born British composers in the classical tradition achieved world renown. The way was led by Elgar, the first Englishman ever to write an internationally acclaimed symphony, as well as a violin concerto and a cello concerto which rank among the greatest of all. He was self taught. A Roman Catholic of humble origin, born in the mid-nineteenth century in what was then a provincial backwater dominated by a snobbish, anti-Catholic squirearchy which was musically (and otherwise) near-illiterate, he never had any prospect of receiving and never did receive any academic musical instruction. He himself said that he could have written his cantata *Caractacus* (1898) ten years earlier if he had not been compelled to earn his living by teaching, by the chores of music and by working

---

(2) A.J.P.Taylor, *English History 1914-1945*, Pelican, London, 1970, p. 727. (First published, Oxford University Press, 1965).

in his father's music shop in Worcester (3). We can but surmise what we may have been deprived of by the circumstances of his early life:- possibly several symphonies, an opera, an oratorio, a piano concerto and perhaps a number of pieces for strings, for which he had unsurpassed feeling.

His Serenade for Strings, to which I have already referred, has a second movement entitled Larghetto. The movement has a theme which has been well described as "a broad stream flowing onward serenely like his own Severn River" and I have particular reasons for liking it.

My mother came from Oldbury Upon Severn, a lovely little village situated near the mouth of what is there the very broad and flowing river. My mother's family had a long connection with the Severn. My maternal grandfather, John Allen, was the captain of a small sailing vessel of a type known locally as a "trow" and he was one of the most skilled and respected navigators of the extremely difficult and dangerous estuary. The Larghetto is a happy reminder of a place with which I feel a strong affinity.

Oldbury is a long way downstream from Elgar's part of the Severn but the ambiance is not unlike that of his birthplace at Broadheath, near Worcester. At the time when he was young, Oldbury too was a remote, squirearchical place where my maternal grandmother, when she was a little girl, was once put to bed early by her mother because she refused to curtsey to the vicar. Both my grandmother and my mother had a lifelong superstition that the colour green was "unlucky" and I have sometimes wondered to what extent that was associated with their upbringing. Green was the colour of the Chartists and, even earlier, of the Levellers and the Diggers. I find myself wondering if in earlier times superstitious dread of the colour green was preached for generations from village pulpits, as part of the business of imbuing the peasantry with fear of progressive ideas as well as deference to the ruling class.

I go straight on to something reminiscent of West Wales, from where my father came. He was born in Pembroke, in the delectable "little England beyond Wales" and I feel an affinity with the whole of what was formerly the county of Pembrokeshire; divided in the

---

(3) Michael Kennedy, (Portrait of Elgar), Third Edition, Oxford University Press, 1987, p. 15.

south by the natural harbour of Milford Haven, sloping up to Foel Cwmcerwyn (Prescelly Top) in what South Pembroke people call "the Welsh parts" and bordered on three sides by the sea, with some of the finest coastal scenery in the world. My father was one of life's survivors. He left school at age twelve and was put to work on a farm; he ran away from the farm to work as a coalminer in the Welsh valleys; he survived both the Somme and Passchendaele in the first world war and service at sea in the Merchant Navy throughout the second world war. He also survived Lloyd George's "land fit for heroes" between the wars, of which he always said that you had to be a hero to live in it. He died peacefully in his sleep at the age of ninety-six, having well outlived all his eleven brothers and sisters. His death was sufficiently unexpected to necessitate an autopsy to ascertain the cause!

My piece of music here is Benjamin Britten's setting of *I was Lonely and Forlorn* or, to give it its Welsh title *Bugeilio'r Gwenith Gwyn.* This is one of a collection of eight British folk songs which Britten arranged in the summer of 1976, only months before he died. For me, the lilting melody creates pictures of the lovely landscapes of West Wales, at their best in warm summer sunshine, but the song also poignantly expresses, very much like the French *Plaisir d'amour*, an eternal aspect of human relationships.

I was lonely and forlorn
Among the meadows mourning;
For I had wooed her oft and long,
Yet others reaped her loving.

Not to me this maid did come
To cure my painful yearning.
Yet I had watched, the fields among,
Her beauty and her blooming.

While the seas do ebb and flow
And minutes do not falter;
And while my heart beats in my breast,
My 'fliction ne'er will alter.

Ne'er shall I kiss her cheeks so fair,
Nor feel her arms embracing;
For I had watched the ripening wheat,
Yet others reaped her loving.

Elgar, in his time, was attacked from within the musical establishment for reasons of class and religion, Britten was attacked for other but equally unmusical reasons. To start with, he was a pacifist. His opera *Peter Grimes* was one of the most historic landmarks in British music yet, as soon as it went into rehearsal with the Sadler's Wells Opera Company in the final months of the second world war, certain leading singers in the company tried to stop the production because the compose; the leading tenor, Peter Pears; and the producer, Eric Crozier; were all conscientious objectors to military service. Fortunately, the singers did not prevail and what they had called "a piece of cacophony" was greeted by the opera-going public with acclamation. (4)

Britten was also victimised because he was homosexual and, in a darkening age of British social attitudes in the nineteen-eighties, there was no shortage of those among whom prejudice against him strengthened rather than diminished after his death. Many of his arrangements of folk songs, like his settings of English verse, were written for his lifelong companion Peter Pears, who created many of the leading roles in his operas. Britten never talked publicly about his private life, he never engaged in "gay lib" activities, but neither was his enduring relationship with Pears any sort of shameful secret. Edward Elgar derived great inspiration from his partnership with his wife Alice - the general's daughter who married the tradesman's son, to the fury of her snobbish relatives. Britten derived great inspiration from his partnership with Pears. The world has good cause to be grateful for both partnerships.

For thirty years, I would have described Beethoven as my favourite composer but passing years have brought realization that you cannot restrict yourself to any single "favourite" composer. Nevertheless, his genius remains for me truly awe-inspiring and deeply moving. The notes on the sleeve of the first record I bought of the choral symphony (5) recount how, when Beethoven conducted the first performance in Vienna in 1824, the work was greeted with unprecedented acclamation, of which he was unaware because of his extreme deafness, until one of the singers turned him round to face the tumultuously applauding audience. For me, that is as moving as the music itself. It must have been a rare moment, an occasion in

---

(4) Michael Kennedy, *Britten*, Dent & Sons, London, 1981, pp. 44-6.
(5) Decca SXL 6233 (1966), Vienna Philharmonic Orchestra; Vienna State Opera Chorus: Joan Sutherland, Marilyn Horne, James King, Martti Talvela; conducted by Hans Schmitt-Isserstedt.

history at which I wish I could have been present. My favourite passage from that stupendous masterpiece is the middle section from the adagio, which touches the very deepest emotions of compassion.

It is Beethoven's noble vision and his vigour in addressing those around him, and through them all of us, from the strength of that vision that is so compelling. He admired Napoleon Bonaparte as an embodiment of his own ideals of social justice and had dedicated the *Eroica* symphony to him. The arrival of the news that Napoleon had had himself declared emperor was a betrayal so unacceptable that Beethoven struck the dedication from the title page with a vehemence that put the pen right through the paper. Four years later, the fifth symphony was a devastating commentary on idealism perverted into absolutism.

A booklet I acquired on a visit to Beethoven's birthplace in Bonn records that an estimated twenty thousand people followed his funeral cortege in Vienna in 1827. The exponent of revolutionary, democratic ideals, expressed in musical innovation far ahead of his time in an age of imperial rulers, had nevertheless been acclaimed in his lifetime in one of the most imperial of European capitals and in death he was at once accorded the reverence he deserved.

To conclude these quasi-musical musings, I turn to Shostakovich, a towering genius of the twentieth century who was inspired by the ideals of the Russian Revolution and victimized by the regime which emerged from it.

By the nineteen-thirties, Shostakovich was already marked out as a composer of exceptional genius and he was a recognized leader in the wave of artistic innovation then centred in Leningrad, his native city. It was a time when artists inspired by a liberal interpretation of the ideals of the Russian Revolution were striving to make a complete break with the past through new, advanced forms of expression.

There was even a Moscow production of *Hamlet* without the ghost, for which Shostakovich composed a scintillating suite and of which he jokingly said many years later that Shakespearian scholars considered it to have been the most scandalous production there ever was of *Hamlet*, the very mention of which still caused them to go pale. But tension was growing between the artists and the political establishment. Shostakovich's opera *The Lady Macbeth of the Mtensk District* (an oddly suitable title in the bureaucratic dictatorship which Joseph Stalin was creating over the dead bodies of idealists) was well received by the Soviet Union's perceptive musical public and it was performed a hundred and eighty times before Stalin attended a performance in January 1936 and was infuriated by what he saw and heard. Within days, the official article *Confusion Instead of Music* appeared in Pravda, attacking the opera as a chaotic noise, unmusical and too modern.

The opera was withdrawn. Shostakovich faced an appalling dilemma. To fulfil his career, he had to produce music acceptable to a totalitarian regime which was betraying all his ideals, although to do so would be a corruption of his own integrity which he could not countenance. He was then well forward with his fourth symphony but he withdrew it during rehearsals. In April 1937, he began his fifth symphony. It was written in only three months, in what must have been a white heat of impassioned inspiration, generated out of those events which could have put an early end to his whole career.

First performed in October 1937 in Leningrad, to celebrate the twentieth anniversary of the October Revolution, it was an immediate and overwhelming success, great music at once recognized as such and acclaimed tumultuously. It is recorded that the applause went on for an hour (a quarter of an hour longer than the symphony itself) and that afterwards, people ran up and down in the streets into the small hours, embracing and congratulating each other on having been there [(6)]. No-one could ignore such a reception. Official circles acclaimed the work as marking the welcome return of one of the Soviet Union's most brilliant artists to the fold of what they chose to call "Socialist Realism." Faced with the reception accorded the work and having as a central tenet of their faith that it was essential for symphonies to have a clear appeal to the people, they could scarcely do otherwise.

By any standards, it is one of the greatest of twentieth century masterpieces. With its sardonic tittle *A Soviet Artist's Reply to Just Criticism*, it is arguably Shostakovich's supreme achievement in the irony at which he excelled. It could be interpreted as a celebration of the ultimate triumph of the people against oppressive forces

---

(6) Julianne Ribke, quoting Mstislav Rostropovich, programme notes, German original translated Mary Whittall, Rostropovich conducting the national Symphony Orchestra of Washington D.C., Deutsch Grammophon 410 509-2 (CD 1983).

during and after the great upheaval of 1917. But it could also be interpreted to refer in disguised form to the Stalinist regime and the need to combat what it was doing to the new society. The finale is of huge dramatic intensity which, in any interpretation, expresses hope for the future. Shostakovich wrote of the symphony that he saw man with all his experience at the centre of the composition and of the finale he wrote "the tragically tense impulses of the earlier movements are resolved in optimism and joy of living." (7)

For him, though, there was to be little joy of living. In 1948, the Central Committee of the Soviet Communist Party passed its devastating resolution, charging him, his great contemporary Prokofiev and others with, among other things "formalism and anti-popular tendencies", effectively ending his teaching post at the Moscow Conservatory and stopping public performances of his work. By 1948, he had written nine symphonies. No more came from his pen until after the death of Stalin (5 March 1953, Prokofiev died the same day). Shostakovich produced his tenth - widely rated as the greatest of all his symphonies - very shortly after Stalin died. But it would be more than a decade after his death before those "tragically tense impulses" which had so moved and inspired him would start to be resolved.

## 4. Finale

Starting from the artistic creativity inspired by the Palestinian struggle and going on to use some favourite music as a basis for a certain amount of rumination may have led some distance from Palestine. Yet, because these thoughts have turned up a recurring theme of the indestructibility of the human spirit, there is an important sense in which they have not left Palestine. For Palestine provides an outstanding example of the indestructibility of the spirit of a heroic people in the face of the most discouraging circumstances.

People in the western world without independent sources of information could have been forgiven for thinking that both the Intifada and the spirit of its people were dying at the start of the nineteen-nineties. On top of the brutal physical measures to crush the Intifada, the Israeli government imposed a rigid censorship to

(7) Quoted, Hugh Ottoway, *Shostakovich Symphonies*, BBC, London, 1978, p.25.

prevent knowledge of the magnitude of its repression, That, in turn, enabled it to sustain an international campaign to depict the Intifada as dying. Although that was the opposite of the truth, it was widely accepted in quarters which were happy not only to accept it but to help it on. As the killings and beatings and repression of the most basic human rights continued daily, the world allowed it to continue, virtually without comment and without action to stop it.

In the Spring of 1990, I wrote to ask the editor of a widely listened to radio current affairs programme why an important statement condemning those practices, made by the former US President Jimmy Carter in Jerusalem on 19 March and reported in detail by the international news agency Reuters, had not been reported on his programme. The reply was that the former President's remarks were not considered to be "particularly newsworthy." In addition, the editor considered such a judgement to be justified because it "was shared by many other news organizations." Further correspondence elicited that "Human rights in Palestine *are* (his emphasis) newsworthy *from time to time*" (my emphasis). It was an illuminating insight into the attitude of the British media.

The human rights violations continued to be perpetrated every day without being reported. When, on 26 April, four Palestinians were shot dead and well over two hundred were injured, it was another of those occasions when human rights in Palestine were not considered newsworthy in the overwhelming judgement of the news organizations. It was not until an Israeli gunman killed eight Palestinians and wounded ten more on 20 May and the Israeli army killed another seven and wounded hundreds on the same day because they dared to protest, that the media considered it newsworthy.

The attitudes of governments also remained unsatisfactory. Powerful support in western countries for declarations of independence in the Soviet Baltic Republics contrasted with their lack of support for the Palestinian Declaration of Independence. The principle was the same. Circumstances clearly altered cases. The USA, notwithstanding a few halting steps forward with the advent of the Bush administration, remained subservient to Israel. Its action, in vetoing on 31 May 1990 an otherwise unanimous Security Council resolution to send UN observers to the occupied territories and following up by "suspending" the dialogue with the PLO, might be proved by history to have marked a disastrous turning point.

For what events in the Middle East then signified more strongly than ever was that only concerted international action could resolve the situation. In the first place, the Palestinian struggle could not remain isolated in a world where, from Moscow to Capetown, issues of human rights and self-determination were receiving universal attention. In the second place, neither in Israel nor in Palestine nor anywhere else, could there be any confidence in the good intentions of the then Israeli leaders. Their real intention was unmistakably to reject reasoned argument and negotiation, to maintain colonial rule by force until the Palestinians could be forced out of the West Bank and the Gaza Strip, so that those areas could then be incorporated into a greater Israel and populated with immigrants from the Soviet Union.

Faced with this prospect, the Palestinian people, more than any other party to the conflict, needed international protection. Yasser Arafat graphically described their situation in a letter in February 1990 to an international Jewish gathering, organized in Jerusalem by the International Centre for Peace in the Middle East. The Palestinians, he wrote, had gone "from crisis to catastrophe, from repression to dispossession, from siege to massacre."

All this was taking place in a region seething throughout with unrest and with the potential for even greater conflict. Despair at western indifference and at the support of much of the West, especially the USA, for Israel, was fuelling what a largely uncomprehending West chose to call "Islamic fundamentalism." Fundamentalism, by rejecting western values and aligning itself with the oppressed throughout the region, was encouraging extreme nationalism and threatening the stability of Arab regimes which were sympathetic to the West and often seen as mere tools of the West, Divided and incompetent Arab governments appeared helpless. Israel's unrestricted build up of nuclear and chemical weapons threatened the whole region.

Meanwhile, Iraq, under the rule of Saddam Hussein, emerging as the strongest military power in the Arab World after its long and bloody war with Iran, was directing its attention back to the Arab-Israeli conflict. This brought threats from Israel, to which Iraq replied by warning that it would retaliate strongly against any attack and would not rule out using chemical weapons. For thereby deploying a strategy of deterrence, so long so much loved in the

West, Iraq was immediately branded as "threatening Israel" and became the target for an international campaign of hate. The escalating atrocities in Palestine resembled the situation which preceded the terrorizing of the Palestinians from their homeland in 1948, while the accompanying propaganda campaign was comparable with those which had preceded the Israeli expansionist wars in 1956, 1967 and 1982.

In such a complex and explosive situation, international action through the United Nations was an urgent necessity. Palestine was at the core of the situation. A solution to the Palestine problem would not necessarily eliminate all the other problems in the region but it would go a long way towards defusing them. The absence of a solution and the lack of international will to move towards a solution could only build up the strength of the impending explosion and bring the flashpoint nearer. And on 2 August 1990, the flashpoint, or more correctly, a flashpoint, came with the Iraqi invasion of Kuwait. It was a flashpoint to set in motion a train of events going far beyond the war which is ignited.

The Middle East in August 1990 was like Europe in August 1914. When Germany invaded Belgium in 1914, there was talk that "it would be all over by Christmas" but, of course, an unstoppable train of events had been set in motion. The existing European order disappeared for ever, centuries old ruling dynasties vanished and mighty empires were extinguished. Among them was the Ottoman Empire, in the ruins of which were planted the roots of all the conflicts which have raged in the Middle East ever since. When Iraq invaded Kuwait, seventy-six years almost to the day after Germany invaded Belgium,. there was also talk of an early settlement and there were efforts to bring it about. Jordan and the PLO in particular made frantic efforts to contain the conflict and bring about an early withdrawal and negotiated settlement. But, as in 1914, there were too many complicating factors arising from events which had gone before, too much was at stake and too many in positions of power had taken up postures from which they could not or would not withdraw. The Jordanian and PLO reward for attempting to mediate and avoid further bloodshed was to be branded in a hysterical campaign, both within and without the Arab World, as supporters of the Iraqi aggression.

Although this is not the place for it, there is room for a study of how domestic politics in the USA have influenced developments in the Middle East. Domestic politics in the USA were a factor as heavily present in 1990-91 as, for example, in 1948 and 1978. In 1948, when President Truman was facing election and, according to all the conventional wisdom, facing defeat, he gave a secret undertaking to the Zionist leader, Chaim Weizmann, that if a Jewish state were to proclaim its existence, he would immediately recognize it. That was contrary to the declared policy of his administration, but when the state of Israel duly proclaimed its existence from midnight on 14 May 1948, he fulfilled his secret pledge. The result was that the Israeli lobby delivered the Jewish vote to him at the November election and he was triumphantly re-elected. In 1978, President Carter, who was firmly committed to peace in the Middle East, was facing damaging losses in the mid-term congressional elections. The idea was conceived that bringing President Sadat of Egypt and Prime Minister Begin of Israel together under Jimmy Carter's mediation might be good not only for peace in the Middle East but also for the elections at home. So it was that the Camp David Conference came to be held and although it proved to be good for the elections, it proved disastrous for the Middle East. The only United States President directly to challenge the Israeli lobby prior to 1990-91 - and at the height of an election campaign - was Eisenhower, at the time of the Suez war in 1956. But George Bush in 1990 was neither an Eisenhower nor a Carter. With the mid-term elections due in November and the 1992 presidential election already on the horizon, he was anxious to dispel his growing image as a weak and vacillating president - in American slang parlance "a wimp."

With the invasion and brutal occupation of Kuwait, the Iraqi dictator Saddam Hussein not only gave Bush the chance to establish the macho image he craved for himself at home, he also gave the Americans the chance they had been seeking for years - the opportunity to establish a military presence to control the Gulf oilfields. The Soviet Union, gravely weakened by its collapsing economy and growing internal conflict, was excluded from any effective role. So the way was open for the United States to manipulate the United Nations for what was in reality an American colonial war. When the supposed United Nations operation was launched, the Secretary General was not even informed, while the Security Council, which should have been in constant session during any genuine UN military action, did not meet at all. The rigid economic sanctions which the Security Council had initiated to coerce Iraq by peaceful means into withdrawal were never given the chance to work. President Bush had made up his mind for war at an early stage, urged on by Margaret Thatcher, out of touch as usual with the rest of Europe and by then living in an isolated world of fantasy, unaware that she would shortly be forced out of power by her own Cabinet because she had become a serious liability for the Conservative Party.

The United States had to restrain the Israeli government from launching its own attack on Iraq. Had such an attack been launched, the fragile coalition of Arab governments which the USA had put together would have disintegrated. With the launching of very limited and largely unsuccessful missile attacks against Israel by Iraq, the Israeli government demanded, and got, hundreds of millions of dollars from the USA in compensation and demanded billions more for its "assistance" to the war effort by its "restraint." In anticipation of chemical attacks, the Israeli government issued gas masks. In the occupied territories, these were issued to settlers but not to Palestinians. In the event, chemical weapons were not used by either side. although the "hi-tech" weapons of mass murder used by the coalition against Iraq were just as horrendous. The damage and casualties suffered by Israel were miniscule in comparison with the destruction and casualties inflicted on Iraq, although they received infinitely greater publicity in the West.

Not least among the tragic ironies of the war was the enthusiastic support for Saddam Hussein demonstrated among the people in the occupied territories. It was the expression of the pent-up feelings of a ruthlessly oppressed people who saw Saddam Hussein as the only Arab leader to challenge their oppressors and to challenge the Americans who had for so long sustained their oppressors, but it was tragically ironic in that Saddam's vicious dictatorship was the very antithesis of Palestinian democracy. Palestinian belief in the accountability of leaders to the people was far in advance of anything tolerated by Arab governments, among whom, for all their regularly proclaimed support for the Palestinian cause, there was deep hostility towards Palestinian democracy. The immediate aftermath of the war brought severe repression of Palestinians living in some Arab countries and the cutting off by the wealthy oil autocracies of political and financial support for the PLO, to the serious detriment of the Palestinian cause. That delighted the Israelis and pleased the Americans but it boded ill for inter-Arab relations and for the future stability of Arab regimes. The war brought massive demonstrations of popular hostility towards the

West in general and towards the USA in particular. It was clear that a very large section of the Arab people were neither in line with the policies of their governments nor with their systems of government.

With world attention focussed almost entirely on the Gulf, the Israeli government even further intensified its repression of the Palestinians and further stepped up the construction of colonizing settlements in the occupied territories. Yitshak Shamir yet again and more strongly than ever reiterated his intention never to relinquish the occupied territories. By then, immigrants from the Soviet Union were pouring into Israel and the annexation of the territories and expulsion of the Palestinians was more on the Israeli agenda than ever. The painstaking but predictably doomed efforts of Secretary of State James Baker to negotiate at least some sort of settlement of the Arab-Israeli dispute in the aftermath of the war, even though it excluded Palestinian self-determination, ran as usual, into the sands of Israeli prevarication and obstruction. Palestine remained the unsolved central issue in the Middle East. The war, like all wars, resolved nothing and created new problems. The nineties loomed as a decade with incalculable potential for instability and conflict.

It is not stretching the imagination too far to compare the needs of the Israeli and Palestinian people as similar and not incompatible. The Israelis seek to be masters of their own fate, independent and secure within protected borders. That is precisely the aim of the Palestinians. The Palestinians have long since recognized Israel's right to a secure and peaceful existence. Apart from the repeated declarations to that effect by their recognized representative body, the PLO, it was nowhere put more poignantly than in a Hebrew language leaflet distributed to Israeli soldiers in the occupied territories by the Palestinians :

> Soldiers, go home. Return to your families and children. Be with them in peace so that we may remain with our families and children in peace. We do not wish to harm you, or your state. We wish to be unharmed in our state.

Unfortunately, those sentiments were in no way reciprocated by the Israeli government and, deeply divided though the country was, they were also not reciprocated by a very large section of the population, for the forces of peace and reconciliation, although growing, remained in the minority.

Not least among Israel's problems is the extent to which it is a country founded in mythology, The idea that certain people have an incontestable right to drive another, indigenous people out of their own land in order to occupy it themselves because their alleged ancestors lived there two thousand or more years earlier is self-evidently preposterous and the more the proposition is examined, the more preposterous it becomes. Zionism originated among Jews living in central and eastern Europe, whose claim to be descended from the Israelites of biblical times is especially dubious. They are the descendants of a Tartar people called the Khazars who, between the first and thirteenth centuries A.D., lived in a great empire in what is now the southern Soviet Union.

The Khazars had no connection with the Jews but, in the eighth century, they adopted Judaism as their religion for political reasons. Their powerful neighbours were Byzantium which was Christian and Arabia which was Islamic. Both made efforts to convert them but such efforts were rejected because they were seen as attempts to extend domination over the Khazars. The Khazars were aware that their own primitive form of religion was regarded as barbaric and backward by both Christians and Muslims. Early in the eighth century, they welcomed Jews who left Byzantium to avoid persecution. Their rulers, noting that the Jews had neither territory nor armies which could give them ascendancy, saw the opportunity to claim spiritual ascendancy over both Byzantium and Arabia by adopting Judaism and so becoming "People of the Book" and "God's Chosen People." A proclamation was issued and the entire Khazar people adopted Judaism in the year 740.

The Khazar empire came to an end in the thirteenth century with the Mongol invasion. The people were scattered westwards, principally into the Ukraine and Poland. From them sprang the modern Ashkenazim who now form the majority of the Jewish people and who established the state of Israel, where they relegated Jews from the Middle East to inferior status, notwithstanding that the latter's claim to descent from the biblical Jews is stronger. [8]

---

(8) I am grateful to Mr P. Lewis for information on this subject in his privately circulated paper *An Alternative Strategy for the Palestinian Struggle*, 1989, pp. 7-10. Major sources are Professsor A.N.Poliak's *Khazaria*, Tel Aviv, 1944 and Arthur Koestler's *The Thirteenth Tribe: The Khazar Empire and Its Heritage*, Hutchinson, London, 1976. See also Henry Cattan, *The Palestine Question*, Croom Helm, London 1988, pp. 17-21.

It is not only in dubious ancient mythology that Israel is founded. A state so founded had to create its own modern mythology from the start. One such piece of modern mythology which has become well rooted in western perceptions is that Jewish pioneers "made the desert bloom", that by their know-how and hard work, they transformed an uncultivable, mountainous, swampy and arid land into fertile and productive fields. Dr Moise Saltiel, a highly qualified and experienced Israeli agricultural engineer, agronomist and water engineer, who emigrated from Greece to Palestine in 1932, has shown that the facts tell a very different story.

Dr Saltiel's researches show that in 1945, according to British Mandatory statistics, the cultivated area of Palestine was 920,000 hectares while, according to a survey in 1946, there were 60,000 cultivable hectares in the Golan Heights. By the 1980's, the total cultivated area of the same land - Israel, the West Bank, the Gaza Strip and Golan - was 650,000 hectares - a third less than at the time of the establishment of Israel.

Exactly contrary to the mythology, cultivated land in the Negev has actually been turned into desert. Before the establishment of Israel, the Bedouin had for centuries cultivated land wherever water was to be found, in even the most arid areas of the Negev desert. Forty years after the establishment of Israel, less than half of the previously fertile land in the Negev was under cultivation. The Bedouin had been displaced and the area became a major base for the Israeli army, for large industrial zones, including the site of the huge complex where the Israeli nuclear weapons are manufactured, and a dumping ground for industrial waste. [(9)]

Another manifestation of the modern mythology is in the myth that Israel was invaded by great Arab armies as soon as it proclaimed its existence. Most of such Arab armies as existed at the time were too small, too ill-equipped and too far away to mount any such invasion. They were only ordered into action by reluctant Arab rulers because of the pressure of opinion in their countries over the atrocities committed to drive out the Palestinians. Such as did see action were no match for the highly-trained and well-equipped, Palestine-based, Zionist forces. The only effective Arab army was the Jordanian, which was then British commanded

---

(9) Moise Saltiel, two articles in Israel and Palestine (Magellan, Paris) No. 152, September 1989 pp, 9-13 and No. 156, March 1990 pp. 19-25.

and trained but which was strictly limited to defending from Zionist attack that land which was within the borders of the Palestinian state delineated by the United Nations Partition Resolution.

Yet another carefully created myth was that Arab radio stations ordered the Palestinian population to leave so that the Arab armies could enter the country. How, one wonders, were armies supposed to enter a country whose roads would be choked with refugees fleeing in the opposite direction? The fact is that detailed monitoring of Arab radio stations at the time by both the BBC and the CIA prove beyond doubt that no such broadcasts were ever made. On the contrary, such broadcasts as were made by the Arab radio, without exception, advised the people to remain. None of that has prevented the endless repetition of this modern mythology, apparently on the basis that the bigger the lie you tell and the more often you repeat it, the more likely it is to be believed - the technique propounded by Hitler's propaganda minister Joseph Goebbels and now distinguished with the name "disinformation."

When Imperial Germany invaded Belgium in 1914 and so took Britain into the first world war, the famous British writer H.G.Wells referred to the Germany of those days as " ....this drilling, trampling foolery in the heart of Europe." Sadly, three quarters of a century later, Israel had become a drilling, trampling foolery in the heart of the Middle East. The state of Israel was born in large measure out of events in that terrible period which only reached its conclusion in 1945. The Balfour Declaration of 1917, which so advanced the Zionist cause, arose directly from the exigencies of the first world war, while it was the Nazi genocide in the second war which created the climate within which Israel could be established and the Palestinians, the victims of its establishment, actually treated as if it was they who were the agressors in Palestine.

Jews and Palestinians now find themselves locked in conflict in the heart of the Middle East which nobody can win. Israelis, no less than Palestinians, are now the victims of an appalling situation. That it is a situation created through the policies of the Israeli leadership in no way alters the requirement for peace and justice with honour for both peoples. The conflict is so wide that it can only be resolved through concerted action by the world community as a whole. There is now almost universal recognition of that and if peace and justice are to be made reality, there is inescapably a universal duty to move from recognition to action.

# INDEX

## A



## B

## I



## J



## K

## N



## O



## P



## Q

## R



## S

# T



# U



# V



# W

# Y



# Z